I0114917

Folklore Figures *of* French *and* Creole Louisiana

Folklore Figures
of French *and* Creole Louisiana

Nathan J. Rabalais

Louisiana State University Press
Baton Rouge

Published with the assistance of the John and Virginia Noland Fund

Published by Louisiana State University Press
www.lsupress.org

Copyright © 2021 by Louisiana State University Press
All rights reserved. Except in the case of brief quotations used in articles or reviews,
no part of this publication may be reproduced or transmitted in any format or by any
means without written permission of Louisiana State University Press.

Designer: Barbara Neely Bourgoyne
Typeface: Whitman

Original illustrations are copyright © Jonathan Mayers and cannot be reproduced without
the express permission of the artist. Mayers may be contacted at jonathanmayers.com.

Cover illustration: Jonathan Mayers, *Lapin, un puits, épuis un feufollet*. Acrylic on panel. 2020.

Portions of chapter 2 first appeared in "Roquelaure: A New Perspective on Louisiana
Folklore's Master Thief," *Louisiana Folklore Miscellany* 27 (2017): 29–52, and are reproduced
by permission of the editor. Portions of chapter 3 first appeared in "Les Représentations de
Jean le Sot dans le contexte francophone," *Port Acadie* 31 (2017): 7–22, and are reproduced
by permission of the editor.

Library of Congress Cataloging-in-Publication Data
Names: Rabalais, Nathan J., author.
Title: Folklore figures of French and Creole Louisiana / Nathan J. Rabalais.
Description: Baton Rouge : Louisiana State University Press, 2021. | Includes bibliographical
    references and index.
Identifiers: LCCN 2020042414 (print) | LCCN 2020042415 (ebook) | ISBN 978-0-8071-7481-4
    (cloth) | ISBN 978-0-8071-7556-9 (pdf) | ISBN 978-0-8071-7557-6 (epub)
Subjects: LCSH: Folklore—Louisiana. | Tales—Louisiana. | Cajuns—Folklore. | Creoles—
    Louisiana—Folklore. | Louisiana—Social life and customs.
Classification: LCC GR110.L5 R34 2021 (print) | LCC GR110.L5 (ebook) |
    DDC 398.209763—dc23
LC record available at https://lccn.loc.gov/2020042414
LC ebook record available at https://lccn.loc.gov/2020042415

Pour ma famille:

Que nous ayons toujours des contes à nous raconter.

Contents

ACKNOWLEDGMENTS xi

Introduction: Origins and Evolution of Louisiana's French
and Creole Folklore Tradition 1

1. Lapin and Other Animal Tricksters 17

2. The Master Thief, a Human Trickster 50

3. The Many Faces of Jean le Sot 72

4. *Un Sacré Conte:* Anticlerical Humor in Louisiana Folklore 92

5. Bayou Belles: The Fairy Tales of French and Creole Louisiana 115

6. Mystery, Magic, and Curses 139

Epilogue: Contemporary Uses of Folklore Figures 178

NOTES 187

BIBLIOGRAPHY 211

INDEX 227

Illustrations

Bouki, Lapin et le poulailler 38

Monsieur le duc de Roquelaure, engraving, 1683 59

Title page of *Histoire curieuse du duc de Roquelaure* 60

Jean Sot et le beurre 76

Rougarou (Loup-garou) 148

Fifolé de la Pointe Coupée 161

Koushma (Cauchemar) 168

Acknowledgments

In many ways, this book is the result of several years of research and many people who contributed their time and expertise to this project. In the early stages of my work on oral tradition, countless friends and colleagues offered their time and advice as I worked through many questions and challenges. André Magord at Université de Poitiers and Elizabeth Poe at Tulane University were particularly instrumental. The Fulbright-Chateaubriand fellowship and the Commission franco-américaine made possible the extended access to archival sources in France. Barry Ancelet, Marlène Belly, Frank DeCaro, Thomas Klingler, and Dana Kress all offered their expertise in the formative stages of my research on folklore. I am grateful to the MIMMOC (Mémoires, identités, marginalités dans le monde occidental contemporain) research laboratory at the Université de Poitiers for its welcome, support, and office space. This project would not have been possible without the support of a twelve-month fellowship from the National Endowment of the Humanities and a research leave granted by William & Mary. I thank the Reves Center for International Studies for its support of several research and conference trips that indirectly benefited my work on folklore. Deans for Educational Policy LuAnn Homza and Jonathan Donahue as well as the Dean of Arts & Sciences at William & Mary generously supported my travel to consult archival sources in Louisiana, France, and Canada. Administrative coordinators Rebecca Bliley, Michelle Sherman, and Melissa Johnson contributed greatly to the successful sponsorship of my research trips. Aleksandra Grzybowska, Flavie-Isabelle Hade, and everyone at the Centre de la Francophonie des Amériques has also greatly supported my work over the years.

The many librarians and archivists deserve much credit for their tireless work and precious knowledge of sound and documentary records. In particular, John "Pudd" Sharp, Chris Segura, and Joshua Caffery at the Center for Louisiana Studies (CLS); Stéphanie Coulais and Sandra Egreteau at the Centre d'études de recherche et de documentation sur l'oralité (CERDO) at the UPCP-Métive in Parthenay; Sean Benjamin and Leon Miller at Tulane University's Louisiana Research Collection (LARC); Rodolphe Defiolle at the Centre de documentation of the Université de Poitiers; Robert Richard and Frank LeBlanc at the Centre d'études acadiennes Anselme Chiasson at the Université de Moncton; and Valérie Asselin at the Archives de folklore et d'ethnologie of the Université Laval. To the many people in Poitiers who made me and my wife feel at home: Jean-Luc Terradillos and Dominique Truco; Stéphanie, Gérard, and Françoise Moreau; and Elodie Gallet, Kelly Fazilleau, Simon Fleury, and Agathe Marie. A special thanks to Du and Philippe Aldon for their friendship and support. This book is also dedicated to the memory of those important cultural figures whom we have lost since this project began: Frank DeCaro, Liliane Jagueneau, and Michel Valière.

One of the aspects of my work that I truly enjoy the most is conversing with dear colleagues and friends with whom I enjoy exchanging ideas regularly. Clint Bruce, Joseph Dunn, Dana Kress, Christophe Landry, and Robin White—your intellectual curiosity and generous spirit are so appreciated. I also thank Rachel Doherty and Ryan Langley for their time and insight. It has been a privilege to have many mentors who have helped, encouraged, and inspired me over the years, including Barry Ancelet, Amanda LaFleur, Kirby Jambon, André Magord, Brenda Mounier, and Ebba and Tom Schoonover.

I would like to thank the professors, colleagues, and university administrators at multiple institutions who have supported my academic career over the years and facilitated the writing of this book in particular. My scholarship in francophone studies would not have been possible without the initial training that I received from my professors at the University of Louisiana at Lafayette, including several whom I am honored to call colleagues today: Barry Ancelet, Deborah Clifton, Fabrice Leroy, Amadou Ouédraogo, and Monica Wright, who were instrumental in encouraging me to pursue my interests in academia. I also extend my gratitude to my former colleagues in the French and Francophone Studies program at William & Mary for their encouragement and friendship: Brett Brehm, Vanessa Brutsche, Magali Compan, Kate Conley, Katherine Kulick, Déborah Lee-Ferrand, Angela Leruth, Michael Leruth, Giulia Pacini, and Julie Hugonny. I thank the university and departmental leadership at William & Mary for the support that was kindly extended to me as a faculty member. Maryse Fauvel and Silvia Tandeciarz, as chairs, were both extremely supportive of my research endeavors. Many other colleagues in the Department of Modern Languages and Literatures have been valuable interlocutors and sources of encouragement: Carla Buck, Veronika Burney, Paulina Carrion, Francie Cate-Arries, Driss Cherkaoui, Michael Cronin, Sergio Ferrarese, Jennifer Gülly, Michael Hill, Robert Leventhal, Teresa Longo, Sara Mattavelli, Mariana Melo-Vega, Alexander Prokhorov, Elena Prokhorova, John Riofrio, Tomoyuki Sasaki, Monica Seger, Stephen Sheehi, Ann Marie Stock, Jennifer Taylor, Jorge Terukina, and Mona Zaki. Thank you to the department's student workers Gabriella and Marianna for your time and help with scanning loaned materials. I am so grateful for the support and friendship of Cindy DuPuy and Eric Christenson in Williamsburg. Finally, I would like to express my gratitude to my colleagues at the University of Louisiana at Lafayette, especially Regina LaBiche, Administrative Assistant, Monica Wright, Department Head, and all of the Department of Modern Languages, the Center for Louisiana Studies, as well as Dean Jordan Kellman and the College of Liberal Arts, for welcoming me into this dynamic program and for promoting the advancement of Louisiana studies.

The scholarship of my generation is built on the seminal work by the outstanding ethnologists of the generation that preceded us; their work offers fertile ground for new methods and greater understanding of French North America's cultures and oral traditions. Barry Ancelet, Jean-Pierre Pichette, Dean Louder, Bruce Duthu, George Arsenault, Laurier Turgeon, and countless others have been so influential in my work. I wish to extend special thanks to all of the storytellers, both in Louisiana and elsewhere in the whole world, who through their memory and creativity have left us with the precious intangible heritage so crucial to understanding our past and our place in the present. David Lanclos and Ronnie Chatelain were particularly generous with their time and keen knowledge of the folktale repertoire of Louisiana.

The art of Jonathan Mayers has been an important element of this project from the time that I began the manuscript. His unique interpretations of the folklore and *mythologies* of French and Creole Louisiana offer a visual manifestation of the region's cultural imaginary that compliments the analysis of the oral tradition. I am thrilled to include some of his original work created for this book. You can find out more about Mayers's work at www.jonathanmayers.com.

Finally, I express my heartfelt thanks to my family: to my late father, Joe Rabalais, who instilled in me the love of storytelling and making "the truth" a little more interesting every time it is told; to my wife, Jessica, for her inspiration, for proofreading my work, and for so often talking through various research conundrums with me; to my daughters, Cécile and Julie, for bringing me joy (and distractions) during long periods of writing and for being an indulgent audience for my own storytelling; to my mother, Gail, and my siblings, David, Rebecca, and Hannah; to Paul Rabalais, Lisa Peyton, Joshua and Katie Cormier, and all of our family and friends who offered their support and encouragement.

Folklore Figures *of* French *and* Creole Louisiana

Introduction

*Origins and Evolution of Louisiana's French
and Creole Folklore Tradition*

Le fond de cette littérature [orale] semble commun à la plupart des peuples: mais c'est une fleur dont les nuances varient selon les pays.

The foundation of this [oral] literature seems to be shared by most peoples; but it is a flower whose nuances vary from land to land.
—Léon Pineau, *Contes du Poitou*

Tout a pour changer. Quand ça arrête de changer, ça crève.

Everything must change. When something doesn't change, it dies.
—Dewey Balfa, cited in Barry Ancelet's *Cajun and Creole Music Makers*

Louisiana is home to one of the most complex and diverse cultural landscapes in the world. As the site of centuries of Native American history, three successive colonial regimes, an integral part of the transatlantic slave trade, and as the eighteenth state of the union, Louisiana continues to attract attention as a unique region of the United States. Since its founding as a French colony over three centuries ago, settlers, refugees, forced immigrants, and enslaved peoples came to Louisiana from many parts of the world. While Louisiana's historical connections with France and Acadia are well known and celebrated through festivals and the state's cultural and educational institutions, the influence of West Africa and Saint-Domingue (present-day Haiti) on the area's culture, cuisine, and language are often neglected. Still other groups of Spanish, German, and Italian origins are even less present in popular representations of South Louisiana, and yet all have contributed to its distinctive culture. The oral tradition of French and Creole Louisiana offers a remarkable reflection of this complexity. While undeniably part of the Deep South, South Louisiana possesses a French and Creole oral repertoire that distinguishes itself from other southern folklore traditions in many respects; language, characters, and subtle racial and cultural palimpsests have noticeably tinged the moral overtones of otherwise familiar tales.

FOLKLORE STUDIES IN LOUISIANA

Unfortunately, many American folklore scholars, unable or unwilling to confront the linguistic challenges posed by Louisiana's French and Creole language, have largely neglected the rich, creolized tapestry of Louisiana's oral tradition. Or they have simply viewed Louisiana's folklore as a subcategory of "southern" folklore, lumping South Louisiana in with other regions of the Deep South. Accessing this repertoire only through English translations has effaced the linguistic and cultural specificities of the region and obscured the diverse influences of the oral tradition and those who have maintained it for generations. For instance, simply framing Louisiana Creole folklore as "African American folklore of the South" obscures the unique slave trade patterns of colonial Louisiana and the relative continuity of West African languages and customs compared to the former British colonies (for example, Virginia or the Carolinas) as well as the vestiges of West African and Caribbean cultures. In a similar way, basing one's analyses of French-language folktales on English translations presents severe limitations in noticing (let alone understanding) the subtle cultural references and performative cues provided by the storyteller.

Scholars from Louisiana undertook a considerable amount of fieldwork during the twentieth century. They were obliged to leave Louisiana to pursue degrees in folklore studies because there was no broad institutional impetus to collect and archive the region's folklore, contrary to Quebec and France, where institutions like Université Laval or the Centre national de la recherche scientifique (CNRS) supported such efforts. Thus, while the recorded repertoire of folktales is modest when compared to other parts of the Francophone world, several large collections of French- and Creole-language tales provide us with a sufficiently comprehensive sampling of the region's oral tradition. Among the larger collections are Alcée Fortier's 1895 transcriptions of Creole folktales from in and near New Orleans, sound recordings and transcriptions from Avoyelles Parish in the 1940s by Calvin Claudel and Corinne Saucier, Elizabeth Brandon's 1955 dissertation on the traditions of Vermilion Parish, and many recordings of songs, folktales, and oral history collected by Barry Ancelet in the 1970s. Bruce Duthu collected the largest sampling of Houma tales. The fieldwork of Catherine Jolicoeur, many master's theses directed by James Broussard at Louisiana State University, and other smaller collections round out the full repertoire available to us today in print form and archival centers.[1]

All of these undertakings fulfilled a pressing need at the time given the rapid erosion of this storytelling tradition, but scholarly work in folklore focused primarily on collection and transcription of the folktale repertoire. Much less attention was paid to the analysis of this body of folktales and how narratives compared to other variants elsewhere in Louisiana or, more broadly, in the Francophone world. A closer look at some of the major folklore scholars, where they were from, and the areas that they studied reveals a glaring limitation: most folklorists from Louisiana studied the folklore of their native regions and seem to have shown little interest in other parts of the state. Furthermore, in an effort to not only preserve this unique storytelling tradition but also to make it accessible to a wider audience, Saucier (1962), Claudel (1979), Duthu (1979), and Brian Costello (2004) published most or all of their collections in English translation only. Basing interpretations on English translations presents its own set of constraints in terms of analyzing the cultural and linguistic content of the oral tradition.

Using the recorded repertoire of French and Creole folktales available from documentary and archival sources, I have taken the logical next step: analysis. More precisely, I argue that this diverse repertoire is a reflection of the region's humor, values, and morality that can be studied as a barometer of sociocultural adaptation in Louisiana. The very nature of oral narrative necessitates a double constant in order to survive: repetition and adaptation. Unless written down or otherwise recorded, narratives irrelevant to a community will disappear from the popular repertoire and fade from collective memory.

TOWARD A NEW UNDERSTANDING OF LOUISIANA'S FRENCH AND CREOLE ORAL TRADITION

Folklorists have long been aware of what Paul Delarue called the *canevas commun*, a common set of themes and motifs seemingly shared by all of humanity.[2] Yet for many cultures, folktales occupy an important place in collective memory and help communities to carve out a definite cultural identity and regional history. The paradox of specificity and universality is what gives readers and listeners around the world the peculiar impression of both familiarity and novelty.[3] Although folklore scholars of the nineteenth century were erroneously focused on discovering the supposed origins of what appeared to be universally shared folk narratives, comparative methodologies have since become the sine qua non of folklore studies.[4]

My approach here is fundamentally comparative in nature. The points of comparison are selected and informed by Louisiana's history and its most important immigration events and cultural influences. By considering the major trends in immigration from France and Acadia, the slave trade's impact, as well as other lesser known examples of immigration in Louisiana's history, I place South Louisiana in a larger Francophone context in order to better understand how specific tales or morals differ from their counterparts elsewhere. I compiled this corpus of folktales with these major immigration events in mind while drawing on folktales from various collections of Caribbean and African folklore as well as from archival materials at the Centre d'études acadiennes Anselme Chiasson (CEAAC) in Moncton, New Brunswick; the Centre d'études, de recherche et de documentation sur l'oralité in Parthenay, France; the Archives de folklore et d'ethnologie at Université Laval; the Center for Louisiana Studies at the University of Louisiana at Lafayette; and the Louisiana Research Center at Tulane University. Variants of selected tale types from France, Canada, Africa, and the Caribbean serve as points of comparison that elucidate examples of cultural adaptation to the Louisiana context.

My objectives here intersect with cultural anthropology, history, and psychology, but my approach is not psychoanalytical. While Bruno Bettelheim and other psychoanalysts sought a universal psychological significance (or "use") of specific folktales whose interpretations could be applied to all children, these scholars disregarded the existence of a multitude of variants of each folktale from oral sources that often differ greatly from the literary adaptations on which they based their analyses. Moreover, the reader will likely observe that this study largely excludes literary folktales written by single authors (for example, the works of Charles Perrault and the brothers Grimm). In order to more closely grasp the cultural changes expressed by storytellers, I have chosen to avoid collections that literize the folktales and/or obscure their specific origins. To the greatest extent possible, the material I use has been extracted directly from folklore archives or from transcriptions produced by folklorists with the goal of accuracy and proper attribution given to the storyteller. On occasion, it has proven necessary to cautiously refer to texts that fall outside of these criteria for the purposes of documenting attestations and regional variation.[5]

In this way, I take quite the opposite approach of many psychoanalysts by restricting this study's scope to oral sources in order to conduct cross-regional comparisons. Taking into account a large corpus in my analyses allows us to identify key differences that can be indicative of sociocultural and even moral differences in tales that can be representative of their respective regions and cultures. In other words, rather than analyzing a quintessential or archetypal version of a particular tale, I focus on the significance of variation between regions and the potential sociocultural implications of those adaptations. In order to better understand Louisiana's French and Creole oral tradition and its place within a larger Francophone context, it is imperative to consider not only the origin of the immigrants who settled there but also the conditions in which they arrived, whether by choice or by force.

A REGION FORGED IN TUMULT

Catchphrases like *joie de vivre* and *laissez les bons temps rouler* embody the popular media portrayal of South Louisiana as a hedonist's paradise; however, this skewed characterization stands in stark contrast to the painful histories endured by many of Louisiana's founding groups. Over the course of several centuries, what began as a French military outpost and place of exile for the

French Republic's undesirables became home to settlers, slaves, refugees, religious exiles, and immigrants from throughout Europe and the Atlantic World. All of these outside influences combined in a region that was already populated by a diverse group of Native American tribes. While for certain groups coming from elsewhere, Louisiana certainly offered some solace as a place of refuge, it was a forced destination for those enslaved, imprisoned, or in political exile. From its earliest beginnings, the French colonization proved difficult, with disease, inclement weather, famine, floods, and problems navigating the intricate rivers, swamps, and mouth of the Mississippi. The French government even resorted to deporting "riffraff"—criminals, prostitutes, and vagrants—to try to populate the colony.[6] Practically every major influx of migration into Louisiana was the result of some form of trauma or conflict.

Perhaps one of the best-known chapters of Louisiana's history is that of the Acadians' arrival to the area beginning in 1764. The Acadian deportation from their native land of Acadie, now the maritime provinces of eastern Canada, followed their refusal to partake in the long-going Anglo-French imperial wars of the eighteenth century.[7] Commonly referred to as the *Grand dérangement* (Great Upheaval), the Acadians' expulsion could be categorized as ethnic cleansing or genocide, as the British meant to prevent the Acadians from ever re-forming as a nation. In order to accomplish this, the British systematically separated the surviving Acadians from their families and forced them onto ships in all directions. Many died at sea or in ports along the New England coast, where they were not permitted to come ashore. Others were imprisoned in England or Nova Scotia or deported elsewhere: maritime France, the American Eastern Seaboard, and the French colonies in the Caribbean.[8] The Acadians who made their way to Louisiana by way of intermediary and temporary destinations did so over several waves of immigration beginning in 1764, during the Spanish colonial period. The newly arrived Acadians underwent a second diaspora in Louisiana due to the Spanish colonial government's practice of placing Acadian immigrants in various strategic locations along the Mississippi River in order to populate as much land as possible, thus forming a strategic buffer zone for the Spanish against potential British invasion.[9]

While the Acadians' influence on the language and culture of South Louisiana is emphasized more than other groups in our popular conception of "Cajun country," the total number of Acadians who immigrated to Louisiana pales in comparison to the significant number of enslaved individuals who were taken to Louisiana in the eighteenth and nineteenth centuries. At various moments in Louisiana's history, the enslaved population made up roughly half of the region's total inhabitants. Compared to other parts of North America affected by the slave trade, namely the British colonies, Louisiana bears some important differences.[10] Although some historians and ethnologists, such as Richard Dorson and Lawrence Levine, have emphasized the utter loss of regional African identities during the slave trade, more recent research forces us to reexamine the unique nature of the slave trade to Louisiana and consequently the ethnic makeup of Louisiana's slave communities. Throughout the eighteenth century, more slaves were taken to Louisiana from Senegambia than from Central Africa; this was the case under both Spanish and French colonial rule. The practice somewhat mitigated fragmentation of language and culture as a result of the slave trade in Louisiana.[11]

The lesser degree of linguistic and cultural fragmentation of the slave and former slave communities of French Louisiana, at least compared to their British counterparts, resulted in a greater level of cultural continuity in the New Orleans area as well as in the plantation country of present-day St. James, St. John, and Pointe Coupée Parishes. Similar to French immigration to Louisiana, forced immigration from Africa reached a high point in the 1720s. Roughly two-thirds of these enslaved Africans taken to Louisiana during the French colonial period originated from Senegambia, and a large majority of them were Bambara from present-day Mali. It has been suggested that this cultural cohesiveness facilitated the subsequent emergence of a significantly large free Black Creole society.[12]

Although much of the scholarship from the last few decades on the historically French-speaking region of Louisiana has largely focused on the Cajuns, the influence of Saint-Domingue on the language and culture of South Louisiana has recently come to light. In terms of sheer quantity of persons brought to Louisiana, the magnitude of the Saint-Domingue Revolution's impact on the population of Louisiana (particularly on New Orleans) and the slave trade at large far outweighs the roughly three thousand Acadians that made their way to Louisiana following the *Grand dérangement*. And yet the French Antillean migration in the Lower Mississippi Valley has been called "one of the most enduring lacunae in Louisiana historiography."[13] As a result of the insurrection in Saint-Domingue, over eleven thousand refugees came to Louisiana between 1792 and 1809.[14] But this group, especially the last contingents, was made up of a mix of refugees composed roughly of one-third White elites, another one-third free people of color, and the remaining one-third enslaved people who were the property of either of the other elite groups.[15] The number of refugees from Saint-Domingue was great enough to permanently alter the Creole identity of New Orleans, with the 1809 influx alone doubling the population of New Orleans within a three-month period.

Beyond simple population growth, the arrival of the Saint-Domingue refugees reinforced the presence of the French language in Louisiana and postponed the process of Anglo-Americanization by a couple of generations. It also reified the Latin-Caribbean triracial system (enslaved Blacks, free Whites, free people of color) that had begun to recede following the transfer of Louisiana to the United States in 1803 and the adoption of the American biracial system of White and Black.[16] The Creole identity remained distinct from a larger African American identity and served as a social buffer for Creoles of color during the oppression of the Jim Crow era.[17] Many Creoles spoke, or still speak, a language distinct from Louisiana French: Louisiana Creole, or *kouri-vini* (a glossonym derived from the distinctive verb forms of *go* and *come*), which has historically been seen pejoratively as a corrupt patois.[18] Association with slavery is also a significant source of some of the pejorative names for the Louisiana Creole language that even some of its speakers use to refer to it—*nègre, français nègre, n*—— *French, kouri-vini.*[19] However, as English became the dominant language in Louisiana in the nineteenth century, all varieties of French in Louisiana became symbols of difference and inferiority. French lost its status as a language of official matters, and in the early twentieth century, French was actively discouraged and stigmatized, particularly in schools.

The rural parishes of southeastern and southwestern Louisiana maintained the French language to a surprising degree given the total lack of resources to develop the language's status and even systematic efforts to erase its presence in the region. Although it is estimated that Louisiana counted as many as one million French speakers as late as 1970, the sharp decline in more recent years is largely due to the linguistic rupture caused by the interdiction of French as a language of instruction in public schools. More than the policy itself, the state constitution of 1921 (and to a somewhat lesser degree, the constitutions immediately preceding it) was only part of a nationwide trend of eradicating non-English languages in the United States. In this sense, Louisiana French met a similar fate as Polish in the Midwest, German in Texas, or Italian in New York during the same period. Despite this larger movement for an English-only nation captured by Teddy Roosevelt's warning against becoming a "polyglot boarding house," the 1921 state constitution is often pointed to as a defining moment at which the balance of power tipped in favor of the English language.[20] Thenceforth, French was rarely offered in schools and only then as a "foreign" language. More important on a social and psychological level, however, this new legislation crystallized an otherwise vague sentiment of disdain for "ethnic languages" in the United States and seemed to legitimize, for those in positions of power, widespread abuse of French- and Creole-speaking children in Louisiana. This practice of humiliating children likely had the most profoundly negative and long-lasting effect on French in Louisiana whose speakers were "eventually convinced that speaking French was a sign of cultural illegitimacy."[21]

Infraction of the English-only rule in Louisiana schools resulted in the physical abuse and humiliation of the schoolchildren in front of their classmates. Such cruel practices solidified Louisiana in a state of diglossia, with English acting as the language of prestige. French's perceived inferiority as well as social and political pressures resulted in a need to assimilate into Anglo-American culture. Not unlike the Louisiana Creole language's association with slavery, the French language took on pejorative connotations linked to humiliation and shame for an entire generation of Louisiana Francophones. The abuse was often severe and nearly systematic throughout the state; corporal punishment like kneeling on grains of rice for long periods of time, verbal abuse, and writing lines on the chalkboard were common well into the 1950s, making public education and learning to function in English a traumatic experience.[22] To this day, most elderly native speakers of Louisiana French can recall enduring or at least witnessing the cruel and humiliating practice implemented by teachers (in public and parochial schools) or principals. A combination of self-stigmatization, a willingness to prevent their own children from this painful experience, and aspirations of upward social mobility (and thus assimilation) contributed to an almost complete interruption of the French language's transmission to younger generations.[23]

CULTURAL TRAUMA AND COLLECTIVE EXPERIENCE

The Acadian deportation, slavery, and linguistic and cultural discrimination are but a few examples of cultural trauma experienced by French and Creole Louisiana's various founding immigrant groups. The flipside of the medallion of South Louisiana's self-indulgent facade seen in tourism or popular media is not at all visible to the casual observer; these painful collective experiences are deeply embedded in the aftermath of cultural trauma and its lingering social narratives. One of my objectives in analyzing this corpus of folktales is to demonstrate how real and collectively lived experiences like slavery and the Acadian deportation, combined with a sustained period of marginalization of the French- and Creole-speaking population of Louisiana, fundamentally affected these communities' worldviews and by extension the morals and humor of their oral tradition.[24]

It is important to note that cultural trauma is quite different from individual trauma, both in its symptoms and development. Cathy Caruth describes individual trauma as "a response, sometimes delayed, to an overwhelming event or events, which takes the form of repeated, intrusive hallucinations, dreams, thoughts or behaviors stemming from the event, along with numbing that may have begun during or after the experience, and possibly also increased arousal to (and avoidance of) stimuli recalling the event."[25] Individuals often repress memories of traumatic events and overcome personal trauma once they are able to surmount this natural psychological defense of denial and acknowledge past events.

Collectivities, on the other hand, address trauma in a remarkably different way. Groups create trauma narratives by constructing a "we" through narrative and coding, and this collective identity experiences and faces the threat to the group. Thus, rather than denial or repression, collectivities rely on the creation of characters, narratives, and symbolic construction and framing.[26] However, cultural trauma does not always follow an instance of social injustice or violence. In fact, whether or not a collective trauma narrative is created is largely unrelated to the gravity or atrocity of the event itself. Rather, "trauma scripts are performed in the theatres of everyday collective life," and transforming suffering into a culture narrative of trauma hinges on speech, public discourse, art, film, and storytelling of all kinds.[27] I am arguing here for a kind of indirect trauma discourse that, rather than explicitly recounting the experience, informs the moral attitude carried by the narrative. No one would deny the relationship between slavery and blues or gospel music, yet one would be hard pressed to find a blues song that dealt explicitly with the trauma of slavery. This same kind of oblique or metaphorical working-through of trauma is evident in African American folklore, most notably in the Tar Baby story adapted and popularized by Joel Chandler Harris, whereby a small creature overcomes a much stronger enemy using his intelligence.[28] In Louisiana, the discrimination and marginalization endured by generations are seldom made explicit in folktales, but I contend that this collective experience fundamentally changed the portrayal and perception of the fool (and trickster) figure in the oral tradition and popular imagination. The collective trauma inflicted on Louisiana's French-speaking schoolchildren beginning in the 1920s is also confronted in other arenas such as music, poetry, and theater.

LOCALIZATION AND PRISMING

The practice of storytelling necessitates a reciprocal relationship between the storyteller and the listener. Storytellers must convey a narrative while negotiating their own experiences and cultural references with those of their audience. It is in this way that tales whose structures might be part of a *canevas commun* take on meaningful specificity. What might be interpreted simply as "local color" often depends on subtle adaptations that may or may not be effectuated consciously by the storyteller. This process, which might result in substituting a dog for a wolf, a bayou for a river, or other elements that are primarily decorative or surface level, is what I refer to as "localization." While localization does not normally affect the narrative structure or the moral of a folktale, it is not to be discounted; its innovations are an integral part of the process of maintaining the relevance of a tale in the oral tradition.[29] Localization is responsible for the relatability of the tale and an affective proximity to its listener. This is not always accomplished by adaptation or substitution; often it is a matter of filtering out seemingly arbitrary details or obsolete cultural references.

Beyond localization in scenery, landscape, or cultural references, a subtler and more profound level of adaptation pertains to the morality of tales. Just as the storyteller wittingly or unwittingly adapts details and setting to conform to his or her audience, the social and moral framework and lessons to be gleaned adapt over time to their new and ever-changing contexts. It is no coincidence that the trickster figure of West African tales to be feared and avoided was transformed into the small but clever folklore hero throughout the American South. Likewise, Jean le Sot (Foolish John) who, in the folklore tradition of France, sometimes prevails despite his dim intellect and clumsiness à la the Three Stooges is only ridiculed and despised in the Louisiana variants. Such mutations in the overall moral message of tales seem apparent on the surface.

I call the process through which these moral shifts occur "prisming." Prisming is what enables a storyteller to portray a thief as hero or an otherwise "immoral" trickster as a model for survival, and it is this moral malleability that makes the folktale an effective indicator of cultural attitudes toward certain kinds of transgressions. As in real life, all people will generally not see human interactions in terms of black and white, good or bad, moral or immoral; they are subject to our many personal and cultural biases. These predispositions are in turn formed by our social realities and personal and collective experiences.

In physics, Snell's law describes how light slows down while passing from the air through the glass of a dispersive prism only to regain speed upon exiting the glass. Light entering the glass at an angle is bent as it travels through the prism to the opposite side of the glass, where it is bent once more before exiting the prism. A storyteller functions in a similar fashion, influenced by his or her own cultural experience and shaping the moral overtones of a given narrative accordingly. The effect of prisming on similar plot structures can result in characters being cast as heroic or diabolic. In my analyses, I distinguish between prisming (relating to morals and cultural values) and localization of smaller elements of a nonstructural order that recalibrate a tale to its context. Whereas localization applies to the substitution of objects or spaces to correspond within a given context, prisming manifests itself, through narration, as an overarching, moral coloring of the narrative. A folktale that praises the merits of hard work for which one will eventually be rewarded would not be applicable to someone who is enslaved. However, a story about a small but clever animal that manages to steal enough food from a larger animal in order to survive would have a deeper and more relevant significance. Despite striking degrees of continuity in terms of characters, narrative, and even insignificant motifs, such tales have discernibly gone through a major shift in morality through social change and a cultural *brassage*. It is precisely this kind of deep and, if not for detailed comparative analysis, imperceptible transformation that is my primary focus in this book.

Memorization gives way to variation in a tale's future performances and also brings to traditional narrative an element of timelessness. In other words, a tale may have lived for a very long time before being attested in a written text, thus becoming for a folklorist the oldest attested version of a tale but by no means the oldest version of the tale.[30] Oral literature depends on its realization through verbal delivery for its survival. While certain narrative structures might lend themselves to memorization better than others, there ultimately must be an opportunity for someone to pass on that narrative.[31] If a story becomes culturally irrelevant or unworthy of passing on, it will die.

If a narrative's survival can be ensured by the preservation of memory, the same cannot be said of its identical reproduction. In fact, preservation and stability are often opposed to one another in oral literature. In order to remain in living memory, a story must adapt to changing social and cultural realities. This phenomenon, for which we can borrow Paul Zumthor's term *false reiterability*, typically includes several major tendencies that take effect over many different iterations of a narrative. One is the modification of a story to fit the performance context (for example, duration, interaction with listeners, [in] formality). Another involves the leveling off of semantic difficulties, which may include archaic vocabulary, confusion caused by the disappearance of prior cultural context, or arbitrary proper names.[32] This instability is responsible for the many examples of substitutions, additions, or transpositions of characters and motifs.[33]

Prisming is not only cultural or generational; it is also individual and neurological. Even in the early twentieth century, studies on individuals conducted by Frederic Bartlett demonstrated syllables or narratives did not just become shorter or less defined over time; there were also additions and modifications influenced by the subject's own past experiences and attitudes. The human brain naturally attaches narrative to existing memories and experiences already stored in long-term memory, and this in turn helps to preserve (and distort) the narrative for a future retelling. In other words, the act of remembering is not as mechanical or straightforward as we might think. It is not, as Bartlett concludes, "the re-excitation of innumerable fixed, lifeless and fragmentary traces" but rather an imaginative reconstruction, "built out of the relation of our attitude towards a whole active mass of organized past reactions or experience."[34] Motivation or interest has also been proven to be an important factor in individuals' ability to retain and pass on narrative.[35] This should not be surprising as it is often the anecdotes and jokes that we find most compelling or humorous that we tend to tell and retell the most.

LANGUAGE, ETHNICITY, AND TERMINOLOGY

It is no secret that the precise definitions of ethnonyms like *Cajun* and *Creole* are the topic of much debate both among scholars and members of those respective communities. *Cajun* and *Creole,* like the labels of many cultural communities, can be difficult terms to define or justify as race or ethnicity. Much of the French-speaking population in southern Louisiana has been lumped together with those of Acadian descent under the euphemistic "Cajun" label. This includes groups who historically were somewhat hostile to the exiles' descendants.[36] Today areas such as Avoyelles and Evangeline Parishes that have historically been identified as "French" or "Creole" have experienced a shift in cultural identity and are now undeniably part of "Cajun country." While I by no means wish to offer my own definition or point of view on the subject here, it would be an error to not at least address this issue insofar as it has guided my choice of this book's title and the use of certain terminology used in my analyses. For example, one need not look further than the titles of the various collections of Louisiana folklore to observe a centralization of French Louisiana's many different ethnic communities around the Cajun label in the latter part of the twentieth century. The linguistic and cultural revival movement known as the "Cajun Renaissance" hastened this "Cajunization of

French Louisiana" and the forging of a regional identity based on the Cajun descriptor.[37]

Fortier, Claudel, Saucier, and others all wrote about and collected "Louisiana folk tales," "Creole folk tales" or "folk tales of French Louisiana." The first collection from the region referring to Cajun folktales was Barry Ancelet's *Cajun and Creole Folktales: The French Oral Tradition of South Louisiana*, published in 1994. I generally avoid the use of the word *Cajun* as an ethnonym in my writing here for three main reasons: there is a problem of anachronism as it was not the adjective used for the majority of the collections from which I draw; the term, for some, connotes a considerably narrower meaning that emphasizes Acadian descent, which is not necessarily the case of much of the corpus; and to the contrary of my second point, in popular parlance, the Cajun label has come to be more or less synonymous with all (White) Francophone culture in Louisiana.

If the Cajun ethnic label presents a certain number of difficulties in how it is perceived and defined, both in Louisiana and outside the region, a universal understanding of *Creole* remains even more elusive as it predates the Cajun identity and is highly dependent on temporal, geographical, and disciplinary contexts.[38] The term was in use as far back as the 1560s in the Spanish new-world settlements, although it was limited to differentiating between enslaved persons born in Africa and those born in the Americas.[39] The earliest understanding of the term in Louisiana shared this connotation of "native-born" or "of the New World" but without any reference to color. This nonracial use of *Creole* was common in the Caribbean islands and was likely transplanted from Saint-Domingue because of the significant influx of refugees that arrived in New Orleans during the Haitian Revolution.[40]

Throughout the eighteenth century, the term was applied to White and Black people in Louisiana and eventually came to denote descendants of those who were in Louisiana before the territory was purchased by the United States. This was also a strong cultural distinction that separated the predominantly Latin (Spanish, French, and Italian) and Catholic Creoles from the newly arrived Anglo-Saxon and Protestant Americans. During the post-Reconstruction era, when being perceived as racially mixed came at an extremely high social cost due to Jim Crow laws, many White Creoles sought to distance themselves from the racial ambiguity of this label.[41] In the Crescent City, this was an attempt to claim the term *Creole* for themselves and separate themselves from Creoles of color; to the west of the city—in the rural, agrarian parishes—this distinction aimed to distance them from the Acadian/Cajun neighbors who were often seen as lower-class, subsistence farmers.[42] For Creoles of color, the Creole identity offered various advantages, most notably a positive distinction from other Blacks within the binary racial system of the Anglo-Americans and a way to maintain their own social and cultural institutions.[43] In the twentieth century, as the Creole label was used more and more by people of color, most Whites shifted toward adopting the Cajun identity regardless of having little or no Acadian ancestry. Today the term *Creole* continues to be employed primarily by people of color, although a number of White Louisianians have retained (or reclaimed) the earlier, nonracial Creole identity.

In sum, the linguistic and cultural reality of South Louisiana presents significant complexities and challenges in describing the cultural artifacts. Who is Creole today? Who is Cajun? Is a folktale included from "French Louisiana" collected in the 1940s but also found in Ancelet's 1994 collection of "Cajun" folktales now Cajun? Surely, there are no simple answers to these questions, nor is it my objective to resolve such debates in this book. In the interest of practicality and clarity, I have opted to rely primarily on a linguistic description. That is to say, tales recounted in Louisiana French are described as "Louisiana French tales" and likewise for those told in "Louisiana Creole." While these two descriptors admittedly refer to idealized language varieties, this method presents considerably fewer methodological problems and anachronisms than relying on ethnonyms such as *Cajun* and *Creole* whose meanings have shifted over time and, even today, are subject to debate.[44] In instances in which more specific demographic or settlement information would be pertinent to a particular folktale or event, that information will be borne out in my analyses.

CHAPTER 1

Lapin and Other Animal Tricksters

Animal tales are perhaps the most prevalent in the folklore repertoires of many cultures. From the fables of La Fontaine to Brer Rabbit, animal tales are probably first to come to mind when the average person thinks of "folktales" today, and it is not difficult to understand their appeal. The most remarkable quality of animal characters is perhaps their "neutrality" and adaptability: they are neither Black nor White; the language they speak in the story is arbitrary; and they can be slyly used to embody (and mock) those in power without explicitly naming them. This slyness is as present in *Le Roman de Renart* as it is in the slave narratives of the American South. The convenient malleability of animal tales is also paired with a capacity for extraordinary precision and specificity. In other words, a region's animals (like its flora, languages, and customs) are not found just anywhere. A creature regarded as the creator of the world in one folk tradition might be insignificant or even absent in another tradition.

As humans, we intuitively attribute certain characteristics to specific animals, anthropomorphizing them in a way that reflects our cultural reality. This practice has even permeated our everyday expressions. One can be "sly as a fox" or "meek as a lamb" and so forth. But again, these interpretations come with a high degree of cultural specificity. Whereas an American might be familiar with the phrase "wise as an owl," a Frenchman would more readily recognize the comparison "curieux comme une chouette" (curious as an owl).

In French- and Creole-speaking Louisiana, animal tales, or *contes d'animaux,* are the result of a mélange of European, Native American, and African traditions. At the same time, they are undeniably rooted in the unique social reality of Louisiana. For the most part, the cast of characters in the animal tales of Louisiana represents a confluence of French and African traditions.[1]

In addition to these two major influences, there are many others, including that of the Spanish as evidenced in the rich folklore of the Isleño communities of St. Bernard Parish. A quick look at a sampling of French and Creole folktales of Louisiana will show that while some characters bear remarkable resemblance to the French tradition (the fox, swan, and rabbit), African and Caribbean folklore influences are equally strong, both with regard to the animals (the elephant, hyena, and tiger) and the character traits associated with them. What is not to be understated, however, is how deeply rooted in the reality of Louisiana these tales are. In fact, most of the animals found in this repertoire—turtles, rabbits, frogs, and deer—are easily found in the bayous and prairies of South Louisiana.

From the very earliest written collection of Louisiana Creole folktales in Alcée Fortier's *Louisiana Folk-Tales* (1895) to collections of contemporary folklorists such as Barry Ancelet, it is clear that animal tales make up one of the largest categories of folktales in the region. The variety of animals is equally notable. But despite this formidable cast of animal characters, two characters have made their way to the forefront: Bouki and Lapin. This dupe-and-trickster duo can be found in Fortier's work and throughout the major folklore collections. The two have even been the subject of much more recent works, such as Susan Spillman's *Compère Lapin voyageur* (2013) and other children's books. Who can say why these two characters have gained such popularity? Perhaps it is the plethora of fieldwork that introduced storytellers like Enola Matthews to a wider audience. Perhaps it is the sheer number of Bouki and Lapin stories that seem to be equally appealing to white Cajuns as they are to Creoles of color. Or perhaps it is their accessibility and similarity to the ever-popular Brer Rabbit stories of J. C. Harris's fictional orator Uncle Remus. Whatever the reason may be, today Bouki and Lapin are emblematic of Louisiana's folklore and are known well beyond the relatively limited circle of folklorists and storytellers.

Scholars of African American folklore such as Richard Dorson and Lawrence Levine have rightfully warned of the pitfalls of placing too much emphasis on African origins, as this repertoire is primarily an American phenomenon. While it is certainly not my intention here to trace uninterrupted transmissions between American and African folktales or identify definitive analogues or their supposed origins, the historical and cultural connections between Louisiana and West Africa are undeniable. There can be no doubt concerning the strong African influence of the Bouki and Lapin stories in Louisiana. The West African roots of much of the enslaved population of Louisiana and the subsequent Afro-Creole society as well as similarities within the characterization of the folktales confirm this Louisiana–West African connection. One of the most salient and indisputable connections to West Africa is the very name of Bouki, the Wolof word for "hyena." In addition to Bouki's analogous casting as the dupe to the clever rabbit in West African and Louisiana Creole tales, the fact that the Wolof word for hyena has persisted in Louisiana is surprising, as very few in Louisiana seem to be aware of the name's original meaning. And while the two characters often appear together in tales, this is not always the case. Lapin is without a doubt an animal trickster. As a trickster figure, Lapin finds himself in a pantheon of complex characters with examples ranging from Greek mythology to Native American folktales.[2] The question becomes, then, what can the representation of the trickster in the folklore of a certain region tell us about that culture?

Regardless of the culture or time period in question, there are a number of overarching traits present in nearly all trickster figures. Tricksters are not simply deceitful; they defy social norms, mock authority figures, disrupt social order, and upset the "normal" order of things. Beyond these common traits, the trickster can display more specific traits (overt or ambiguous sexuality, an affinity for disguise, and so forth). In the case of Lapin or other animal tricksters of Louisiana folklore, there is no single legend or story cycle associated with him, as is the case of African characters such as Anansi, Eshu, Legba, and Ogo-Yurugu.[3]

The linguistic origin of the Bouki character makes clear the West African origins of the hyena and hare tales; however, the genre's exact passage into Louisiana's oral tradition cannot be known for sure. This is because similar tales are found elsewhere in the Caribbean, namely in modern-day Haiti. Furthermore, the traits of Bouki and Lapin are essentially analogous to those of *le loup et le renard* (the wolf and the fox) in the French tradition. No early written evidence exists of the name Leuk/Lëk (Wolof for "rabbit") in Louisiana, although it certainly persists in West African folklore today. Curiously, the character has retained its animal identity in Louisiana folklore, as his French appellation of Lapin indicates. Today in Haiti, the tales of *Bouki ak*

Malis (Bouki and Malice) are still well known among children. As is the case in Louisiana, the original meaning of *bouki* is mostly unknown, even among Haitians who are very familiar with the tales, suggesting that the association with its Wolof origin was lost before the character's arrival in Louisiana. In Haiti, the animality of the rabbit has also been either lost or morphed in favor of a personification of the hare's deceitful nature. In place of Lapin or Lëk, Bouki's counterpart is known simply as "Malice." It is logical that the Wolof term *bouki* would have been preserved in Louisiana folktales, as opposed to translating it to English or French, given the absence of hyenas in Louisiana. As an abstract dupe-like character, *bouki* became a somewhat arbitrary name for a stock folklore figure.[4] Unfortunately, without any attestation of the tales in Louisiana before the Saint-Domingue Revolution, it is impossible to say with any certainty whether the character was imported directly from the West African tradition or by way of Saint-Domingue. A third and perhaps more likely explanation would be that the influx of Saint-Domingue refugees into Louisiana reinforced a recent but already present repertoire of Bouki and Lapin tales from the transatlantic slave trade.

The earliest examples of Creole folktales in Louisiana were recorded after the end of the Civil War, as is the case for Black folklore in general in the United States.[5] Alcée Fortier, a member of the White Creole upper class of New Orleans, was a linguist and professor of French at Tulane University when he published *Louisiana Folk-Tales* in 1895. Fortier's position with the Black Creole community is complicated, to say the least. In fact, it is difficult to determine his exact feelings toward the Creole language as he marvels in a condescending tone at "how the ignorant African slave transformed his master's language into a speech concise and simple, and at the same time soft and musical," but he also argues that Louisiana Creole was "not a corruption of French" but rather "a real idiom with a morphology and grammar of its own."[6] To add to the ambivalence of Fortier's writings, he asserts that some of the tales are "without doubt, of African origin" but also admits that he has made little or no attempt at cataloging or comparing these tales to those found elsewhere in other oral traditions.[7]

The African influence and didactic nature of the tales in Fortier's collection are particularly salient in the animal tales. More significant than mere vestiges of African tradition, animal tales remained popular and socially relevant in the New World for a number of reasons, coexisting and often melding with their counterparts of European and Native American origin. Animals in these folktales, while perfectly recognizable as such, are also thoroughly anthropomorphized. In Louisiana Creole folklore, as in most oral traditions, animals typically have assigned characteristics (cleverness, strength, or stupidity) or roles (the trickster, the dupe, or the glutton), making the morals not only easy to understand but also universal enough to transpose or mix with the animals and repertoires of other communities.

For the Black Creoles of Louisiana, animal tales had several uses, both during and after the period of slavery. The lack of proper names, or even human beings, made it easier to implicitly criticize the power structure without the knowledge of outsiders. Because animal characters are based so heavily on paradigms, animal tales remain the most accessible and relatable. The casting of animals as the primary characters, especially those characters who upset social order, allowed animal tales to appear innocuous to outsiders or to those in power who may otherwise try to censor or outlaw stories critical of the status quo. The narrative structure and characterization of many animal tales are of African origin, at least on a fundamental level, although certain changes in the narration or interpretation of these tales would have occurred in their transition into what one might call a "slave narrative."[8]

One illustration of this phenomenon, presumably of African origin, that lends itself easily to interpretation as a slave narrative is "Chien avec tigue" (The Dog and the Tiger) from Fortier's collection.[9] Not surprisingly, the tiger's principal trait is normally that of physical strength. The dog is more seldom seen in the folktales of Louisiana and generally does not exhibit the qualities of cleverness or trickery. One day the dog purchases one hundred hens and one rooster, while the tiger buys one hundred roosters and one hen. It is not long before the dog has a basketful of eggs from his chicken house every evening, while the tiger only finds one every so often. Instead of realizing his own foolish error, the tiger grows angry with the dog: "Tigue dit chien volé li, et li taché li, li metté li dans in brouette et li parti pour vende li" (The tiger accused the dog of robbing him, and, tying him up, he put him in a wheelbarrow and took him along to sell him).[10] On the road, the tiger meets a deer and asks him if he is correct in selling the dog. The deer argues with the tiger, claiming that he has no right to sell another animal, and the tiger immediately becomes enraged and kills the deer. Next the tiger comes across a lion, an animal typically associated with brute strength, who also states that the tiger is wrong to sell the captive dog. The tiger replies, "Vous parlé comme ça pasqué vous connin vous plis fort qué moin" (You speak that way because you know that you are stronger than I).[11] The tiger continues on his way to sell the dog until he makes the mistake of leaving his wheelbarrow unguarded. Soon thereafter, a few hunters pass by and ask the dog what he is doing there. After the dog relates his story to the hunters, they pursue the tiger (presumably killing him), and the dog is never bothered again.

When interpreted as a slave narrative, the moral of the tale is clearly one of impending liberation: "Tigue la té pair comme djabe, et dépi temps la chien jamin pair béte sauvage" (The tiger was terribly frightened, and from that time dogs have never been afraid of wild beasts).[12] Although Fortier makes no mention of any possible symbolism or allusion to slavery, from a present-day perspective, such analogies seem difficult to ignore. Simply in the casting of the dog as the victimized protagonist, there is an implication of domestication or servitude. Despite his logical choice to purchase more hens than roosters, the dog, much like the slave, is not compensated for his labor. He then faces the terrible prospect of being sold by the tiger, who is less intelligent but physically stronger. One can imagine that the deer and the lion might represent other factions opposed to slavery during the rise of the abolitionist movement leading up to the Civil War.[13] As in many tales considered to be slave narratives, there is a marked absence of physical violence committed by the characterized slave. Patience and, perhaps to an even greater extent, cleverness consistently outweigh physical strength.

Another tale from Fortier's collection with similar undertones evoking slavery, featuring a clever tortoise that offers such an example. is "Tortie" (The Tortoise), recounted to Fortier by a storyteller noted only as "Julia, 7 Prytania Street, New Orleans."[14] In this tale, a *michié* (*monsieur*, or "gentleman") finds a tortoise on the banks of a bayou one day and proceeds to invite some of his friends to dinner. The gentleman's son, in his father's absence, goes to the cage where his father put him. The tortoise begins to whistle to the astonishment of the boy, who says, "Comme to sifflé bien!" (How well you whistle!).[15] The tortoise assures the boy that he could whistle even better if the cage were open. After proving his point with the second round of whistling, the tortoise convinces the boy that if he were to set him on the floor, he could dance and sing. Finally, the boy, marveling at the tortoise's ability to dance and sing, is persuaded to set him back on the banks of the bayou so that he can continue to impress the boy. The duped child then watches the tortoise disappear into the water. It is the tortoise that pokes his head above the water to deliver the first moral of the short tale: "Apprende pas fié moune to pas connin" (Learn not to trust, hereafter, people whom you do not know.)[16]

Structurally, the tale offers a mirror image of the Aarne-Thompson-Uther (ATU) tale type 6, *Animal Captor Persuaded to Talk,* whereby a human protagonist tricks his animal captor into opening his mouth by speaking, allowing the trapped human a chance to escape.[17] The moral, which appears at the very end of the first and penultimate paragraph of the tale, is similar in form and nature to others found in the folklore of Africa, where animal tales are told not only for entertainment but also especially for didactic purposes. The use of animal tales from the African oral tradition to convey moral teachings to children continues in the New World even though some animals cast in the stories have been adapted to the geography of the American South. Similarly, Isidore Okpewho observes that in many traditional African cultures, it is precisely through songs, narratives, proverbs, and riddles that young members of society "absorb the ideas that will guide them through life and the older ones are constantly reminded of the rules and ideals that must be kept alive for the benefit of those coming behind them."[18]

It is ironic that the moral of distrusting strangers in this Black Creole tale is directed to the young White child. Perhaps the tale would have been presented as such to a White audience, in a situation like Fortier describes: "It is a strange fact that the old negroes do not like to relate those tales with which they enchanted their little masters before the war."[19] What is more intriguing than the moral itself is the manner in which it is woven into a larger narrative with quite a different message, becoming apparent at the story's end. The first half of the tale easily lends itself to a metaphor wherein the soon-to-be slave is taken from his or her place of origin (the bayou), here representing Africa. Removed from his or her home and placed in a foreign land, the slave is held captive by the oppressive European colonial system, much like the tortoise in its cage on a figurative level. There are a number of non-African elements of localization such as the bayou, the upper-class household structure of the gentleman, the cook, and the silverware. In "Tortie," being trapped in a cage on the white man's estate serves as a clear analogy for slavery.

If the first half of the tale provides us with a representation of slavery, the second half leaves itself open to the audience's interpretation. It cannot be known if the second part is tacked on from another tale from the African tradition or if the entirety has been adapted to the Louisiana experience. This sort of sequencing in which two different tales about the same animal are juxtaposed and made to function as a single narrative is common in Creole tales. The addendum offers a glimpse of what happened after the tortoise's escape.

For fear of his father, the boy places a stone in the cage where the turtle had been. Thinking it was the tortoise, the cook began to cook the stone and was astonished to see that it remained hard for so long. The master then ordered the cook to put it upon the table where he attempted to cut it. The storyteller recounts the narrative's curious ending: "He took the carving-knife, in vain. He took the hatchet, in vain. He took the axe, he broke the dishes, the table, but the tortoise remained intact. He then saw it was a stone, and to this day he has not understood how his tortoise was changed into a stone."[20]

There is an inherent structural symmetry within the narrative. Intensification and repetition are tools for the storyteller to give balance and interest to the content. The three physical spaces representing the path to freedom (the cage, the floor, and the bayou) are mirrored in the second part by the three tools used by the master in his attempt to break the stone (knife, hatchet, ax). The master does not realize that the turtle (or slave) is missing until it affects his own well-being, as symbolized by the dishes and the dinner table. As in many animal tales from the African tradition, food (as sustenance) can be equated with physical survival and thus plays an important role in the Black Creole trickster tales.

In addition to what we might consider a commentary on the detriment to plantocracy following the slave's escape, the second half of the tale focuses more squarely on the condition of the enslaved. The tortoise's metamorphosis into stone, at least in the eyes of his former master, at the end is significant because he is fortified and transformed, physically and metaphorically, by his flight to freedom or a Maroon space. By the same token, the tortoise's petrification renders him useless to the master in that he is no longer the source of physical nourishment.

Finally, it is interesting to note that in this instance the trickster is represented by the tortoise and not the rabbit or fox (which would be typical of the African or European tradition, respectively), as is so common in other animal tales. The tortoise outsmarts the boy through cunning and by biding his time. Like in so many Louisiana tales, physical strengths are subverted here. Unlike the speed of the rabbit or the brute strength and size of the elephant, patience and cleverness enable the tortoise to gain his freedom.

"Tortie" bears a striking resemblance to a passage in Alfred Mercier's 1881 novel *L'Habitation Saint-Ybars*. In the novel, Mamrie, the most important domestic slave on the plantation and very much a maternal figure to the young master Démon (Édmond), tries to impress upon the boy the sadness that must be felt by the larks he has captured in a small cage. Although Mamrie does not explicitly mention slavery, the reader nonetheless understands the parallel between captive animals and enslaved humans. The boy eventually releases the larks out of compassion, not for having been deceived, as in "Tortie."[21]

Many such metaphors for slavery can be found in the folktales of the South. The folktale's capacity for conveying secret information among slave communities and Maroon spaces has been observed by numerous historians. Tales served as an important communication tool for the enslaved, who used them to rehearse tactics, poke fun at their masters, and teach their children the strategies they would need later on for survival.[22] In this sense, such a tale could have served as a hidden message for potential escapees to wait until plans to revolt were finalized.

In "Tortie," the tortoise plays the role of trickster, reminiscent of the trickster Ajapa in the Yoruba culture of West Africa. More frequently, however, the rabbit or hare is cast in this role in Louisiana's oral tradition. The trickster figure, found almost universally in folklore, takes on a special significance in the African American and Black Creole oral traditions of Louisiana. As a result of slavery, oppressed slave communities found in the trickster figure not only a form of amusement but also a means by which they could be victorious through cunning and cleverness, despite a lack of physical or political power. The trickster also filled a void in the cultural and moral gap between Africa and White-controlled plantation society. In a sense, the trickster enabled enslaved individuals to justify their need to lie or steal while keeping these actions separate from their conventional model of morality. This is not to imply that they created a counter-morality but rather that in their interactions with Whites their moral values could necessarily be absent if it were a question of survival.[23] Although the perception and the interpretation of the trickster figure may have taken on different connotations as a result of the slavery experience, the trickster genre was already "perhaps the most common type of tale in the African repertoire."[24]

Trickster figures often possess their own "cycles" of tales and appear in the myths and folktales of many traditional societies, sometimes as a god but more frequently as an animal.[25] African tricksters border on the mythological and are not dissimilar to certain Native American traditions such as the Winnebago Hare Cycle.[26] In contrast to these loftier representations, the typical trickster of French and Creole Louisiana exhibits no godlike characteristics and relies solely on his wit to trump his opponent. In this way, he more closely resembles the *renard*, or fox, of the French tradition.

While I have argued against the conflation of the Louisiana Creole and other Anglophone African American folklore traditions of the American South, there are nevertheless many similarities with the African American folktales collected by or commented on by Alan Dundes, Richard Dorson, Lawrence Levine, and others. One particularly salient commonality is the prevalence of the trickster figure: "Despite all of the changes that took place, there persisted the mechanism so well developed throughout most of Africa, by means of which psychic relief from arbitrary authority could be secured, symbolic assaults upon the powerful could be waged, and important lessons about authority relationships could be imparted. Afro-Americans in the United States were to make extended use of this mechanism throughout their years of servitude."[27]

In practically all of the trickster tales analyzed in this chapter, we see evidence of a typically African patterning of trickster tales, which can be described as a progression from *contract* (friendship or family) to a *deception*. The violation of the contract represents the destruction of the social bond and all of its implications. This formula can be extrapolated in such a fashion that the narrative structure of the trickster tale is likely a reflection of the cultural trauma caused by slavery. In other words, the state of contract is broken or violated through the slave trade, and the trickster serves as a reaction to the dissolution of the human and social bond, which does not necessarily imply a "counter-morality" but rather a means of survival that is made possible through adeptness and social dexterity.

Given the significant West African influence on the Creole population of Louisiana of the period, particularly from the Senegambian region, an analysis of certain key motifs is warranted. Dembo Fanta Bojang and Sukai Mbye Bojang present a trickster tale entitled "Hare Gets Hyena and Elephant to Work on His Farm" in the second volume of *Folk Tales and Fables from the Gambia*.[28] Similar to the two preceding Louisiana Creole tales from Fortier's collection, the motif of food and specifically the cultivation of crops plays a large role in the story. In both of these contexts, food represents not only strength or power but also the continued survival of the characters.

The story begins with the hyena and the hare talking about a plot of land that the hare has acquired in the Sare Alpha region. As is customary in the Louisiana variants of Bouki and Lapin, the characters are first introduced as "two friends."[29] The rapport between the two animals and their human-like traits are further underscored by their designation as *Maube*. The word, *maubeh* is a derivation of the Fula *mawbe* or *maodo,* meaning "wiseman" or "elder."[30] In fact, the word is still used today among the Fulani to refer to the chief elders or council.[31] The use of such a title is analogous to that of *compère* used in Louisiana Creole animal tales, most frequently used to refer to Compère Bouki and Compère Lapin. I argue that the use of a humanizing term like *compère* represents both a holdover from the African tradition as well as an adaptation to the sociocultural context of Louisiana. Both *compère* and *maubeh* elevate the status of the animal characters and impart a human quality to their respective roles of dupe and trickster in the narrative. Such titles also testify to a common vision of animal tales as didactic tools among African and Creole communities. The Old World, African understanding and practicality of animal tales and the need to give their characters human titles obviously persisted and is apparent not only in the Louisiana Creole tales but also in the African American tradition of the English-speaking colonies. This is more widely known in the form of "Brer" (Brother) Rabbit, popularized by the *Uncle Remus* tales of Joel Chandler Harris. This story even specifies the characters' motivation for starting their own farm: "The two would spend hours talking a lot with admiration about the ways of life of human beings. They marveled at the system of government and their various means of earning a living."[32] The storytellers' explicit connection between the animal and human kingdom is telling of the African understanding of the universe and underlines the didactic utility of the tale.

The two animals decide that millet would be the best yield for the first crop and decide to clear the land as soon as possible in light of the oncoming monsoons. As in many West African and Louisiana tales that feature the hyena and hare duo, the two animals set off more or less on equal footing. However, the hare is determined to see his crops sown and harvested without doing any of the work himself. He decides to enlist the help of the elephant. It is worth noting that the presence of other animals in tales that one could otherwise simply classify as "Hyena and Hare" tales is not uncommon in West African tales nor in the early Black Creole tales collected by Alcée Fortier. However, the hyena and hare appear much more exclusively in later collections, especially among White Creole or Cajun communities. In this tale from the Gambia region, the elephant's minor role in the genre is made evident in the manner in which the teller refers to him simply as "Elephant," without such a distinction as Compère or another title.

As one might expect, the hare bests his fellow animals, not by force but by his cunning and wit. In this tale, the hare dupes both the elephant and the hyena into working the plot of land in exchange for a share of the harvest. The hare first visits the elephant, offering to work the morning shift if the elephant will work during the afternoon. Against the advice of his wife, the elephant agrees, without even settling the details of their business arrangement. The hare then proceeds to visit the hyena, offering to work during the afternoon if he will take the morning shift. After three days' time, the land is completely cleared, and the hare has never touched a hoe. Just before finishing the clearing, Maubeh Hare provides the elephant and Maubeh Hyena millet seeds for sowing, doing so separately as "they were both ignorant of each other's toil in the farm although they innocently competed over performance on their daily output in the farm."[33]

After the plentiful rains, it is not long before the millet is ready to be harvested, and Maubeh Hare is determined to have his gullible friends reap the crop for him. The hare recounts to the elephant a false rumor of Maubeh Hyena planning to steal their crop during the night. The hare then tells a similar falsehood to Maubeh Hyena about Elephant's scheme to raid the millet the same evening. Thus, the elephant and hyena catch each other at what they believe to be theft. Although Maubeh Hyena escapes, to be deceived another time by the hare, Elephant is caught in a trap set by the hare and is left hanging from a tree. The unfortunate Elephant eventually falls from the tree and dies.

The motif of theft or at least trickery resulting in the acquisition of food by the trickster figure seems to be a common theme in the oral traditions of West Africa and French and Creole Louisiana. However, the death of the dupe—most often the hyena, elephant, or monkey—is generally a trait found only in the African tradition, rarely occurring in the Louisiana corpus. The final and often morbid endings of many African animal tales are part of the realism that pervades many folktales. The dupe's fate also underscores the very different moral of such African tales. Whereas the Louisiana Creole tales celebrate the cleverness of the trickster, the otherwise similar African tales warn of the dangers of the trickster, who is to be avoided at all costs.

Motifs involving crop theft are by no means unique to African or Louisiana oral traditions. Motifs like K171.1 *Deceptive crop division: above the ground, below the ground* can be found in *Le Roman de Renart,* and Louisiana French and Creole versions of such tales seem to be quite common. Ancelet's *Cajun and Creole Folktales* (1994) includes a typical Louisiana variant of ATU 9B *In the Division of the Crop the Fox Takes the Corn* entitled "En haut la terre ou en bas la terre," told by Martin Latiolais of Catahoula, Louisiana.[34] This variant features Bouki and Lapin, who are surveying their crop of potatoes. Similar to the hyena and hare tales in the Bojang collection, the storyteller begins the tale by mentioning the "friendly" relationship between the characters, alluding to the regularity of their visits with each other: "Then, another time (they were associates, you see) they made a crop. So, the first year, they planted potatoes. Oh, it was beautiful to see those potato vines."[35] The once peaceful relationship between Bouki and Lapin, or Hyena and Hare, is consistently iterated in both Louisiana and African traditions. This trait harks back to an older African convention whereby the storyteller reminds the audience at the start of the narrative that everyone and everything in nature was in harmony. The peaceful state before the trickster's arrival is often captured in a short opening line that storytellers can use to create a dramatic contrast with the impending chaos caused by the trickster.[36]

Deciding how to divide the crop, Lapin gives Bouki his choice of whether he would rather have what was above the earth or below, expecting Bouki to foolishly be tempted by the beautiful sweet potato vines, and he was. Here Lapin gives Bouki the illusion of being in control while anticipating his stupidity, as in motif J1731.9.1 *Ignorance of which part of plant is the fruit (crop)*. While Lapin enjoys the potatoes throughout the year, Bouki is stuck with the useless flowers and vines of the potato plants and nearly starves. The following year, the two plant a crop of corn. Determined not to be outsmarted once again, Bouki insists on taking his share of the harvest from below the ground, saying, "You won't fool me this year. I'll take what's below the ground."[37] Of course, Lapin happily obliges, enjoying his plentiful harvest of corn, while Bouki is once again left with nothing.[38]

Calvin Claudel offers an almost identical variant of ATU 9B titled "The Farm," also featuring Bouki, here spelled Bouqui, and Lapin in his collection *Fools and Rascals*. Although the body of the tale is the same, Claudel's informant adds, "During the winter Bouqui went to ask Lapin for something to eat. Lapin refused him. Bouqui almost died from hunger that year, and he decided not to work on shares with comrade Lapin anymore."[39] Despite such seemingly definite endings, these tales constitute an implicit cycle, and therefore the characters are continually reappearing in subsequent variants.

In another tale from the Senegambia found in the Bojang collection, "The Hyena and the Hare," the hare repeatedly outwits the hyena.[40] The narrator of this particular tale casts the two animals as brothers-in-law. Like Fortier's "Tortie," this tale could be interpreted as two separate narratives fused together. The story begins when the hyena and the hare leave their village Sutura early in the morning in order to visit their in-laws. Each animal carries with him a bag of rice meant as gifts for the family. Along the way, the hyena feels the need to relieve himself and wishes to do so with some privacy, so he walks away from the path. The hare deceitfully assures the hyena that he is still visible from the path and encourages him to walk farther and farther away. While the hyena is at a distance and out of sight, the hare plays his first trick on the hyena. Noticing that the hyena's bag contains clean and well-sieved rice and that his own rice still contains husks and was not clean, the hare decides to switch out the rice from the two bags, leaving the hyena with the lower-quality rice. "This will serve him right. If he thinks he's smart in his effort to win over our in-laws, he's making a big mistake. [. . .] I intend to be, and must be, the favorite son-in-law."[41] As this tale attests, although hyena is cast as the typical dupe of the tale, he is sometimes the more logical and prepared of the two characters.

Upon arriving at the home of the father-in-law Pa Juma, hyena is shocked at how poor his rice looks since he has last seen it. Pa Juma assures both hyena and hare that he loves them equally, but just before their departure, he gifts the hare with a large bull and gives to hyena only a meager goat. Halfway along their journey home, the hyena becomes hungry and suggests to the hare that they kill and eat the goat and the bull. The hare replies, "Perhaps you didn't notice how much I ate during lunch. You know when it comes to food, I have my fill no matter who is present. I'm not hungry. [. . .] If you want you can kill your goat and eat it."[42] Here the gluttony displayed by the hare earlier at his father-in-law's resembles the hyena character of Louisiana tales like "Dans la grosserie," and "Dézéf zozo," which I will describe later. In this African tale, hare is devoid of any redeeming qualities, while hyena is duped despite his good moral judgment.

While the hyena is hardly even full after eating his skinny goat, the hare parades his bull into the village, "determined to show everybody in a quiet way that his in-laws held him in higher esteem than the hyena that came home with nothing."[43] To further humiliate the hyena, the hare sent meat to all of the villagers, and since the hyena had no food left over from the father-in-law's gift, his own family had nothing but the bones sent to them by the hare. Not unlike other hyena and hare tales of Africa and Louisiana, this tale includes a second part, which takes place five months later, that could very well be considered a separate tale altogether or even a variation on the first, as it also takes place at the father-in-law's home.

After a morning of working on the farm and lunch, the father-in-law asks the hyena and hare to retrieve some honey from a large beehive "in a big tree separating this village from Tambakoto."[44] The location of the tree is evocative of the liminal nature often associated with the trickster figure, as he is often portrayed as being at the border between friend and foe, part of society and yet marginalized.[45] The hare offers to retrieve the honey for the hyena, saying: "I know you are very weak with sweet food. [. . .] We'll be very embarrassed if we don't take back any."[46] Much in the same way that Lapin gives Bouki first choice of the two crop divisions in two Louisiana variants of ATU 9B, here, too, the hare lets the hyena set his own trap.

When the two arrive at the beehive, the hare decides to go first, putting his head in the hole, staying there for ten minutes while he licks up the honey. The hyena grows impatient during this time, and when the hare finally takes his head out of the tree, the hyena eagerly pushes his large head into the hole and is nearly unable to remove his head at all. The narrator states that "as he pulled with force, the top skin of his head came off and remained on the bark of the tree trunk."[47] Although the hyena does not die in the tree, the scenario is otherwise identical to motif K.1020.1 found in type ATU 41 *The Wolf Overeats in the Cellar,* found in another variant from Claudel's collection seen later.

Pa Juma, unsatisfied with the pitiful amount of honey that he received, is obliged to return to the tree himself to get enough honey for his family. Upon his arrival at the tree, he is amused to find the hyena's scalp stuck near the opening of the hole and carefully carves it out with his knife and returns to the farm. Pa Juma then instructs his wife to cook the skin separately with palm oil, and that night, he and the hare eat only the rice and porridge, while the hyena feasts on everything, including his own skin. Unaware of what he is really eating, the hyena asks: "Where did you get the meat? It tastes very nice and my mother-in-law is a very good cook. I really envy you."[48] When the hyena is informed that he is eating his own skin, he tries to regurgitate it but to no avail. The motif of eating one's own flesh, identified as G60 *Human flesh eaten unwittingly,* is found elsewhere in the oral tradition in North America, Asia, Africa, and Europe.

The meaning of such a motif in this tale could be found in its relationship to the motif K1856.1 *Human flesh substituted for eaten (lost) meat.* The hyena's ingestion of his own skin is meant to serve as a punishment for his eating honey that was not his to consume. In this sense, he compensates for his debt to society incurred by eating the taboo honey from the tree. Once again, the role of food is one of utmost importance. Here not only is food a representation of one's survival but also, by extension, it is a sort of social currency that, once borrowed or stolen, must be repaid. Pa Juma, true to his role as the village elder, acts as the authoritative figure fit to administer hyena's punishment and restore balance to the social order. On a structural level, the hyena eating his own flesh can be viewed as an intensification of what has already taken place in the narrative. Each time that the hyena is deceived, it is through his own fault or negligence, first by leaving his bag of rice in the hare's keeping, second by allowing the hare to enter the tree first, and third by being the only one at the table to serve himself his own skin.

This tale seems to be mostly didactic in nature against greed, as the hyena is consumed, both figuratively and literally, by his own gluttony. However, a closer reading reveals that the hare is just as much or even more of a glutton than the hyena. Perhaps the real cultural lesson here is one of the values of intelligence and social comportment. In other words, the hare is successful not because he manages to avoid overeating, which is not the case at any rate, but because he possesses the social finesse to remain in good standing with the villagers as well as his own father-in-law. The tale also suggests a natural order of things, implying that the hare will always outwit the hyena.

It would appear that one of the most striking differences between African and Louisiana animal tales is the manner in which African tales include not only a greater variety of animal characters but also the implication of a greater society (villages, families, tribal origins). Obviously, the relation between the individual and the community, as well as many other societal structures, was upended by the violence of slavery. Koffi Konan, a native of the Ivory Coast, speaks of the African philosophy of the union between man and nature and the polyvalent nature of the folktale in African society: "Indeed, the folktale is the reflection of society as a whole. It is the life of our people, of our traditional civilization with our social structure, its political and economic life, its cultural system. The folktale offers us a society in which man and beast live in symbiosis. The folktale makes us understand the people's civilization, more specifically, its culture, that is to say a heritage of customs, of knowledge slowly attained over the course of centuries, and beliefs."[49] On the other hand, Bouki and Lapin are often the only characters in many of the tales in which they appear in the Louisiana repertoire, and animal tales seem to exist in a spatial and temporal frame removed and independent from the real world. This difference between the two traditions suggests a decline in the didactic need for folktales in the New World, with a more institutionalized system of education as well as a greater distance with the source culture of Africa.[50]

In "Compair Bouki, Compair Lapin et dézef zozo" (Bouki, Lapin, and the Bird's Eggs) from Fortier's collection, we see a relatively common beginning in both Louisiana and West African tales, whereby Bouki (the hyena) is hungry and asks Lapin (the hare) to show him where he finds his food. This tale also starts with an abbreviated version of the description of the Edenic natural state present in most African trickster tales: "Compair Bouki and Compair Lapin were neighbors."[51] What is curious in this tale is that Bouki exclaims to his neighbor consecutively his extreme hunger and his terrible toothache. Admiring his kettle of food on the fire, Bouki is keenly intent on finding out what Lapin is preparing for dinner and repeats his two ailments: "What smells so good in that kettle, Compair Lapin? Oh! what a toothache I have!"[52] From the very beginning of the tale, Bouki demonstrates the paradoxical nature of his character that we find to be so prevalent elsewhere in the West African and French and Creole Louisiana oral tradition; he is both starved and gluttonous, famished but unable to eat. Michel Cazenave notes that "the teeth are the symbol most often used for vitality, procreation, and the strength of the sperm. [. . .] 'A dream wherein the teeth fall out, much like a toothache, is related to the expression of impotence.'"[53] The relationship between teeth, vital mechanisms for the consumption of food, and physical survival is extended by Cazenave's assertion that the symbol of teeth encompasses the possibility of future progeny. This symbolic relationship will reappear in another tale from Magel's collection, "Hyena in the Well."

Lapin informs Bouki that he is cooking birds' eggs, and Bouki is convinced that this is just what is needed to cure him. Giving Bouki a few eggs, Lapin even promises to take him the next day to the place where he finds them. Bouki returns home to his mother, who upon smelling her son's breath, insists on scraping particles of the eggs off his teeth with a piece of wood. Impressed by the smell, she says to Bouki, "You must get me some!"[54]

As promised, the next day Lapin shows Bouki where he had been finding his eggs but warns Bouki that he must not take more than one egg from each nest, lest the birds realize that they have been stolen. Of course, Bouki does not heed Lapin's advice, and it does not take long for the birds to notice that their eggs are missing. Similar to what can be found in the African tradition, Bouki and Lapin are not the only animals present, as the ox and the horse are suspected of having taken the eggs, but they answer that they only eat grass and hay, respectively. A similar tale of African origin would presumably include a series of animals interrogated one by one about the possibility of their having eaten the eggs, each one declaring their innocence and what they eat. When Bouki is finally interrogated, he foolishly replies, "Yes, it is I who ate your eggs."[55] Immediately thereafter, the birds put his eyes out and nearly tear him to pieces. Here again, consistent with the other Louisiana tales (and in contrast with many African tales), the dupe does not die at the end of the tale.

In both the West African and Louisiana oral traditions, many tales of Bouki and Lapin, or hyena and hare, consist of narratives that depend heavily on the dupe's role of glutton. "Dans la grosserie" (In the Grocery Store), told by Elby Deshotels, in Ancelet's collection, is one such example that has made its way into the repertoire of White Francophone storytellers. Elby, like his twin brother, Edward, was a gifted musician and storyteller who learned many tales from their father, Marcellus. The family was from the Mamou and Reddell area in Evangeline Parish, where relatively few Acadians settled. French Creoles mostly settled the area, which is located on the northern part of what is now called Acadiana.[56] The tale is just one example of how the characters of Bouki and Lapin have been integrated into the communities of White French speakers and also exhibits motifs similar to those of the West African tales in our corpus. Similar forms of the tale type 41, *The Wolf Overeats in the Cellar,* can certainly be found elsewhere in the oral tradition, but the characters' names suggest sustained contact with elements of West African folklore. Although the principal motifs and character names of this tale are reminiscent of Africa, the setting is adapted to the context of twentieth-century Louisiana. *La grosserie* is the common term in Louisiana French for "food store, grocery store," where people historically bought their goods *en gros,* or in bulk.[57] The majority of ATU 41 tales take place in a forbidden place, in this instance the grocery store, where live animals are generally not welcome.

The opening of Deshotels' tale deserves some consideration as it embodies several of the nuances that are the subject of our analysis. "There were these two rascals, once. One's name was Bouki and the other was Lapin. And Lapin was always fat. He was in good shape, and Bouki was always, always skinny."[58] Once again, this first sentence of the tale reaffirms a certain degree of preexisting complicity between the two characters, suggesting that they are both *malfaicteurs.*[59] The distinction between the two characters seems to be mostly a physical one, and no emphasis is placed on one being more intelligent or clever than the other at the opening of the narrative. Moreover, Deshotels' telling of this tale draws the listener's attention to the similar ambivalence found in the preceding tales with regard to the dupe's tendency to overeat despite explicit factors that would suggest the contrary (a persistent toothache, skinniness, eating less than the hare). Lapin eventually shares his secret source for food with Bouki and decides to show him that night the grocery store from which he often steals. Deshotels describes the scene: "They arrived at a grocery store. The moon was bright. And Lapin crawled under the grocery. He arrived just under the middle of the floor. There was a plank that had come unattached. So, he pushed the plank and he crawled into the grocery."[60]

Like the tree separating the two villages in the "The Hyena and the Hare" from the Bojangs' collection, Bouki's gluttony also takes place in a liminal space, "under the middle of the floor," that the animals are only able to penetrate in order to enter the next part of the narrative. The two find a big box with a jar inside full of cream. Lapin begins to eat the cream, but Bouki is so greedy that he begins to stuff his face with both hands, despite Lapin's warning to him that the storekeeper will open soon and catch them.

After a while, Lapin has enough sense to leave the grocery store, but Bouki stays behind, eating so much cream that he is unable to pass through the hole through which he first entered and is trapped. It is interesting to note that Bouki, although he is so thin, is the one who is caught, whereas Lapin is capable of both being "tout le temps gras et en bonne condition" (both fat and in good shape) and also able to enter and exit the grocery unimpeded by his size. The grocery store represents more of a narrative space than a physical one. In this sense, Bouki's folly is that he is not able to sufficiently navigate the liminal space that he is forced to inhabit. His lack of self-control and inability to leave the store in time make him a prisoner in that very narrative space.

Calvin Claudel offers another variant of ATU 41 from Avoyelles Parish, a region located north and northeast of Evangeline Parish, another area settled largely by French Creoles. True to the form seen thus far in this study and resembling the early phase of the structure that Dundes refers to as the "contract" between the two characters, the storyteller of "Bouqui et Lapin dans la boucanière" (Bouqui and Lapin in the Smokehouse) introduces Bouqui and Lapin as "two fellows who were very fond of each other."[61] Here again, the representation of food seems to be particularly malleable in this tale type, and it is not surprising that the "forbidden place" should be a *boucanière,* or smokehouse, in this area of Louisiana.

"Bouqui et Lapin dans la boucanière" begins much like "Dans la grosserie," with Bouqui asking Lapin where he gets all of his good meat. Lapin replies that he gets it from "the smokehouse of the Frenchmen."[62] The designation of the smokehouse owners as "Frenchmen" here is perhaps a way of distinguishing the human from the animal characters in the tale but also raises the question of whether the storyteller heard this tale from Black Creoles, as would be suggested by the presence of Bouqui cast as the dupe.[63]

Lapin cautiously agrees to show Bouqui the location of the smokehouse, saying: "Come here tonight after midnight. You must not come before the roosters crow for midnight, when all the lights are out because we will get caught."[64] In contrast to the bright moonlight in "Dans la grosserie," in this variant the two animals take advantage of the darkest moment of the night to sneak into the smokehouse. Bouqui agrees to return to Lapin's home that night but quickly grows anxious and returns well before the agreed meeting time with a blanket under his arm and a stick. Bouqui, in a futile attempt to make time go by faster, begins to poke the chickens with his stick, saying: "Crow! Crow for midnight!"[65] Lapin comes outside, startled by the cries of his chickens, and urges Bouqui to go back to bed, as it is still too early to go to the smokehouse without being detected. In what may be either a departure from the West African oral tradition or rather a European influence, here it is Bouqui, and not Lapin, who transgresses the contract between the two characters, to borrow once more Dundes's term. As in "Dans la grosserie," Bouqui is unable, or unwilling, to abide by the temporal, and liminal, space allotted to him in the narrative. Midnight, between night and day, "l'heure du crime," is the only time during which the theft can be successfully executed, a detail that only Lapin seems to understand.

After going back to sleep, the two wake up again at midnight and set off for the Frenchmen's smokehouse. Once inside the smokehouse, the storyteller explains: "Bouqui spread his blanket upon the ground. He began piling up meat, sausage, in fact, all sorts of good things to eat that were in there. Lapin himself cut off a piece of meat and then went out, leaving through the hole by which he entered."[66] Unlike the "greedy" Bouqui, Lapin cuts off one piece of

Bouki, Lapin et le poulailler. Digital illustration. Jonathan Mayers, 2020.

meat and then leaves the smokehouse. Bouqui stays, taking the four corners of his blanket and tying them together to fill it with meat. He later tries to squeeze his bundle through the hole they had entered, but it will not pass, and when the sun rises, the Frenchmen discover Bouqui stuck in the corner of the smokehouse "still tugging at his bundle," and they give him "a big beating then they gave him a large piece of meat, saying to him, 'Go home and eat now!'"[67] It may seem illogical that the Frenchmen should throw yet another piece of their remaining meat at Bouqui; it is a similar punishment to the one administered by Pa Juma. Bouqui's transgression, the theft of food, can only be remedied by the consumption of meat that is forced upon him by a higher social authority. Although Bouqui is not forced to eat his own flesh like in Bojangs' "The Hyena and the Hare," the punishment inflicted upon him is still one of forced consumption as recompense for eating forbidden food.

This kind of punishment is contrary to what one finds in the Judeo-Christian tradition, whereby Adam and Eve are punished by God for eating the forbidden fruit of knowledge, not by forcing them to eat more but by banishing them from the Garden of Eden, threatening them with starvation rather than forced feeding. "To the man [God] said: 'Because you listened to your wife and ate from the tree of which I had forbidden you to eat, cursed be the ground because of you! In toil shall you eat its yield all the days of your life. Thorns and thistles shall it bring forth to you, as you eat of the plants of the field'" (Gen. 3:17–18). Similar warnings against gluttony are found elsewhere in the Old Testament, including two references in the book of Proverbs: "And put a knife to your throat if you have a ravenous appetite" (Prov. 23:2); and "Consort not with winebibbers, nor with those who eat meat to excess; For the drunkard and the glutton come to poverty and torpor clothes a man in rags" (Prov. 23:21). The motif of forced eating, or even self-cannibalism, as a punishment for greed or gluttony contrasts dramatically with these biblical passages, indicating a vestige of a different set of customs and moral values.

A similar example of auto-cannibalism can be found in "The Hare and Hyena in the Well," from Emil Magel's collection of forty-five Wolof narratives from the Gambia. This tale begins with the hyena and the hare banding together to set traps. Upon returning to their traps later, they find very few animals, and the hare persuades the hyena to let him take their meager catch to his own village, promising to let the hyena have all of what they would catch the next day. However, this went on for days and days until the hyena grew skinny and weary. Angered, and under increasing pressure from his household, hyena seeks revenge by beating the hare and throwing him down a well. The hare quickly finds a way to obtain food, even at the bottom of a well.

The sheep is the first who falls prey to the hare, who cries to each passing animal: "You are very bad. [. . .] You, since I have been sick, until today, you have not visited me." When asked how to enter the well by each passing animal, the hare responds, "If you go this way and then that way, you will arrive here."[68] This ruse enables the hare to surprise and kill the sheep, the goat, the bull, and other animals until he himself grows bigger than a cow. Because of the hare's cunning, he actually thrives in the well in a scenario that, on a basic level, resembles that of Brer Rabbit in motif K581.2 *Briar-patch punishment for rabbit.*

Expecting him to have starved to death, the hyena is surprised to find the hare so big and healthy when he goes to check on him. As the hyena grows envious of all the food the hare is able to acquire at the bottom of the well, it is not difficult for the hare to persuade him to switch places with him. The hare explains to the hyena his method of enticing the passing animals to descend into the well; however, the hyena lacks the intelligence to execute the scheme properly, saying to each passerby, "You only have to walk here and then there, fall into this hole and I will devour you."[69] Not surprisingly, none of the animals are deceived by such a poor attempt at copying the hare's trickery. The hyena eventually begins to starve and hallucinate from lack of food. The storyteller, Malik Boye, recounts how the hyena "no longer knew what he was doing. He began to salivate whenever he looked at his own testicles. He said, 'HUMMM it is honey. If I devour you, you will know it.' [. . .] Then he seized them into his mouth and said, 'Hai! They are on me . . . they are part of *me!*'" The hyena eventually dies from starvation at the bottom of the well, for "what else could he do but just hold the testicles in his mouth?"[70]

It is significant that this tale combines aspects of motifs G60 and C221.3.1 *Tabu: eating animal's genitals,* as it juxtaposes auto-cannibalism as a penalty for gluttony with castration. In this sense, there is a direct link between food, which has been seen in each tale thus far in the corpus to be a symbol of survival or power, and the loss of virility or sexual power. The end of this tale also suggests a certain sexual ambivalence of the hyena, which is likely connected to popular beliefs about the hyena in West Africa. Doubts surrounding the sexual nature of the hyena may have had an influence on the representation of Bouki in Creole Louisiana folklore. The hyena's unusual sexual organs make the female hyena resemble the male, at least until puberty, which is likely the source of certain superstitions surrounding the hyena in Africa.[71] Although the sexual ambivalence of Bouki is not expressed in the Louisiana French and Creole tradition, the figure remains both marginal and liminal. He is systematically humiliated, emasculated in a way, and often held captive in border-like spaces as demonstrated in the above analyses. It is remarkable that although Bouki's original meaning of hyena has been almost completely lost in Louisiana, the character's ambivalent and liminal role has remained intact.

Due to a high degree of overlap with African and European motifs and tale types, attempts to determine with accuracy the origin of certain tales always become problematic, especially where similar narrative structures exist in multiple traditions that have intersected, such as the trickster and dupe scenario (for example, the European *loup et renard* and the African hyena and hare). Levine finds that "a roughly similar percentage were tales common in both Africa and Europe, so that, while slaves may have brought the tale type with them, its place in their lore could well have been reinforced by their contact with whites."[72]

Another tale type that is very prevalent in French and Creole Louisiana folklore as well as elsewhere in the French American oral tradition is type ATU 15, *The Theft of Butter (Honey) by Playing Godfather*.[73] Martin Latiolais from Catahoula, Louisiana, one of Ancelet's most prolific informants, offers a version found in *Cajun and Creole Folktales* titled "Le Gros baril de beurre" (The Big Barrel of Butter).[74] The body of this tale exhibits minimal variation from the majority of cataloged variants throughout North America and the West Indies. Similar versions are found in Louisiana in French, Creole, and English and are relatively uniform in their structure. While Bouki and Lapin are out working in the field, Lapin repeatedly pretends to be called away by someone to name or baptize a baby, although he is actually stealing food (such as butter or honey). Each time Lapin returns, Bouki inquires about the name he has given the newborn child. The first "child" is named "Commencé," the second "Un quart," the third "La moitié," followed by "Trois quarts" and "Fini."[75]

The beginning of Latiolais's rendition of this tale puts into question the nature and identity of the Lapin character as well as the storyteller's ability to place him in different roles. Latiolais recounts: "Now, when they worked together like that, Lapin posed as a priest, you see? He baptized children. But they had bought a barrel of butter, a big barrel of butter."[76] Moreover, Lapin's faculty as a trickster is intensified here, as he is not only called to name the children (as in the Congo variant) or act as godfather, but he is also capable of disguising himself as a priest and performing baptisms. Lapin's "transformation" is carnivalesque in the Bakhtinian sense insofar as the trickster dons a religious costume in a momentary mockery of the baptismal rite in the interest of his own gluttony. Furthermore, the animals' purchase of the large barrel of butter seems to have little relevance to their agricultural endeavors. It would seem that the contents of the barrel, or the well, are of little importance and represent another example of how easily food can be adapted, or localized, to a given geographic or cultural context.

Several Acadian variants of ATU 15 can be found in the Centre d'études acadiennes Anselme Chiasson (CEAAC) at the Université de Moncton. These tales feature a much more European-influenced casting of characters, the fox as the trickster and the wolf as the dupe. In "Le Loup et le renard," told by Alyre Maddix of Abrams Village, Prince Edward Island,[77] the first half of the tale is basically identical to that of Martin Latiolais's. The fox pretends to be called off to play godfather to a child and gives the imaginary children names like "Bien Commencé," "Mi-Vide," and "Cu-Frippé." The fox proceeds to trick the wolf several more times, enticing him with clams and lobsters, yet another example of localization in how food is adapted to fit the cultural environment of the storyteller. The fox finally convinces the wolf to play dead on the side of the road, wait for a traveling fisherman to pass by with a load of lobsters, and take him by surprise: "Jump up, and take what you want! He'll never notice!" However, when the man passes by, he picks up the wolf with a pitchfork, throws him atop his load of lobsters, and takes him away, leaving the fox safe and sound.

Joseph Carrière includes two variants of ATU 15 featuring Bouki and Lapin in *Tales from the French Folk-Lore of Missouri* (1937), suggesting continuity between the greater Louisiana Territory to West Africa, but the type is also widely found in the French tradition, such as with Renart and Isengrin in the *Roman de Renart*. May Klipple, in her doctoral dissertation "African Folk Tales with Foreign Analogues" (1938), only mentions four African attestations of ATU 15, which differ considerably from most Louisiana variants. The first variant from South Africa, which casts the jackal and the hyena as trickster and dupe, includes the motif of smearing fat on the hyena's tail to incriminate him.[78] Only one of the tales from Klipple's catalog features the name-giving motif, an integral trait of the Louisiana variants. Given the importance of the slave trade linking Louisiana to the Congo, it is probably not coincidental that this variant was collected in the Congo region in Richard Dennett's *The Folk-Lore of the Fjort*.[79] Of the four African variants provided by Klipple, "The Rabbit and the Antelope" is the only one that bears significant resemblance to the Louisiana variants beyond the most basic structure of the tale type. In this

Congo variant, the rabbit and the antelope set out to dig a well, and the rabbit leaves, saying that he is being called to name someone's baby. Upon the rabbit's first return, he informs the antelope that he named the child "Uncompleted one" and then "Completed" the second time.

Although Klipple's summary does not cover the entire tale, the ending in Dennett's full transcription is quite intriguing. When the antelope discovers that the rabbit has been stealing food, he challenges him to a truth test (motif K981), which, as Ancelet notes, is also present in the two French Missouri variants collected by Carrière.[80] The truth test consists of both animals eating the *casca* (truth bark), an emetic, in front of all the villagers. Whoever's tail is wet after eating the bark is the liar.[81] The rabbit is found guilty and flees, but sometime thereafter, a bird tells the antelope that the rabbit is still in the habit of drinking water from the well every day. The antelope is enraged by this news and devises a small figure out of sticks about the size of a rabbit, sets it near the well, and smears it with birdlime, an adhesive substance used for trapping birds. What ensues is basically a variation of type ATU 175 *The Tarbaby and the Rabbit.* The rabbit is annoyed by the presence of this strange figure near the well and asks repeatedly who he is and what he is doing there. When the figure does not respond, the rabbit punches the figure with his right hand, then his left. With both hands stuck in the birdlime, he then kicks the figure with his right foot and then his left. When the rabbit begins to cry for help, the antelope finds him "helplessly fastened to the figure," laughs at him, and then kills him.[82] Klipple gives thirty-nine African variants of ATU 175, although the cast of characters and the manner in which the trickster is caught differ greatly from the Louisiana variants.[83] In several instances, the leopard is cast (either as trickster or dupe), and a number of variants do not include a sticky figure but rather a tortoise shell into which the jackal jumps and becomes ensnared.

What is significant here is the fact that among the thirty-nine variants of ATU 175 comparable to the Louisiana French and Creole variants, none of the African tales exhibits a successful trickster. At best, the rabbit is able to escape, but only in a few of the African variants listed by Klipple is this the case. In the vast majority of the cases, the trickster (rabbit, jackal, monkey, or other animal) is killed and sometimes eaten. A similar trend is found in the African oral tradition, in which, according to Klipple, nineteen of the thirty-nine versions of ATU 175 pertain to a pairing with at least one other tale, including ATU 15 *The Theft of Butter (Honey) by Playing Godfather.*

The practice of combining with another tale type is certainly an important commonality with the Louisiana variants of ATU 175; however, an important distinction lies in the absence of motif K581.2 *Briar-patch punishment for rabbit,* in the African variants. In fact, Klipple gives only three instances of motif K581.2 from Africa, each one showing noticeable dissimilarities from the typical scenario associated with Louisiana Creole Bouki and Lapin tales or the Brer Rabbit tales of the English-speaking American South.[84] The astounding prevalence of the trickster's victory following the briar patch motif (K581.2) in the southern United States, compared to its relative absence in the continental African corpus provided by Klipple, implies more of a new-world phenomenon than a holdover from the African tradition.

Even in the earliest examples such as in Fortier's 1895 collection, "Fillèle Compair Lapin" (Compair Lapin's Godchild) concludes with the dupe giving the trickster the choice between being thrown in the fire or into the briars.[85] I argue that the change in how the briar patch motif plays out is a reaction to the cultural trauma of slavery. Familiar with Bouki's malice and lack of intelligence, Lapin pleads for the fire, the opposite of what he really wants. To spite Lapin, Bouki throws him into the briars, to which Lapin retorts, "Thank you, my good Bouki; you placed me exactly where my mother resides."[86] So, although the hyena and hare have penetrated the cast of characters of French and Creole Louisiana as Bouki and Lapin, the inherent moral values and social implications of the tales have changed on a fundamental level.

Conclusions similar to motif K581.2 are found in later tales among predominantly White Francophone communities of Louisiana. An intriguing example is found in Calvin Claudel's doctoral dissertation "A Study of Louisiana French Folktales in Avoyelles Parish" (1948). Like many of the tales in the study, "Bouki et Lapin et le 'tit bébé Godron" (Bouqui, Lapin, and the Tar Baby) is told by A. E. Claudel, the author's mother.[87] The narrative structure and motifs present in this tale are admittedly typical of most African American variants of the tar baby story; however, the most remarkable feature of this tale is completely obscured in the monolingual English translation of the story appearing thirty years later in Claudel's *Fools and Rascals.* Only by consulting the original sound recordings from the early 1940s for the purposes of Claudel's thesis can one discover the systematic code-switching between French and Creole. Mrs. Claudel consistently narrates in her native French of Avoyelles Parish, but when speaking for Bouqui or Lapin, she seamlessly transitions to Creole, as in the example that follows (with the forms most indicative of Creole in bold): "Ça fait, il y avait les quatre pattes. 'Mais, **ma boqué** toi dans ton trayon avec ma tête!' Pah! Il lui fout sa tête, ça reste collé. 'Lâche-moi, 'tite fille ! Lâche-moi, **mo dis** toi!' La 'tite fille grouillait pas. Il dit, '**Mo va boqué toi** avec ma queue asteur'" (So, there were the four paws. "Well, I'm gonna punch you in the belly with my head!" Pow! He headbutts it, and his head sticks. "Let me go, little girl! Let me go, I tell you!" The little girl didn't budge. He says, "I'll hit you with my tail now").[88] While it is not uncommon that morphological elements typical of Louisiana Creole should be found in the dialects of Louisiana French speakers, this phenomenon is more common in St. Martin and St. Landry Parishes, not in Avoyelles Parish. Moreover, the animal characters' dialogue in A. E. Claudel's story is clearly distinct from the narrative voice by way of code-switching between French and Creole. At several points in the narrative, the storyteller seems to forget to speak for a character in Creole and "corrects" herself. Clearly, this is a conscious decision made by the storyteller that indicates a custom of performing identity—and in this case, performing the "other." It has been suggested that it is through narrative that we construct identity.[89]

These linguistic peculiarities raise several questions. Did the storyteller consciously associate these tales (and more specifically the characters within them) with Black Creoles? Given that Avoyelles Parish is not typically regarded as an area with a strong presence of Creole speakers, did she learn these tales elsewhere? In addition, the final words howled by Lapin as he is soaring through the air toward the briar patch are uttered in English: "You set me free, now watch me go!" Does the abrupt switch to English (the only complete sentence in English in the entire recording) at the end indicate some contact with English-language versions of Brer Rabbit? Whatever the exact explanation may be, it is clear that the characters are others as can be surmised by the linguistic difference from the narrated portions of the tale. This kind of "doing" or performance of identity is borne out by recent research on narrative identity construction that suggests performed identity is dynamic rather than fixed, contradictory and situational, as it is developed through interactions with people.[90]

Corinne Saucier includes a similar example in her collection *Folk Tales of French Louisiana*, first published in 1962 and based largely on tales collected in predominantly White Creole communities of Avoyelles Parish in the 1940s and 1950s. Tales 30 and 31 of her collection demonstrate striking similarities to the Congo variant collected by Dennett with regard to the narrative structure but end in a manner much more typical of the new-world briar patch scenario. "Brer Turtle" is quite similar to Dennett's tale of the rabbit and the antelope, and it does feature the familiar "forbidden well" scenario representative of the African corpus.[91] As one might expect, Brer Goat decides to place a tar baby near the well to which Brer Turtle becomes attached after his bout with the sticky figure. Much like in "Fillèle Compair Lapin" in Fortier's collection, Brer Goat gives the turtle his choice of punishment: to be thrown in boiling water or thrown into the river. The choice between heat (fire or boiling water) and the cool river (or the shade of a briar patch) seems to be a recurrent trait of the Louisiana variants of ATU 175. Moreover, we can consider the goat or wolf's punishment that he bestows to the trickster as a fitting recompense for his transgression. In other words, it is fitting for him who has stolen water to be thrown in the river, just as the glutton in the African tales is forced to eat more. Although the structure and motifs of the Louisiana and African variants of type 175 are largely the same, it is the effect of the trickster's punishment that has morphed into a victory of cleverness over brute force. Furthermore, the characterization of "Brer Turtle" from Saucier's Avoyelles Parish informant lucidly displays the confluence of European and African traditions as well as the resulting fluidity and interchangeability within the animal paradigm of trickster and dupe.

Tale types ATU 15 and ATU 175 are also prime examples of the problems encountered when attempting to trace certain types or motifs to the African or European oral traditions. This is even more so the case with type 175, which is one of the most prevalent animal tales in the oral tradition. In effect, the confluence of these contrasting cultures is rendered even more opaque due to the significant degree of commonalities between them. Naturally, when a given motif is present in two oral traditions that have been mixed together in a culturally diverse environment like Louisiana, it becomes impossible to ascertain the origin of such a motif or if it is simply a shared trait. However, what is more important than points of origin in my approach here is the analysis of the tales' meaning and function. The strong presence of Bouki and Lapin in the oral tradition of White Francophone communities of Louisiana demonstrates that these tales were equally pertinent to their social reality. Of course, because of the oral nature of the transmission and diffusion of folktales, there is a lack of written documentation of the tales' African origins.

For instance, the significant number of Saint-Domingue refugees would have been sufficient to influence the body of animal tales in Louisiana, not only in New Orleans but in the rural parishes as well. The 1810–20 Census Reports show that 22 percent of the Saint-Domingue refugees settled in Louisiana's rural parishes.[92] Most of those refugees who settled outside of New Orleans went to the area comprising Lafayette, Vermilion, and St. Martin Parishes and the river parishes, from Pointe Coupée to St. James.[93] Therefore, it is not surprising that the majority the Bouki and Lapin tales from Ancelet's collection were found in St. Martin Parish. In addition, Alcée Fortier collected numerous tales from the plantation region in St. James Parish, two of which are credited to "'an old negro at *La Vacherie,* St. James Parish,' the site of the plantation where Fortier had been raised and of the St. James Sugar Refinery which was also on his grandfather's property."[94] The social divide across South Louisiana's different communities may have been less marked than in other American states if the shared repertoire of folktales is any indication.

The slave trade affected Louisiana in many significant ways—culturally, demographically, and socially—and also allowed for the integration of folktale repertoires from Africa and the Caribbean into the European (mainly French) paradigm of animal tales. Perhaps as a direct result, the trickster figure takes on an especially important role in Louisiana Creole folklore. The augmented prestige of the Louisiana trickster figure, exemplified by Lapin, is a reaction to the cultural trauma caused by slavery and its conditions. In this sense, the Lapin character of Creole Louisiana is comparable to other tricksters found in English-speaking slave communities elsewhere in the American South, such as Brer Rabbit. Within the context of slavery, a trickster figure became essential on a psychological level, as "antebellum slaves manifested a central feature of the consciousness graphically and dramatically through the medium of trickster tales featuring the victories of the weak over the strong."[95] Ernest Jones confirms folklore's role in the expression of social consciousness in saying that "the material studied in folklore, whether it be customs, beliefs, or folksongs. [. . .] is the product of dynamic mental processes, the response of the folk soul to either outer or inner needs, the expression of various longings, fears, aversion, or desire."[96]

Although the notion of slavery as being traumatic is not unusual, I propose that cultural trauma likely had an effect on the adaptations of folktales among slaves and former slave communities. Again, cultural trauma differs from personal trauma in the sense that "as cultural process, trauma is mediated through various forms of representation and linked to the reformation of collective identity and the reworking of collective memory."[97] Therefore, folklore can be considered one such form of representation, and I would argue that the perseverance of the trickster figure in Black Creole folklore played a role in forming a certain collective identity. In the case of African American identity, Ron Eyerman examines the trauma of slavery "not as institution or even experience, but as collective memory, a form of remembrance that grounded the identity-formation of a people."[98] The cultural trauma of slavery resulted in the need for (and thus the prevalence of) a trickster figure, and some animal tales also lent themselves to hidden slave narratives, as seen in tales like "Tortie" and "Chien avec tigue" from Fortier's collection.

Through cultural contact between Black Creole and White Francophone populations, the African animal paradigm (specifically the hyena and the hare) has demonstrated its ability to superimpose itself onto typically European tale types, as is the case with ATU 15, *The Theft of Butter (Honey) by Playing Godfather*. Because of the paradigmatic simplicity of the trickster and dupe scenario, the characters of Bouki and Lapin were able to transplant themselves into narratives that fit a basic structure, regardless of the supposed origin of more specific motifs. Another example is the motif K581.2, in which we see a dramatic shift from the African tales in Klipple's catalog. Instead of being killed and eaten, the trickster anticipates the malice of the dupe by tricking him into throwing him into his own home (the river or briar patch).

While the animal trickster tales of West Africa are generally more didactic in nature, serving to warn their audience against the wiles of the trickster, the trickster of Louisiana is celebrated for his cleverness and victory over his opponent's physical strength. The lesson, or moral, of these stories has shifted to reflect a new social reality and collective experience. Furthermore, the propagation of trickster tales (especially those featuring the animal trickster) into White Francophone communities was facilitated by a certain shared experience. It is not difficult to imagine such "underdog" tales being both relatable and psychologically satisfying among White groups who did not undergo the trauma of slavery but who were nonetheless marginalized through exile (as with the Acadians), extreme poverty, and lack of political representation.

CHAPTER 2

The Master Thief,
a Human Trickster

Throughout much of the nineteenth century, rural Louisiana was not so different from other portions of the United States where popular myth reflected the
notion that bandits represented the poor or disenfranchised parts of society.
The frontier "offered ample violence and disorder as a background," and because these marginalized elements of society often found themselves preyed
upon by those in power, outlaws' offenses were validated, if not fully justified.[1]
Given the historically marginalized status of French- and Creole-speaking
communities in Louisiana, it is not surprising that an outlaw figure who is
also a trickster figure would be an appealing folk hero. The plethora of jokes
involving poor or simple characters who outwit police officers, priests, professors, or other symbols of authority or intellectualism is telling of a culture that
has survived despite a historical lack of access to political power and prestige.[2]

The Catholic Church, colonial authorities, and law enforcement all represent an official set of laws. However, much of what a community may perceive
as just or unjust depends on other unwritten laws that we can consider folk
laws. These are "the deep-seated rules of behavior particular to a locale or to
a tight-knit group communicated orally or by firsthand experience, and they
carry with them the punishments meted out by members of the groups that
hold them as laws."[3] In a sense, people's everyday actions and sense of morality
are dictated more strongly by folk law, which in some places existed before
the official law, thus causing it to be perceived as more important.[4] Often folk
laws within a community can be both dynamic and imperceptible to those
from outside—what spot one is permitted to fish from, at what point one's

steps become "trespassing," or where one gang's territory ends and another's begins. All of these folk laws are unofficial, yet they can be deadly serious in the realm of folk law.

On a basic level, outlaw heroes owe their attractiveness to a friction between folk law and official law. Because folk laws are so dependent and indicative of the values, fears, and identity of the community to which they belong, heroes that defend folk laws can act as an extension of these values. In other words, an outlaw hero expresses "the deep-seated experiences people have shared" and "acts as a monument to the past and as a representation of a people within a place."[5] In the case of most outlaw hero narratives, the community strongly identifies as poor or oppressed. There is also an implicit understanding that the community is generally good; it possesses folk laws that are not only just but that also go beyond the official laws of repression dictated by the king, prefect, or other symbol of authority. The outlaw hero is necessary to transgress boundaries, defy existing rules, and upset the existing social order.[6] Social bandits are distinguishable from common criminals in that they are peasant outlaws regarded as criminals by the established authority, but they remain in peasant society and are considered as heroes and admired by the people.[7] This is, in essence, the Robin Hood legend, although few examples from the oral tradition specifically describe the thief giving to the poor. In this sense, Robin Hood is both the quintessential bandit and also rather atypical.[8]

One of the most prevalent examples of the outlaw hero in folklore is ATU 1525 *The Master Thief,* in which the protagonist is depicted as more of an outlaw hero than a generic trickster.[9] This tale type enjoys wide popularity in the French-speaking world; a considerable number of Master Thief tales have been attested in France, Acadia, and Louisiana. The Master Thief, often called *Le Fin voleur* or *Le Franc voleur* in Francophone folklore, is generally associated with ATU 1525, and it is found not only in French and Creole oral traditions but also in English-language tales elsewhere in the southern United States.[10] In Louisiana, Elizabeth Brandon, Calvin Claudel, and Corinne Saucier all collected variants of ATU 1525 involving a Master Thief–like protagonist by the name of Roclore or Roclos.[11] These tales feature a villainous authority figure, often a king, who opposes the Master Thief. In an attempt to rid himself of the thief, the king challenges him to perform daring acts of theft that become progressively more difficult. The most commonly found motifs consist of some variation of the following actions, usually in this order: stealing horses from a guarded stable, stealing cows or sheep while they are being guarded by the overseer's field hands, and stealing the sheets from the authority figure's bed during the night.[12] In many variants, including "Der Meisterdieb" (The Master Thief) in the Grimms' *Kinder- und Hausmärchen,* Roquelaure's capacity to disguise himself reinforces his identity as a trickster figure, according to Jung's description of the archetype.

One of the most prevalent motifs in the Louisiana variants of ATU 1525 and similar thief tales is motif K842 *Dupe persuaded to take prisoner's place in a sack: killed.*[13] This motif invariably occurs at the end of the narrative and consists of the thief, finally trapped by the king and placed in a sack, duping an unfortunate passerby into switching places with him by crying: "I won't marry the princess! You can drown me, but I won't marry the princess." In most variants, the two exchange places while the king is distracted. When the king returns, he throws the sack into a lake, believing that he has finally rid himself of the thief. Later the king sees the thief on horseback and exclaims his disbelief in seeing the rascal alive. At this point, the thief cleverly responds to the king in anger for not having thrown him far enough into the lake, supposedly where the best horses could be found. Upon hearing this, the gullible king then pleads with the thief to throw him into the lake so that he might see the finest horses. The Master Thief gladly obliges the king, who never resurfaces. An underlying commentary of the king's ignorance about basic matters of rural life and self-sufficiency is particularly salient in such scenes; although he may be wealthy and powerful, he is sufficiently gullible to believe that horses are sold at the bottom of a lake. This last-ditch effort for survival using one's wit and a form of reverse psychology parallels the rabbit's briar patch punishment (motif K581.2) found in ATU 175 *The Tarbaby and the Rabbit.*

In most Master Thief tales, theft is warranted because the king is unjust and greedy. The peasants surrounding his land are all aware that the king's actions are the cause of their poverty. However, only the Master Thief (himself a member of the community) dares to defy the king. In this sense, the Master Thief is a true outlaw in that he operates outside of the king's land and set of laws. This constitutes an important distinction from a "criminal" who commits a crime yet remains subject to, possibly, but also protected by official rules, proceedings, hearings, and so forth.[14] An outlaw, on the other hand, is completely removed from both the protections and punishment of official law. In the Master Thief tales of French and Creole Louisiana, one finds considerable vestiges of old-world monarchy: a king, a queen, a castle, and peasants living on the king's land. This is remarkable because, for the most part, the folklore repertoire of Louisiana is devoid of such holdovers, having adapted to storytellers' current realities. Because the "hero" is in fact a thief, Master Thief tales can provide insight into a culture's moral outlook with regard to social justice and class difference. The Master Thief is "an amoral tale with a moral hero," wherein the protagonist, "normally the embodiment of his society's more positive values—is here asked to do the work of a sociopath, performing a series of robberies to win his fortune."[15] The casting of an otherwise "good" character (invariably of lower social status) as a thief results in a moral tension that storytellers are obliged to negotiate. This is why variants of ATU 1525 typically feature "a greater number of subjective statements and narrative asides," thus making the tale "more volatile, and cultural differences emerge more quickly and clearly."[16] The Master Thief tales force us to ask questions such as "When is theft socially or even culturally permissible for an otherwise moral hero and why?" Faced with this ethical tension and fundamental dilemma, what is at stake for the storyteller and his or her audience on a moral, social, and even cultural level? The Master Thief tale type responds indirectly to these questions in ways that are as variable as the names, places, and characters found alongside them. As variants of this type are attested around the world, specific needs for an outlaw hero who transgresses common moral boundaries can differ greatly from one community to another. Likewise, the justification for the hero's immoral acts are subject to the storyteller's own moral perspective informed by his or her feelings toward theft and attitude toward authority.

Calvin Claudel's collection includes a tale from Pointe Coupée Parish entitled "Frank Rascal," likely a translation of *Franc voleur* found elsewhere in the French oral tradition.[17] Frankness in this sense serves as justification for the hero's immoral actions later on. In this case, the young thief consoles his disappointed mother, saying: "Don't worry, Mama. I am a frank rascal. I don't have to do anything bad."[18] Being *franc* in overtly admitting that he is a thief renders his actions less reprehensible. This implicitly contrasts to the established authority figure, such as the king, who unjustly appropriates money through taxation or oppression. Another common motif is juxtaposition of theft (as a trade) with more respectable professions, here represented by his two brothers.[19] In Claudel's tale, one brother goes to college to become a doctor, while the other goes to law school.[20] Later on in the tale, when the thief attempts to steal the king's horses, Frank Rascal does not dress up as an old woman, as in "Der Meisterdieb," or as a Capuchin monk, as seen in the Lorraine variant. Rather, he chooses to "dress himself as an old Negro" and offers the guards a flask of whiskey in order to subdue them.[21] These instances of localization demonstrate not only the thief's capacity to disguise himself but also his penchant for adopting the opposite of his true appearance.[22]

The moral of Claudel's tale even denigrates the choices of the older brothers: "When he arrived, he found his town brothers who had finished school. Neither the one nor the other was earning money. The doctor had no practice, and the lawyer spent all his time reading. Of the three brothers, only he who had learned to steal made money."[23] The moral meant to be derived here might illustrate a strong mistrust of formal education and conventional ideas of financial success or possibly the sentiment of marginalization of French and Creole speakers and an awareness of social barriers that would prevent them from being upwardly mobile in society.

Stanislaus Faul of Cankton performed the longest and most robust versions of the Master Thief, or *Fin voleur*.[24] As in "Der Meisterdieb" and "Le Franc voleur" from Cosquin's collection, Faul's begins not with the protagonist but by accentuating the family's poverty.[25] While it might appear to be insignificant background information, this overture underscores a crucial element of the tale. The *Fin voleur*'s social standing and familial situation is paramount in justifying the crimes that he will commit later on in the narrative. For this reason, he is at first rejected when the two older brothers decide to leave in order to learn their respective professions to support their family. Eventually, the two older brothers permit the youngest to accompany them on their quest. The brothers quickly come to a three-way fork in the road, at which point each brother takes his own path, agreeing to meet each other in one year's time at that very spot.[26]

Liminal imagery, like M301.12 *Three fates,* is a recurrent motif in ATU 1525 variants and conveys the volatility of the protagonist's upbringing while also effacing the thief's agency in his progression from peasant to outlaw.[27] Another common motif is the father's death ahead of the narrative. Storytellers subtly use these motifs to remove any fault that might be placed on the thief and instead attribute his misdeeds to the circumstances or people surrounding him.[28] The group of thieves that the protagonist meets early on in the narrative functions as a sort of "donor" in the Proppian sense, as they supply the hero with the necessary skill, or "magic."[29] In this way, the storyteller is able to distance himself from the negative qualities associated with the hero's questionable profession because the art of theft is learned outside of the community. Furthermore, it is understood that the Master Thief's victims—for example, the king—will also be far away.

The king gives *Fin voleur* several tasks under the threat of death by hanging should he refuse or fail. The *Fin voleur*'s final challenge, stealing the queen's wedding ring and bedsheet while she sleeps, is decidedly carnivalesque in how he fashions a manikin out of a pig, fitted with a spring in order to mimic a human, thus inciting the gunshots of the king's guards, who mistake it for the thief. Disguise is an integral part of the *Fin voleur*'s modus operandi.[30] When the thief is believed to be shot, the king races down to order his men to bury him fifteen feet deep. Meanwhile, the thief seizes this opportunity to climb up to his room and steal the king's wife's sheet and wedding ring, symbolizing the reversal of power and the upside-down world described by Mikhail Bakhtin (a veritable "dethronement" in which the fool becomes king).[31] But despite these overtly Bakhtinian traits, Louisiana variants ATU 1525 remain relatively tame and devoid of the sexual and scatological elements found in the French oral tradition. In some variants of France, for example, the thief takes advantage of this furtive moment in the king's chamber to have intercourse with the queen (pretending to be the king in the dark), urinate in the bottle on his nightstand, and defecate in his boots.[32]

While some outlaw heroes or Master Thief figures remain nameless, others possess emblematic names, sometimes based on real-life individuals known as cunning figures. In such cases, the line between "history" and "folklore" becomes considerably blurred. Here I focus on one specific manifestation of this figure, Roquelaure, who has carved out a significant place in Louisiana's oral tradition. However, it is important to view this character in a larger context both in terms of geography, as the character is found practically everywhere in the Francophone world, and narrative, as an expression of a larger archetype of outlaw hero.

Few characters in Louisiana's oral tradition exemplify this conundrum better than the master thief Roquelaure.[33] Nearly all of the attestations of Master Thief tales recorded in Louisiana indicate that the protagonist is named Roquelaure, with some varied spelling. Usually appearing as a Master Thief figure, Roquelaure is also found elsewhere in the folklore of French-speaking North America and France, and although nearly identical representations of such characters have been attested throughout the world for centuries, the Master Thief has a way of representing a specific culture's identity and values.

Several inquiries have been made pertaining to the origin of the name Roquelaure and its relationship to the Master Thief tale type, and it is understandable that such a question has baffled folklore scholars for some time. One theory is based on the fusion of *râteler* (to rake), which would be pronounced *râcler* in certain dialectal forms, and *or* (gold).[34] These words together would supposedly convey the notion that the protagonist greedily hoards gold. Germain Lemieux's collection of Franco-Ontarian tales *Les Vieux m'ont conté* contain variations on the spelling that might support this theory.[35] However, I argue that this is highly unlikely for several reasons: the name's spelling with *qu* rather than *c* is too consistent across regions; the proximity of the vowels *o* and *â* is not as acute elsewhere in the French-speaking world as it is in Francophone Canada, where a confusion between those two vowels could actually occur; in the majority of Master Thief tales, the thief is not motivated by greed, and rarely is gold one of the objects that he is compelled to steal; and most important, there is a significant number of links in the documentary record to strongly suggest a connection to historical figures of the Roquelaure family of French nobility. The origin of the family, the community of Roquelaure, still exists in the Gers region of southern France. As I will lay out in some detail, several members of the family achieved notoriety in France for their mischievous and cunning reputations.

As a surname, there seems to be no evidence that Roquelaure ever existed in Louisiana; however, one does find an entry for *rôquelaure* in the *Dictionary of Louisiana French*. As a noun, the word refers to a "good-for-nothing," although this is more likely a result of the folklore figure's mischievous persona.[36] Based on this similarity to the noble surname, Louisiana folklore scholar George Reinecke drew attention to a specific motif found both in the folktales of Louisiana and in a rather obscure text that recounts comic episodes purportedly from the life of Gaston-Jean-Baptiste de Roquelaure, a duke and military officer under Louis XIV.[37] The book, entitled *Le Momus françois*, was published in 1727.[38] Because it seems that Reinecke's knowledge of references to the Roquelaure family in France was limited to this one text, the notion remained in the realm of conjecture.

What I aim to present here is a more complete historical perspective of Roquelaure, the character as well as its potential links to historical figures. Further investigation of theater and literature from the eighteenth century reveals sufficient evidence to prove that one (or several) of the members of the noble French Roquelaure family had already entered into the popular imagination as somewhat of a legend as early as the seventeenth century, beginning in courtly society and later spreading to the general population of France. Comparing episodes described in these period sources with Louisiana variants of the Master Thief tales sheds light on the significance of the name Roquelaure and its connection with the Master Thief tale type.

Attestations of a character named Roquelaure (Roclore or Roclos) cast as a Master Thief figure in ATU 1525 *The Master Thief* or ATU 1535 *The Rich Peasant and the Poor Peasant* are found in Louisiana, maritime Canada, France, and Reunion Island. Despite similarities with the English-language Jack tales, the character of Roquelaure appears to be limited to French and Creole oral traditions.[39] It is likely that the uncommonness of this name (unlike Jean or Jack) has led a few scholars to suggest a possible connection between the Master Thief figure and the noble Roquelaure family.

It has been pointed out that the name Roquelaure can refer to several men of a noble Gasconian family widely recognized for their wit and their closeness to kings from Henri IV to Louis XIV.[40] Perhaps much of the family's mystique—and consequently the difficulty of establishing a veritable link between the Roquelaure family and the clever thief of Louisiana folklore—derives from a considerable array of anecdotes and references beginning in the sixteenth century and the conflation of numerous references to members of the Roquelaure family. Among these historical references are the elder Antoine de Roquelaure (1543–1625), his son Gaston-Jean-Baptiste (1615–1678?), and his grandson Antoine-Gaston de Roquelaure (1656–1738). Both Gaston-Jean-Baptiste and his son Antoine-Gaston de Roquelaure, often referred to by his title Chevalier, were known in the social circles of the French nobility for their wit and flamboyant personalities. However, much distinction among these three figures is lost due to the common use of the simple reference of "Roquelaure" as well as the fact that multiple members of the family shared several of the same titles (*marquis, duc, maréchal, chevalier*). Moreover, the Roquelaure family's roots in the Gascony region are frequently mentioned in historical accounts. Perhaps this detail was a source of exoticism, otherness, or even a pretext for the kinds of erratic behavior that they displayed toward other members of the French nobility at the court. I mean to demonstrate here that additional sources from the period prove that a notion of Roquelaure, or at least a conflation of one or more members of the family, had already attained a somewhat legendary status in French popular culture. Furthermore, the numerous historical accounts and theatrical works featuring a character named Roquelaure persisted in France well into the nineteenth century.

Gédéon Tallemant des Réaux's (1619–92) *Historiettes,* a collection of short biographies of notable figures of society, including some of the more scandalous tales, gives some insight into the reputation of the dukes of Roquelaure.[41] The first duke Antoine, Baron de Roquelaure (1543–1625), also known as *le maréchal de Roquelaure,* is most noted for his military prowess, although Tallemant also notes his humor, which was much appreciated by King Henri IV. Antoine's son Gaston-Jean-Baptiste de Roquelaure became a duke in 1652. He later inspired T. de Robville's *Histoire curieuse du duc de Roquelaure, surnommé l'homme le plus laid et le plus gai de France,* published in 1861. In the preface to this colorful and pseudo-biographical work, Robville draws attention to Gaston de Roquelaure's notoriety as a fixture of popular culture: "Gaston, Duke de Roquelaure [. . .] is a popular character; the salons and studios know him at least by name, and he is celebrated like a friend who is awaited to return."[42] One finds a lengthier description in the earlier text, *Le Momus françois, ou le portrait et les aventures divertissantes du duc de Roquelaure,* mysteriously attributed to S.L.R., perhaps Sieur Antoine Le Roy. The "Portrait of the Duke of Roquelaure," or "the ugliest man in the world," begins, "This Duke had dark little eyes, commonly called pig eyes; he had broad and thick eyebrows, a dark complexion [. . .]; a nose that was so flattened between his two eyes that it was difficult to even discern."[43] Gaston de Roquelaure's physical singularity echoes many portrayals of the trickster figure in the oral tradition, which is "always a marked creature, an anomaly among animals or humans."[44] In a

Monsieur le duc de Roquelaure,
engraving from 1683, Bibliothèque Nationale de France.

HISTOIRE CURIEUSE

DU DUC DE

ROQUELAURE

SURNOMMÉ

L'HOMME LE PLUS LAID ET LE PLUS GAI DE FRANCE

SES AVENTURES GALANTES INCOMPARABLES, SES RUSES
EXTRAORDINAIRES, SES FACÉTIES, IMPROMPTUS,
RÉPARTIES, BONS MOTS, JOYEUSETÉS DE TOUT GENRE, ETC., ETC.,
RECUEILLIS A LA SUITE DE NOMBREUSES RECHERCHES
ET MIS DANS UN NOUVEL ORDRE,

Par M. DE ROBVILLE

Tout pour rire, est notre devise.

Vengeance des dames de la cour. (Page 37.)

PARIS

LE BAILLY, LIBRAIRE

Rue Cardinale, 6, et rue de l'Abbaye, 2

Faubourg Saint-Germain.

1861

Title page of *Histoire curieuse du duc de Roquelaure*,
Bibliothèque Nationale de France.

number of Master Thief tales, including the Grimms' "Der Meisterdieb" and Lazard Daigle's "Fin voleur," collected in Louisiana by Barry Ancelet, a mark on the forehead or shoulder is a significant feature by which the thief's family recognizes him when he returns home as an adult. The anonymous author of *Le Momus françois* also makes note of Roquelaure's humor and wit: "Regarding his mood, he was joyful with a satirical mind, farcical and mocking, his manners civil, insinuating, natural and noble. [. . .] He loved the pleasures of life, even to the point of debauchery and sometimes excess. He was as brave as a soldier and generous as a prince, quick to the aid of his friends. [. . .] His primary vice was that of satire, which he pushed too far at times until it degenerated into slander. One might say that if he had many fine qualities, he also had his faults."[45]

This description of the duke of Roquelaure includes some of the most salient characteristics of the Master Thief figure, including the Roquelaure of Louisiana folklore. Most notable are his civil and charming demeanor, particularly toward the king, and his ability to maintain his courteous manners all the while slyly mocking the king. And yet this portrait of Roquelaure does not depict an utter scoundrel; he has friends and is happy to be of service when he is needed.

The member of the Roquelaure family that most resembles the human trickster figure of French and Creole Louisiana folklore, however, is Antoine-Gaston de Roquelaure. Remembered as one of the "representative figures of libertinage" of seventeenth-century France, he is often referred to as Antoine Chevalier de Roquelaure, perhaps to distinguish him from the more respectable reputation of his grandfather, with whom he shared the first name of Antoine.[46] Antoine-Gaston, or Antoine Chevalier de Roquelaure, has even been described as a "gentleman from a powerful family, a blasphemer and famous debaucher," and it is likely blasphemy that led to the trials and eventual incarceration of the chevalier de Roquelaure in 1646 in the Conciergerie de Toulouse, from which he later escaped by bribing a guard.[47]

Stories of the chevalier de Roquelaure's antics were apparently widespread enough to become the inspiration for the "Pauper scene" of Molière's 1682 play *Dom Juan*.[48] In Molière's play, Dom Juan offers a louis d'or to a downtrodden hermit begging for alms in the street, provided that he will "swear."[49] After the man repeatedly refuses to blaspheme, Dom Juan gives the pauper some money "pour l'amour de l'humanité" (for the love of humanity). In this way, Dom Juan slyly invents a profane variation of the common phrase "pour l'amour de Dieu" (for the love of God).[50] Clearly, this scenario was inspired by a nearly identical real-life episode, which became the subject of the chevalier de Roquelaure's trial in 1646.[51]

The significant number of anecdotes, literary examples, and historical records prove that the name Roquelaure was, to some degree, a fixture of popular culture from seventeenth- and well into nineteenth-century France. The popularity attributed to the name Roquelaure, based on a reputation of being remarkably clever, is not surprising as the outlaw hero mantle is often attached to figures who show wit, style, or sympathy that sets them apart from common criminals.[52] However, the case of Antoine-Gaston de Roquelaure stands out from many other legends because early biographical accounts so closely resemble folklore motifs associated with a specific tale type (ATU 1525). Tallemant des Réaux's description of Antoine-Gaston de Roquelaure in his *Historiettes* contains several such motifs:

> The chevalier of Roquelaure is kind of a madman who is also the greatest blasphemer in the kingdom. It is said that he has corrected his ways a bit. In Malta, he was put down a well where he was left for some time as a punishment. In the navy, the Count of Harcourt was prepared to throw him into the sea with a cannonball on his foot. That did not change his behavior; as several years later, having found people just as crazy as he was in Toulouse, he said Mass during a game of tennis . . . , baptized and wed dogs, and all manner of impiety imaginable. The authorities were notified. [. . .] Several days later, he corrupted the prison guard with a bribe of six hundred pistols: the jailer escaped with him though misfortune later found him, because the chevalier stole his money and sent him away like a rascal.[53]

This description evokes several motifs found in variants of Master Thief tales, including Roquelaure tales in Louisiana. Tallemant des Réaux's description of the chevalier de Roquelaure is one of someone who consistently defies authority. Furthermore, this excerpt contains multiple instances of escaping from confinement. It is clear that Roquelaure is accustomed to regaining his freedom through his wit when he faces punishment or imprisonment by figures of authority. Even the reaction of the count of Harcourt, willing to throw Roquelaure into the sea, is reminiscent of motif K842, the sack exchange motif.

ROQUELAURE AND THE SPANISH SOIL TRICK

An 1836 vaudeville play, *Roquelaure, ou l'homme le plus laid de France*, provides further evidence that the name Roquelaure maintained a place in the collective imagination of nineteenth-century France. In this curious theatrical work, Roquelaure is banished from the country by the king (presumably Louis XIV) and is forbidden to set foot on French soil. He manages to return, however, in a small *charrette* (cart) filled will Spanish soil, pulled by two men. The choir announces his return to France with a song composed on the air "Le Curé de Pomponne" that relates Roquelaure's clever trick to avoid the king's wrath by remaining on Spanish soil that he has loaded onto a cart. Roquelaure's song continues:

> Quoique exilé je ne crains rien
>   D'un roi que je révère;
> Je suis toujours, je le maintien [*sic*],
>   Sur la terre étrangère;
> Car cette terre, mes amis,
>   En tous lieux m'accompagne . . . ,
> Dans mes souliers j'en ai mis,
>   Et je suis
> Sur les terres d'Espagne![54]

> Although exiled, I fear nothing
>   Of a king that I revere;
> I am still, I maintain,
>   On foreign soil;
> For this earth, my friends,
>   accompanies me everywhere . . . ,
> In my shoes I have placed it,
>   And I am
> On Spanish land.

This image of Roquelaure proudly standing on a bed of Spanish soil is yet another symbol of the character's precarious status between hero and criminal. Moreover, the striking similarity between this episode and Roquelaure tales from France and Louisiana suggest that Roquelaure's adventures and conflicts with authority entered into the popular consciousness of France and left a lasting impression, considering that this play was written nearly a century after the lifetime of the last duke of Roquelaure.

Beyond historical and literary examples outlined here, multiple tales in the oral tradition well outside of the Parisian region attest to the far-reaching renown of Roquelaure and similar motifs. For instance, two tales from the South of France collected by Paul Barrié from the region of Pays de Sault depict similar scenes.[55] The storyteller, sixty-six years of age and from Carcanières (Ariège), France, describes a nearly identical story of an exiled Roquelaure returning to the king's court in a stagecoach (*carrosse*) filled with foreign soil (*terre étrangère*). Although the Spanish origin of the soil is not made explicit in this variant, the following tale in Barrié's collection depicts Roquelaure defeating a Spanish general in a sword fight.[56]

The "Spanish soil trick" has even been attested in the Creole folklore of Reunion Island. Marie-Christine Decros includes a tale called "Roklor é le roi" (Roklor and the King) in her 1978 thesis, "Contes réunionnais: textes et traductions." Although not technically a variant of ATU 1525, this tale is nevertheless similar in that it consists of a series of tricks that Roklor plays on the king.[57] As in the French variant collected by Barrié, Roklor is banished from the land and returns to the king in a wheelbarrow (*saret la ter* or *charrette de terre*) filled with Spanish soil.[58]

These multiple references to the same name from distant geographic zones are difficult to explain through mere coincidence. Are these similar episodes reflective of the chevalier de Roquelaure's exile in Spain? Or is it, rather, a question of confusing the chevalier with other members of the Roquelaure family, especially the elder Antoine Maréchal de Roquelaure, who completed several military campaigns in Spain? Whatever the origin of this scenario involving Roquelaure transporting himself on a layer of foreign soil, it seems that the story had become a sufficiently stable fixture of the French oral tradition to survive in Louisiana through various waves of French and Francophone immigration.

Elizabeth Brandon collected a Roquelaure tale told by a native of Abbeville in Vermilion Parish, Edgar Boudreaux, in 1953. Typical of Roquelaure variants in Louisiana, the character is cast not as the king's servant but simply as "living with the king."[59] After humiliating the king by succeeding in two assigned tasks, Roquelaure is banished from the king's domain that, curiously enough, is in Louisiana. Roquelaure decides to return to Louisiana after a year and aims to do so by filling up his buggy with Spanish soil, just as is described in the vaudeville play *Roquelaure, ou l'homme le plus laid de France*.

The significance of the earth's Spanish provenance in Boudreaux's tale is ambiguous. Is the motif merely a holdover from French folklore, as several elements would suggest? For example, transporting soil in a cart from Spain to France is much more plausible than hauling soil from Spain to Louisiana, which would involve crossing the Atlantic Ocean. The fantastical image of a king's court in Louisiana also points to an old-world vestige simply transposed directly onto a Louisiana context. Such direct transposition would contradict Zumthor's notion of false reiterability—which in oral narrative serves to level off semantic difficulties, archaic words, or ambiguities from a defunct cultural context—and arbitrariness of proper names.[60] Although folktales generally do find a way of adapting to their cultural contexts, certain vestiges seem to persist. The monarchy could certainly be considered a defunct cultural context in 1950s Louisiana, and Roclore had undoubtedly become an arbitrary proper name. At the same time, this variant contains a remarkable degree of localization.

Unsurprisingly, this tale ends with the sack exchange, motif K842, during which Boudreaux specifies that Roclore's mules are from Kentucky and Roclore's true motivation for returning from Spain is an important football game. Other Louisiana variants have Roclore retrieving the dirt from his own land or from a neighboring parish.[61] It is possible that Spain remaining the source of Roclore's soil in some Louisiana variants signifies some kind of historical relationship to Spain. After all, it was during the Spanish colonial era (1763–1800) that the majority of Acadian refugees arrived in Louisiana. This time period also coincides with the performances of *Le Momus françois* and *Un Tour de Roquelaure* (1799).

Newly arrived Acadians were effectively placed by the Spanish government in a stretch of settlements along the Mississippi River from what is now St.

James Parish to where the town of Vidalia is presently located. The Spanish government, eager to populate the Louisiana Territory newly acquired from France, did provide refuge to the Acadians. However, their frustration grew over the Spanish government's practice of strategically placing the Acadians in areas that were demographically sparse, subjecting them to what has even been referred to as "a second diaspora."[62] Because Vermilion Parish, where Brandon collected this variant, became home to a particularly large number of Acadians, it is possible that the notion of Spanish soil could have retained a certain connotation as a middle ground between refuge and place of exile, or home and foreign land.[63]

The attestation of this Vermilion Parish variant casts doubt on one of Reinecke's principal remarks on the Roquelaure tales of Louisiana, which is their presumed exclusivity to Avoyelles Parish.[64] It would seem, therefore, that Roquelaure tales in Louisiana are not necessarily typical of Acadian heritage or of Avoyelles Parish but are simply common to French popular culture and oral tradition. To further illustrate the widespread popularity of Roquelaure tales in French-speaking North America is an Acadian variant collected by Jean-Pierre Pichette in Richibucto, New Brunswick, told by the prolific storyteller Séraphie Daigle-Martin.[65] In this tale, the protagonist is named Roquelaure, and the theft motifs are very similar to the Louisiana variants, including the theft of the queen's ring and bedsheet by raising a sort of scarecrow to the king's window. The tale even ends with motif K842, the sack exchange. The Master Thief of this tale is rather peculiar because unlike most variants, in which the thief is forced by the king to steal, this Acadian variant depicts Roquelaure as relentlessly plaguing the king of his own accord. Daigle-Martin includes a variation of the "Spanish soil trick" that is highly reminiscent of the scene from the French play Le Momus françois: "Roquelore s'en va le lendemain, [. . .] il garrochait une pelletée de terre puis il marchait dessus, il passait. . . . Le roi a dit: Roquelore, je t'ai pas dit que je voulais pas te voir sur ma terre? Sire le roi, il dit, c'est pas votre terre; c'est la terre d'Irlande, il dit. Il avont comprit là, il pouvait pas le tuer, vois-tu, c'était pas sur sa terre" (Roquelaure leaves the next day, [. . .] he would throw a shovelful of dirt, then he would walk on it and pass by . . . The king said: Roquelore, didn't I tell you that I didn't want to see you on my land? But sire, he said, it's not your land, it comes from Ireland, he said. He understood at that point that he couldn't kill him because he wasn't on his land).[66]

Although the name of the thief, the structure of the narrative, and the stolen items are more or less identical to what is found in the French variants, the soil comes from Ireland rather than Spain. The attestations in various regions—France, New Brunswick, and Louisiana, for example—of Master Thief tales featuring a character whose name is Roquelaure, or a variation thereof, completing a variation of the "Spanish soil trick" strongly suggests a historical connection with one or more members of the noble Roquelaure family of France. The intermingling of history and myth is particularly common in the case of outlaw figures, like the Master Thief. One reason for the ambivalence of the noble thief figure is its capacity to straddle opposing realms of myth and reality. While some outlaw heroes are purely fictional, most are rooted to some extent in historical figures.[67]

Whether or not it is made explicit, the audience understands that the hero will not steal from his own community. Some would argue that it is for this very reason that he can be considered a hero at all.[68] One can understand the nearly universal appeal of this tale type and how the Master Thief figure has maintained a prominent status both in the Francophone world and throughout the American South. Because such figures emerge when social, cultural, ethnic, or religious groups feel oppressed and mistreated by some other more powerful group(s), the Master Thief's appeal is understandable in the cultural context of French and Creole Louisiana, which identifies itself to a large extent in opposition to mainstream Anglo-Saxon American culture.

Therefore, the Master Thief tales represent a way to place the oppressed culture on equal footing with figures of authority or oppression. Much like in the tales of Bouki and Lapin, this is accomplished through cleverness, adaptability, and wit. In this way, the Master Thief genre also represents a parallel with the slave narratives of the American South. Levine notes how "slave tales document the distinction many slaves made between 'stealing,' which meant appropriating something that belonged to another slave and was not condoned, and 'taking,' which meant appropriating part of the master's property for the benefit of another part."[69]

Several Louisiana Creole variants attest to this observation, including "Jean des Pois Verts" (John Green Peas), collected by Alcée Fortier in late-nineteenth-century New Orleans.[70] The protagonist's name evokes a pantheon of folk heroes such as Ti-Jean, or Petit Jean, of the French- and Creole-speaking oral traditions explored in the next chapter. However, this tale also corresponds to what Lawrence Levine calls a "slave trickster cycle" that features a trickster figure often named John: "In John, slaves created a figure who epitomized the rewards, the limits, and the hazards of the trickster. He could improve his situation through careful deception, but at no time was he really in complete control; the rewards he could win were limited by the realities of the system within which he existed, and dangers he faced were great. Time and again the more elaborate schemes of the slave trickster failed, and he saved himself only by last minute verbal facility and role playing—two qualities which these stories emphasized were crucial for all slaves to cultivate."[71]

Jean des Pois Verts enjoys the king's infinite trust, although the neighbors all suspect Jean as a thief. As the king's chickens, geese, and gold are repeatedly stolen, each time he entrusts Jean with finding a better place to hide his riches. As we find in countless slave narratives, Jean steals objects that are directly related to his physical survival as an act of resistance against oppression. Similar to the animal trickster stories, acquiring food was "a primary goal for the slave trickster."[72] This is quite different from the Master Thief of the French tradition, in which the thief is challenged to steal objects based on the difficulty in acquiring them, such as the king's horse or the queen's bedsheet and wedding ring. Another key difference between this variant and the majority of the Master Thief tales of the European tradition is that Jean des Pois Verts is trusted by the king, even to the point of being charged with the task of finding the thief. This scenario seems much more indicative of a relationship in which the subject (or slave) has spent his entire life on the king's (or master's) property, whereas in most European variants of the Master Thief, the robber leaves at a young age to learn his craft and returns as an adult to antagonize the king. When the king finally understands that Jean is the thief, he orders him to be placed in a sack and thrown in the river. As is typical, motif K842 *Dupe persuaded to take prisoner's place in a sack: killed* follows, and the king later jumps into the river and drowns. Essentially, motif K842 fulfills the same narrative function as motif K581.2 *Briar-patch punishment for rabbit* in the Creole animal trickster tales. In both cases, the protagonist, unable to free himself through force, relies on his wits and especially his words to dupe his captor into freeing him through a changing of places.

The Master Thief tale's ability to remain relevant in colonial contexts in which slavery played a prominent part in society is further demonstrated by variants in the Antilles. Jean Noël Stanislaus Priméon of Trois Rivières, Guadeloupe, tells two versions that were collected by Elsie Clews Parsons.[73] Among the variants found in the French- and Creole-speaking oral tradition, these tales featuring a "Maît'e volé' (Master Thief) named Félicien, who most closely resembles the Grimms' "Der Meisterdieb." The village abbot, Félis, is cast as the thief's opponent, and as in "Der Meisterdieb," he is also the thief's godfather. One of the challenges set forth by the abbot is for Félicien to kidnap the abbot's clergyman and sacristan, which plays out in a nearly identical fashion to the Grimms' tale. Félicien releases into the cemetery a sackful of crabs with candles on their backs. This example of ATU 1737 *The Parson in the Sack to Heaven* demonstrates a greater resemblance with the European tradition than the Louisiana variants.[74] Furthermore, Félicien's cry to the abbot is practically a direct translation into Guadeloupian Creole of the Meisterdieb's exclamation: "Every day you hear talk of the end of the world, the end of the world! Look at the cemetery and see how the dead are burning. Whoever wishes to go to heaven with me, crawl into my sack!"[75] It is curious that ATU 1737 should have survived in the Creole tradition of Guadeloupe but not, at least according to the resources available, in Louisiana. Conversely, the sack exchange scene of motif K842 is very prevalent among the Louisiana variants but not in succession with the motif of going to heaven in ATU 1737. Such a filtering out of this motif would be in line with the complete lack of blasphemy in the Roquelaure tales of Louisiana, whereas it was an element closely associated with the Roquelaure tales of France.

꙰

If the prevalence of Compère Lapin and other sly animal characters in its folklore repertoire is any indication, French and Creole Louisiana displays a remarkable affinity for the trickster figure. The human trickster tales resemble the animal trickster in many ways, but while storytellers typically rely on perceived characteristics of specific animals to exude certain qualities like strength or cunning, these distinctions are more explicit in tales of the human trickster. Social status, poverty, and wealth give the impression of moral clarity even with the protagonist's thievery, shrouding our perception of justice in ambiguity despite clues and narrative asides offered by storytellers. Because each community is in need of a figure to transgress social boundaries and rock the established order, Master Thief tales are appealing to a wide range of groups from Europe to the Antilles.

The numerous attestations of the Master Thief tales throughout the world, including the Creole variants of Louisiana and Guadeloupe, show that the Roquelaure family is by no means at the source of the Master Thief tale types ATU 1525 and 1535.[76] However, the abundance of specific scenarios and motifs found in literature, oral tradition, and theater of France confirms that the name Roquelaure became associated with a sort of trickster figure in the French popular imagination as early as the seventeenth century and that the connection with the name was prevalent at least until the latter part of the nineteenth century.[77] These numerous references from various types of sources—from Tallemant des Réaux's *Historiettes* to folktales in the South of France—suggest that this name was known both in and outside of courtly society in France. With the wide reach of French colonization in North America, the Antilles, and well beyond, the association between the trickster figure and the name Roquelaure spread throughout most of the French- and Creole-speaking world.

The historical reference among storytellers linking the trickster figure Roquelaure (whatever the variation in spelling) of Louisiana folklore and a member of the French nobility by the same name was undoubtedly lost long ago, not unlike the character Bouki, whose original Wolof meaning of "hyena" is unknown to many of the most prolific Cajun and Creole storytellers. However, its survival in Louisiana as a noun meaning "rascal" or "good-for-nothing" certainly suggests that the association with the name was once known. In addition to restoring meaning to nearly lost signification of characters' names in the oral tradition and their origins, research into written sources also problematizes a prevalent misconception that rural Francophone Louisiana was almost entirely isolated from the literary and popular culture of France. The existence of the name Roquelaure as well as striking similarities with regard to motifs found in the oral tradition of France suggest a linguistic, narrative, and cultural continuity. Put simply, the Roquelaure name seems to have been fused to the tale type ATU 1525 in much of Francophone North America, especially in Louisiana. Roquelaure the human trickster figure became part and parcel of a preexisting Master Thief tale type and represents a testament to the fluent exchanges between Louisiana, the Caribbean, France, and Acadia.

CHAPTER 3

The Many Faces of Jean le Sot

The mythologist Joseph Campbell titled his 1949 study of what he believed to be the quasi-universal "hero's journey" *The Hero with a Thousand Faces*. While heroes' names and the cultures that celebrate them may differ greatly, most share a basic narrative structure.[1] In contrast, in Francophone folklore, the figure Jean appears in a wider variety of scenarios. Jean tales can be found throughout the Francophone world, and there exist multiple variations on the name: Jean le Sot (Foolish John), Jean-sans-peur (Fearless John), Ti-Jean (Little John), Jean de l'Ours (John the Bear), and others. These characters display tremendous variability both with regard to their names and the characteristics and morals associated with them. Jean, as an exceedingly common first name, is not unlike other prevalent folklore traditions, including the Jack tales in North America and the John slave trickster cycle. The commonplace nature of the name Jean highlights the ordinariness of the character and allows storytellers to create a sense of proximity between the character and their audience. Whether Jean is portrayed as a fearless hero or bungling fool, he is always depicted as a member of his community. While there is a great deal of variation between these extremes within the larger Francophone folklore repertoire, I will focus here on Jean le Sot, his representation in Louisiana, and how this relates to other portrayals elsewhere in the French-speaking world.

Jean's ambivalence and wide range of characteristics is reflected in the name's history and etymology. At its origin, the Greek Ιωαννης was derived from the Hebrew, *Yochanan* (יוֹחָנָן), meaning "Yahweh is gracious." Compassion, sympathy, and generosity are the protagonist's defining traits in the majority of Jean tales. In the case of Jean le Sot specifically, he is often generous to a fault with his misplaced empathy causing his downfall. We might wonder why the name Jean has lent itself to such a wide range of tale genres. It is, of course, an extremely common first name in the French-speaking world, but could the same not be said of Pierre or Jacques? It is possible that the name's meaning(s) in Christian culture gave rise to interpretations (or parodies) of certain traits that infiltrated popular culture and the oral tradition.

The Bible contains two important figures bearing the name in the New Testament: John the Baptist and the apostle John. John the Baptist, an ascetic who directly opposed the authority of Herod and also spent much time in the wilderness, represented a marginalized group of Jewish society. Moreover, he is the only character in the New Testament whose physical appearance receives any attention at all. John the Baptist is described as wearing a leather belt, nourishing himself on a diet of locusts and wild honey, and donning a garment of camel's hair around his waist.[2] In many cultures throughout the biblical tradition, hair was associated with an intimacy with nature and nonconformity, which is reflected in John the Baptist's role in a marginalized community outside of regular society. In a similar way, Jean le Sot of the Francophone oral tradition invariably exudes a distinctive quality of unconventionality and is generally rejected from the normal society of the village. He is often described at the beginning of tales as having a different appearance than those around him.[3]

Jean le Sot, or Foolish John, as he is commonly called in English translations, is the numbskull par excellence of Louisiana's French and Creole folklore.[4] There is some variation with regard to spelling and pronunciation; in Louisiana, Jean Sotte is the most commonly found version of the name.[5] Jean le Sot is also one of the most prevalent folklore figures of France, and he can be found virtually everywhere in the French-speaking world, including the Antilles, Acadian communities of eastern Canada, and Francophone Missouri.[6] The most common spelling in France is *Jean le Sot;* however, much regional variation exists throughout the French-speaking world and even in France (Jan le Pec in Gascony, Joan le Piot in Aude, and Jouan Nesci in Auvergne).[7] These tales seem to be particularly prevalent in Poitou and the neighboring regions. Considering the geographical provenance of the Acadians and other early settlers of Louisiana mentioned in the introductory chapter of this book, it is not surprising that Jean le Sot tales are also common in Acadian communities of maritime Canada and Louisiana.

Many variants involve Jean le Sot's mother sending him on several errands that he later fails to execute due to his clumsiness or misunderstanding of the instructions. Because the narrative structure hinges on a series of errands, Jean le Sot tales lend themselves easily to interchangeable episodes that storytellers can chain together much in the same way that several Bouki and Lapin tales can be told in succession.

Another prevalent trait in Jean le Sot tales is language; puns, malaprops, and riddles are often the root of Jean's collapse or (more rarely) triumph. Again, a correlation with the name's biblical connotations comes into play. The Gospel of John has been described as poetic and mystical as it places an emphasis on the Word.[8] This notion is exemplified by the opening passage of his gospel: "In the beginning was the Word, and the Word was with God, and the Word was God."[9] The contiguous relationship between the word and existence—saying and doing—is subverted in the Jean le Sot tales. It is the "word," along with an utter lack of worldliness, that serves as a catalyst for Jean's misadventures. Unable to penetrate the underlying meaning of words and understand his mother's orders, Jean is impeded by the literal meaning of her words. Jean le Sot's problem is that he dutifully attempts to follow instructions to the letter, but he lacks the common sense to interpret the orders he receives. On a structural level, such antics manifest themselves through motifs like J2460 *Literal obedience* and J2259*(p) *Fool's action based on pun.*

The use of puns and wordplay in Jean le Sot tales can be traced to the French oral tradition. Many such examples can be found in the UPCP-Métive/ CERDO archives in Parthenay, France. One common type found in France and Louisiana is ATU 1006 *Casting Eyes*, wherein Jean le Sot, following a friend's advice to "cast eyes" at girls to get their attention, tosses eyeballs plucked from a sheep or another animal's head.[10] This kind of wordplay can also be observed in various dialects. Emile Caillon, a storyteller from the Deux-Sèvres region, tells a variant of ATU 1204 *Fool Keeps Repeating His Instructions So As to Remember Them*, in which Jean le Sot, on an errand to purchase salt in the village, continuously mutters to himself, "Sàu, sàu, sàu" ("salt" in Poitevin-Saintongeais dialect). A man that he crosses along the way believes the murmuring to be an insult directed toward him and beats Jean le Sot.[11] Jean le Sot's personage calls into question the word through his repeated literal obedience.[12]

Variants from France, Louisiana, and Acadian communities of maritime Canada all display a remarkable degree of similarity with regard to the specific motifs used. Because the tales' structures rely on consecutive errands, these episodes are largely interchangeable and function independently of one another. As they are often linked together in succession, the structure of many Jean le Sot tales can be interpreted as alternating states of disequilibrium and equilibrium. The tension between need and resolution are common basic structural elements in folktales: something once abundant may have been lost, then recovered; something lost may be found; and so on.[13] Dundes viewed this rubric of moving from disequilibrium to equilibrium as two essential "motifemes," which under his classification were dubbed Lack (L) and Lack Liquidated (LL).[14] While this basic structure is found throughout the oral tradition, typical Jean le Sot tales, particularly those found in Louisiana, place this structure at the forefront of the narrative and include minimal elaboration. The state of disequilibrium in Jean le Sot tales is often related to a lack of household supplies, particularly food. Frequently found examples in the oral traditions of France, Louisiana, and maritime Canada involve an initial lack of food (usually evoked at the beginning of the narrative) or Jean le Sot wasting food or other goods. Because Jean le Sot usually fails at acquiring the necessary resources, the motifeme of Consequence (in the form of the mother's disappointment, scolding, or physical punishment) is a typical conclusion.[15]

Jean le Sot's tendency to waste food is often associated with his affinity for nature, which sometimes causes him to place inanimate elements of nature above the needs of his mother or family. The following tale, told by Revon Reed, evokes the character's awkward attraction to nature and exhibits the typical [L + LL + L + Consequence] narrative structure.

> Jean Sot avait le cœur, on conte, beaucoup sensible. Il aimait tout le monde. Il aimait tous les bêtailles. Il aimait jusqu'à la nature, les arbres, les fleurs, la terre. Il avait un grand sentiment pour tout ce qui existait. Un jour, sa mère lui a donné un gros quart de beurre pour aller vendre à la boutique et *trade* ça pour des marchandises, des grosseries, mais en allant là-bas, Jean Sot était fier et bien associé avec la nature. Il sifflait, il chantait, mais tout d'un coup, tandis qu'il traversait un marais sec, il a vu des craques dans la terre, des grosses craques. Et il croyait que c'était des gerçures, ça. *Chapped,* on dit

en anglais. Alors, il a ouvert la jarre de beurre et il a commencé à graisser les crevasses dans un effort d'essayer de les guérir. Et il pleurait. Il trouvait beaucoup mauvais que la terre était après gercer comme ça. Et quand tout le beurre a manqué, il s'est vite retourné chez sa mère pour d'autre. Après qu'il a conté qui il y avait eu, naturellement, elle lui a pas donné d'autre beurre. Puis elle l'a bien fouetté pour ça, mais c'était trop tard.

Jean Sot had, it is said, a very sensitive heart. He loved everyone. He loved the animals. He loved even nature, the trees, the flowers, the land. He had deep feelings for everything in existence. One day, his mother gave him a big quart of butter to go and sell at the store and to trade for supplies, groceries, but on the way there, Jean Sot was proud and close to nature. He was whistling, he was singing, but all of a sudden, as he was crossing a dry swamp, he saw cracks in the ground, big cracks. And he thought they were chapped marks. So, he opened the butter jar and he started to butter the cracks in an attempt to heal them. And he wept. He thought it very sad that

Jean Sot et le beurre. Digital illustration. Jonathan Mayers, 2020.

the land was chapped so. And when the butter ran out, went quickly home to his mother for more. After he explained what had happened, naturally, she didn't give him any more butter. And she whipped him well for that, but it was too late.[16]

Calvin Claudel's collection includes a similar variant from Avoyelles Parish in which Jean Sotte's mother sends him to town to fetch some cotton cloth and thread. While returning home with the requested items, he crosses a small gum tree (*un copal*) shaking in the wind. Out of pity for the tree, Jean uses all of the newly purchased cloth to cover up the tree. As in Reed's tale, the mother beats the boy after he explains what happened, corresponding to the [L + LL + L + Consequence] narrative structure.[17]

In addition to food and other necessary resources being wasted, there is a recurrent theme of killing farm animals in Jean le Sot tales. One example is the shooting of the cow, accomplished through the motif J2259*(p) *Fool's action based on pun*, when Jean Sot shoots the family's cow after misunderstanding his mother's orders to *tirer* (to milk) instead of its homonym *tirer* (to shoot).[18] Other examples include the crushing of the mother goose's eggs—sometimes after killing the mother goose—while he attempts to brood following her death.[19] For a context like rural Louisiana, the death of domestic and farm animals and the wasting of food could represent significant losses in livelihood for families. This brand of black humor implicitly designates Jean le Sot as a true threat to his family's well-being despite the comedic backdrop of the story.[20]

A comparison of the motifs found in the Louisiana variants with those from the Poitou region of France reveal the greatest degree of cross-regional overlap of any of the tales analyzed in this book. We can see that nearly all of the motifs of lost objects—needles in the haystack, the butter or lard spread in the dry earth, the brooding of eggs—exist in both the Louisiana and Poitou repertoires. Upon closer analysis, however, a point of divergence becomes clear. The Jean le Sot tales found in the Louisiana repertoire are limited to the [L + LL + L + Consequence] narrative structure. However, in the French oral tradition, these nearly identical tales constitute but one of several possibilities for Jean le Sot. It would seem that tales from Poitou are more disposed to cast Jean le Sot as a "hero in spite of himself" rather than exclusively as a simpleton with no redeeming qualities at all.[21] Whereas the Jean Sotte of Louisiana is always depicted as a hopeless young boy, the Jean le Sot of France can be seen as a hero who marries a princess at the end of the tale.

"Jean le Sot, Jean le Fin, Jean le Rusé," told by Marie Vidaud of Turgon, France, is an example of the kind of heroic qualities of the Jean le Sot character within the French oral tradition that seems to be entirely absent in the Louisiana corpus.[22] In this variant of 513B *The Land and Water Ship* a king calls for a suitor for his daughter, offering her hand to whoever can fashion a boat that can travel on land as well as water.[23] Jean le Sot is one of three brothers who set out, one after the other, to complete the task. Shortly after departing from home, each of the sons encounters the Virgin Mary, who asks them to share with her some of the meager rations that their poor mother prepared for their respective travels to the king's court. Despite the intelligence that their names might imply, Jean le Fin (Astute John) and Jean le Rusé (Clever John) show no generosity toward the Virgin Mary, who, in turn, does not grant them help in their impossible task. Only Jean le Sot, who has the least amount of food, offers to share with the Virgin Mary, although she politely declines the boy's humble gesture. As recompense, each time Jean le Sot strikes the tree from which he aims to construct his magic vessel an entire portion of the boat is produced. Even after having constructed the boat requested by the king, Jean le Sot is asked to perform several more seemingly impossible challenges, including collecting a handful of millet cast into a bushel of heather and retrieving the castle keys from the bottom of a lake.

Functionally, these motifs have the opposite effect of those found in the Louisiana variants, in which Jean le Sot repeatedly loses needles, keys, or cloth. In this French variant, it is Jean who finds the lost objects. Furthermore, Jean le Sot is depicted as a character to be emulated because of his generosity, not toward nature but to the Virgin Mary. Vidaud encapsulates the moral of the tale's end by saying: "So, you see, it isn't about being clever, it's about being good! You see, he was good, so he succeeded, and the brothers who were more clever were actually more foolish! There you have it. And Jean le Sot got to marry the king's daughter."[24]

While Louisiana's Jean Sotte does not possess any of the heroic traits seen in the French tale, this does not mean these tale types are absent from the Louisiana repertoire. "Jean l'Ours et la fille du roi," told by Elby Deshotels of Reddel, Louisiana, is a variant of ATU 513B included in Ancelet's collection.[25]

Corinne Saucier also collected a more localized variant of this type, "The Millionaire, His Daughter, and Her Suitors," in which a rich man replaces the king. Therefore, it is clear that legendary tale types like 513B did indeed remain culturally relevant in French and Creole Louisiana, but not as Jean le Sot tales. Positive and heroic characteristics are invariably reserved for Jean l'Ours, Ti-Jean, or other variations of the figure. In contrast, the Jean le Sot figure of the French oral tradition is associated with a much wider variety of traits and tale types.

A significant number of similar variants in which Jean le Sot marries the king's daughter at the end of the tale can be found in the archives of the UPCP-Métive/CERDO in Parthenay, France. Particularly prevalent in Poitevin-Saintongeais are variants of ATU 853 *Hero Catches the Princess with Her Own Words*, wherein Jean le Sot succeeds at the queen's task of making her daughter laugh and thus acquires her hand in marriage.[26] The fantastic deeds demanded of Jean le Sot in the French variants—creating a boat that moves on land and water, acquiring the hand of the king's daughter in marriage—contrast with the menial tasks given to the character by his mother in the Louisiana Jean Sotte variants. The oral tradition of France consists of a much wider gamut of representations of Jean le Sot, ranging from fool to hero.[27]

EDUCATION, LANGUAGE, AND IDENTITY

It is clear that despite the high degree of similarity between the French, Acadian, and Louisiana variants with regard to specific motifs such as buttering the cracks in the ground or losing needles, Jean le Sot's more heroic qualities have not survived in Louisiana's oral tradition. What sociocultural factors could be at the root of the total absence of admirable traits associated with the fool figure in the Jean Sotte tales found in the Louisiana repertoire? It is plausible that difficult conditions of rural life and the need for a cohesive community would have made Jean le Sot, who is based on the fool archetype, an undesirable medium for heroic traits. Moreover, linguistic and cultural discrimination against French and Creole speakers put non-English speakers at odds with the process of Anglo-Americanization, which began with the Louisiana Purchase but accelerated following the Civil War. The strong stigmatization of French- and Creole-speaking communities was eventually formalized through systemic changes in linguistic legislation and mandatory public education.

The state-governed educational institution was already viewed as a foreign concept to many French speakers of the region, who viewed education as the work of the Catholic Church. This was particularly true for those of Acadian descent; not only was this the experience of their forebears in Acadia and France, but it was also their own experience in Louisiana as is reflected in the early history of education in southwestern Louisiana represented by Franklin College of Opelousas and St. Charles College and Sacred Heart Academy of Grand Coteau.[28] However, with the advent of mandatory education came an opportunity to advance the English-only trend toward homogenizing the linguistic landscape of the United States.

The Louisiana State Constitution of 1921 remains a pivotal moment in history for the French language in Louisiana, often cited by historians as a major factor in the decline of the language's transmission.[29] The nationalistic pressure to assimilate into English-speaking American society was met with much tension in primarily Francophone Louisiana and resulted in the widespread stigmatization of the French language, instilling a sentiment of linguistic inferiority in the generations to come. The school system advanced the notion that the monolingual Francophone population of Louisiana was backward and "un-American."

Contrary to popular belief, the constitution of 1921 did not explicitly outlaw the use of French, but it did make English the only acceptable language of instruction. The underlying intent of the legislation, however, was made clear through its brutal implementation, which took advantage of the legal gray area in the constitution. In other words, the 1921 constitution in itself neither obligated nor authorized school officials or educators to punish children for speaking French at school, particularly outside of the classroom. This widespread practice played into a much larger national Zeitgeist meant to eradicate non-English languages throughout the country.

Personal accounts of how this policy was enforced vary greatly; some Louisiana Francophones claim to have received no punishment for speaking French at school, while others describe humiliation and both physical and emotional abuse. Again, because none of these practices were actually condoned by the law, its effects were largely dependent on those in power. One punishment that has penetrated the collective consciousness more than others is forcing children to write on the chalkboard, sometimes over a hundred times, "I will not speak French on the schoolgrounds."[30] The nearly across-the-board and sometimes violent enforcement of the English-only language policy in Louisiana schools following the 1921 legislation resulted in a collectively shared trauma narrative that appears in Louisiana's cultural production such as Jean Arceneaux's "Schizophrénie linguistique," in *Je suis Cadien,* and Hadley Castille's song "200 lignes," among other examples.[31]

The presence of this collective experience in poetry, music, and oral history is reflective of a cultural trauma at the core of the collectivity's sense of identity.[32] The psychological scar inflicted on practically an entire generation of French speakers at a young age was irreversible because it instilled a sense of shame and a feeling of ignorance and inferiority within the community's very identity. These scars manifested themselves in folktales and humor dealing with foolish characters through prisming in two distinct ways. On one hand, "real-life" intelligence and common sense are valued above all because the community's livelihood depends on it. Errands and other essential tasks must be accomplished. On the other hand, the stigmatization of Louisiana's Francophone identity that was created by the public school system is often appropriated and subverted in jokes and folktales. As formal education became a marker of Americanization, intentionally distancing oneself from it became a characteristic trait of the community.

The association between a Francophone identity and ignorance gave way to a host of jokes and anecdotes that link formal education to linguistic or cultural confusion. The following narrative (presented here in half-jest as a "true" story) told by Larrell Richard of Ossun, Louisiana, is a well-known joke in South Louisiana: "My father sent me to school in the first grade and I came home after only twenty minutes. When my father asked me why I wasn't in school, I told him, 'I came home because that's all there was. The teacher said everybody had to talk only English. There were a few who understood, but most of us didn't know what she was saying. Then she said something about numbers and said, 'Say one.' A few people around the classroom said, 'One.' Then she said, 'Say two.' So, we all got up and left." The punch line is based on the misunderstanding of two bilingual homonyms, "Say two" and "C'est tout" (That's all), and plays on "the assumed eagerness of Cajuns to be rid of schooling as soon as possible."[33] Thus, the implicit reality of linguistic inferiority becomes the source of humor and defiance of educational authority.

Another example that pits formal education against a Francophone identity is found in "Jean Sot à l'école" told by Clotilde Richard of Carencro, Louisiana, in 1974.[34] Jean Sot is cast as the young boy in this variant of ATU 1628 *The Learned Son and the Forgotten Language*.[35] Jean has gone to school to study English and, upon returning home, pretends to have become so "educated" that he has forgotten how to speak French. That is, until he accidentally steps on a rake and is struck in the face, causing him to exclaim, "Mon fils-de-putain de rateau!" / "You son-of-a-bitch of a rake!" The mother quips, "My son, I see your French is coming back to you!"[36]

A similar tale was recorded in Civray, Vienne department of Poitou-Charentes. Baribeaux Marcelle was recorded in 1984 telling the following tale in Poitevin-Saintongeais dialect.[37] The young boy, having studied in Paris, attempts to impress his family and neighbors by employing the word *rastelle* in an effort to show off his knowledge of Latin.

> L'aviont un vosin qu'était parti à Paris. Pi au bout de quèques temps, l'est de retour au péyi. Alore l'a velu. Et pi le fasait dau chiqué le velait épater.
>
> O n'avait un qui manquait, l'était dans les prés à minme rateler dau foin. Pi alore [le vat le trouver], ét pi le dit tout d'un cop:
>
> De quoi que tu te sert là? C'est bien une "rastelle"?
>
> Une "rastelle"? qu'o dit le vieux.
>
> Bé oui.
>
> Le se revire, le marche su lés pues dau ratâ. Le yi revint peur le nez. Le se revire, le dit:
>
> Cré fi d'guiarce de ratâ! L'm'a fait dau mau![38]

> They had a neighbor who went to Paris. After a while, he came back to the country. So, he went to visit his neighbors. And he was showing off; he wanted to impress.
>
> But one of his neighbors wasn't home. He was out in the field raking hay. So, he goes out to meet him there and says:
>
> What have you got there? A *rastelle* (rake)?
>
> A *rastelle?* says the old man.

Well, yes!

He turns around and steps on the teeth of the rake. It pops up and hits him right on the nose. He turns around and says:

Damn, son of a bitch rake! That hurt![39]

Poitou-Charentes and Francophone Louisiana are both regions that have historically been home to a considerable degree of diglossia. In Clotilde Richard's rendering of the same tale type, the structure is almost identical to the Poitou-Charentes tale, although the languages in question differ. Whereas the young Poitevin boy has studied Latin and presumably the Île-de-France, or Parisian dialect, the young Cajun has gone off to study English at school. French occupies the status of the low language in Louisiana but the high language in the Poitevin variant. Each of these tales implies that in their respective contexts, formal education should not necessarily be perceived as true intelligence. In Francophone Louisiana, this tale takes on a larger dimension, bringing to the forefront the struggle to maintain a linguistic identity despite the encroachment of the dominant Anglo-American culture.[40]

Both tales offer an incisive commentary on formal education's value (or lack thereof) in traditional society. Both narratives highlight a direct link between language and a traditional, agricultural lifestyle. In both cases, the boy "loses" contact with his mother tongue by distancing himself from the countryside and migrating to the city. Upon returning, it is the rake, a simple agrarian tool, that literally knocks him to his senses, reminding him of his "forgotten" first language. There is a striking carnivalesque aspect to this scene, in that the low language in both diglossic contexts (symbolized by the rake) unexpectedly rises up, temporarily displacing the high language from the boy's mind, bringing back his true identity. Such imagery is reflective of how language and agricultural imagery manifest themselves through traditional carnival celebration in Louisiana. The carnivalesque is a form of resistance as it places the popular culture (*culture populaire*) in a central position.

A number of Jean le Sot variants collected in Acadian communities in maritime Canada exhibit many of the same motifs found in the Louisiana corpus. "Jean le Sot," told by Siphrone d'Entremont of Pubnico West, Nova Scotia, consists of a series of motifs similar to the variant told by Revon Reed. This variant of tale type 1696 *What Should I Have Done*, collected by Helen

Creighton, includes the buttering of the cracks in the earth, losing needles in a haystack, and Jean le Sot, who attempts to brood eggs after killing the mother goose.[41] Although the Acadian variants found in the Centre d'études acadiennes Anselme Chiasson folklore archives generally portray Jean le Sot as a marginalized and ignorant young man, there are several instances of more positive traits attributed to the character despite his lack of intelligence. Catherine Jolicoeur collected a variant including tale types 1691A and 1653 wherein Jean repeatedly fails at household tasks yet manages to unwittingly protect his home from burglars.[42] "Jean le Simple," told by renowned story-teller Exelda Hébert of Richibucto, New Brunswick, includes a character who cunningly tricks the king into firing his guards, appointing Jean le Simple as his new counselor.[43]

In sum, the repertoire of Jean le Sot tales from Acadian communities in maritime Canada seems to represent a sort of intermediary between the tales found in France, where positive character traits for Jean le Sot are most prevalent, and Louisiana, where only negative characteristics are attested. This would suggest that the harsh reality of rural Louisiana resulted in a collective disinclination to cast the fool figure in a favorable light or to portray him as a model for children. Such an example of prisming would be understandable, particularly in Louisiana's French and Creole communities, where cohesiveness would have been paramount in adapting to a different environment and challenging rural lifestyle.

A possible and notable exception to the overall lack of heroic traits associated with Jean Sotte in Louisiana is a Black Creole tale collected by Alcée Fortier in 1895 that seems to portray a protagonist similar to the Master Thief figure, which is also common in the Antilles. As seen in chapter 2, cultural contact and sustained interaction between Black Creoles and White Francophones have resulted in the introduction of the character Bouki into the Cajun folk repertoire. In a similar way, Alcée Fortier's collection confirms that the character of Jean Sotte had entered into the Black Creole oral tradition of New Orleans at least by the end of the nineteenth century and likely much earlier. Contact between White French Creoles and Black French or Creole speakers in the Crescent City during the nineteenth century resulted in a cast of characters that was heavily influenced by the African oral tradition (the hyena, elephant, monkey) but also included traits of French folklore.[44]

Highly paradigmatic characters with easily recognizable narrative functions or human-like traits were especially interchangeable as the African and European traditions converged. Both the hyena and the hare of the West African repertoire and the *loup et le renard* (the wolf and the fox) of France were easily identifiable in their respective roles of dupe and trickster.

Fortier's transcription of "Jean Sotte" represents a hybrid with typical attributes of African animal tales over a substratum of the Jean le Sot tales originating from France. In this sense, the tale's characterization can be likened to the Creole language itself, lexically based in French but creolized through linguistic contact with African languages. The diegesis of Dorlis Aguillard's "Jean Sotte" is a world in which the protagonist meets and interacts with Compair Bouki and Compair Lapin.[45] The tale is creolized in such a manner that the boundary between the animal and human kingdoms is fluid or even absent.

Aguillard describes Jean Sotte as a young man who does everything incorrectly, wearing a heavy coat in the summer yet walking around nearly naked in winter, lighting his lamp in the daytime and carrying an umbrella only at night. This Jean Sotte is not only out of sync with nature, but he is also marked by his physical appearance, drawing stares as he looks so "gauche" (awkward). As in many of the Jean le Sot tales from the French tradition, the hero of this Creole variant is challenged by a higher authority: the king who is searching for a suitable groom for his daughter. King Bangon, upon first encountering Jean Sotte, asks him if Compair Lapin is his father. When another person in the king's audience cries that Compair Bouki is actually Jean Sotte's father, the protagonist responds by affirming that they are both his father. Jean Sotte's misunderstanding comes from his literal interpretation of verbal messages: "All of them; they are all my fathers. Every time one of them passes by me he says, 'Good-morning, my child.' I must believe them, then, that they are all my fathers."[46] Jean Sotte's response is not without comedic value; however, his reaction is significant in that it forces the listener to consider the character's ambiguity and his liminal position between fool and trickster. Jean Sotte is, in a figurative sense, the progeny of Compair Bouki and Compair Lapin, in that he embodies the characteristics of both figures.

Amused by Jean Sotte's simple nature, King Bangon decides to give him a chance at winning his daughter's hand in marriage. He first challenges Jean Sotte to bring him a bottle of bull's milk the next morning as a remedy for his daughter, who is bedridden with a backache. When Jean Sotte fails, the king goes on to challenge Jean a second time, inviting him to return in one month, on the first of April, to answer a question within three guesses. If Jean should succeed, he will win the king's daughter in marriage, but should he fail after three attempts, the king will have him beheaded. The mention of the first of April as a suitable day to trick someone—April Fool's Day—suggests a strong connection with the French tradition.[47]

The symbolism of the bull's milk can be interpreted in at least two ways. One interpretation is as a euphemism for sperm and, by extension, a suitable husband for his daughter and heir to the throne,[48] but it could also be seen in a more obvious way as what Dundes calls a "fool's errand." Moreover, the mention of April Fool's Day in itself evokes the pranking ritual. False quest objects are often localized according to specific occupations, such as a carpenter's apprentice being sent for a board shortener, a painter for a bucket of striped paint, and so on.[49] In this instance, the king seems to be attempting to take advantage of Jean Sotte's reputed lack of knowledge of nature and sexuality.[50] An important detail in this narrative, as the reader discovers later, is that Jean Sotte is only pretending to be tricked by the king. Therefore, although he verbally agrees to leave the king's court in search of the bull's milk, his lack of intelligence is only an illusion.

When Jean returns home from his first encounter with the king, he recounts the day's happenings to his mother: "Quand li rivé coté li, li raconté tout ça so moman, et vié femme prend crié, crié, pasqué tout sotte so garçon té yé moman la té laimin li quand méme, pasqué c'était jisse ein piti li té gagnin. Li défende Jean Sotte couri, ménacé li marré li ou ben fait sheriff jété li dans prison" (When he reached home, he related to his mother all that had happened, and the old woman began to cry, and could not be consoled, because, however foolish her boy was, she loved him, as he was her only child. She forbade him to go to the king, and threatened to tie him in her cabin, or to have the sheriff throw him in prison).[51] It is interesting to note the compassion that the mother shows Jean, which is quite different from the image of the scolding mother, ashamed of her son, that one finds in nearly all of the Cajun variants. Jean Sotte leaves his mother's house armed with an ax, intent on boldly challenging the king's authority. Even early in the story, it is clear that Jean Sotte is much unlike the typical Cajun representation of the amiable

Jean Sot described by Reed. In this Creole tale, Jean Sotte's provocation of the king is more akin to what one finds in other "Jean" characters of the French tradition, such as Jean l'Ours, 'Tit Jean, or the Master Thief.

Upon arriving at the king's property, Jean Sotte climbs up an oak tree just in front of the king's door and begins to chop away, purposely attracting the attention of the watchman and eventually drawing out the king himself. To the contrary of the French and Cajun variants, the Jean Sotte of this Black Creole tale insists on speaking directly to the king, affronting him both by his presence and his words.

Whereas the other Louisiana variants discussed thus far describe a character lacking the ability to effectively use language and understand his mother's instruction beyond the literal meaning of her words, in this tale Jean Sotte is quick-witted and facetious. The angry king demands that Jean Sotte explain what he is doing to his tree, to which Jean retorts that he is cutting the bark to make tea for his father, who has just given birth to twins. The king answers back: "For whom do you take me, Jean Sotte? Where did you ever hear of a man in childbirth? I think you mean to make fun of me."[52] Jean Sotte reminds the king that a man giving birth is no more ridiculous than his earlier request for a bottle of bull's milk. In this way, he shows him that he does understand the simple nature of basic sexuality. Jean Sotte's audacity is respected and even rewarded by the king, who invites Jean into the kitchen for breakfast.

One of the more surprising elements of the tale is that when Jean Sotte returns to the king one month later, on the first of April, Bouki and Lapin present themselves into the narrative. This tale is unique among the major collections of Louisiana tales in that Jean le Sot is found alongside Bouki and Lapin in the same tale. Bouki, who is described as *traite* and *malfaisant* ("deceitful" and "evil-minded"), plots to sabotage Jean Sotte's mission and plans to leave a basket of poisoned cakes on the road as bait in order to steal his horse once he is dead. The villainous representation of Bouki is a departure from the African tradition, in which the hyena is often portrayed as a victim to the hare's ruses.

The tale illustrates that not only does Jean Sotte inhabit the same narrative world as Bouki and Lapin, but there is a preexisting complicity between Jean Sotte and Lapin: "Compair Lapin té laimin Jean Sotte, pasqué ein fois li té trouvé li méme dans grand nembarras, li té trouvé dans prison dans ein la trappe et Jean Sotte té laché li. Pou ça Compair Lapin dit li méme: Mo va protégé pove ninnocent la" (Compair Lapin liked Jean Sotte, because one day, when he was caught in a snare, Jean Sotte had freed him. He did not forget that, and said: "I want to protect the poor fellow").[53] Having overheard Bouki's malicious plans, Lapin decides to wait for Jean Sotte on the road as early as daybreak and, upon their encounter, warns him not to eat or drink anything on his way to see the king. Lapin effectively save Jean's life, but he does not expect this good deed to go unrewarded, saying, "Don't forget me when you marry the king's daughter; we can have good business together."[54] In this way, Lapin recognizes Jean Sotte as a peer, even a fellow trickster.

Jean Sotte heeds Lapin's advice but nevertheless tests the validity of his warning by feeding a few of the cakes to his horse. The horse drops dead immediately, and Jean throws it into the river just before three buzzards alight on it. Jean Sotte continues on foot, recalling Lapin's advice to him to listen, look, and remain quiet. By the time Jean Sotte arrives at the castle, the tyrannical King Bangon has already killed fifty men for guessing incorrectly at his riddles. In light of Jean Sotte's reputation as a half-wit, the court attendants are surprised to see Jean return to make an attempt to answer the king's riddle: "What is it that early in the morning walks on four legs, at noon on two, and in the evening on three legs?"[55] Reminding the king of his promise to give his daughter's hand in marriage should the riddle be solved, Jean responds that it was "a child who walked on four legs; when he grew up he walked on two, and when he grew old he had to take a stick, and that made three legs."[56] The crowd is astonished by Jean Sotte's correct response, and Bangon, not to be outdone, proclaims that if anyone present should stump him with a riddle of their own that he would relinquish to them his crown and fortune. In a scenario much like what is found in the Master Thief tales, Jean Sotte composes a riddle based on his journey that day: "I saw a dead being that was carrying three living beings and was nourishing them. The dead did not touch the land and was not in the sky; tell me what it is, or I shall take your kingdom and your fortune."[57] When the king proves to be unable to respond, Jean Sotte explains: "My horse died on a bridge, I threw him into the river, and three buzzards alighted on him and were eating him up in the river. They did not touch the land and they were not in the sky."[58]

At the end of the tale, Jean Sotte seems to undergo a transformation whereby his name is replaced. Once everyone saw that Jean Sotte was much more clever than he had appeared, he married the king's daughter and appointed Lapin as his first overseer and hanged Bouki for his *coquinerie* (rascality). Jean's change of name is noteworthy in a number of ways. First, the character's new name of Jean L'Esprit (Clever John) represents a clear shift in his identity and, perhaps more important, in the way in which he is perceived by others. With regard to the characterization of the Jean le Sot genre, the eventual conflation of the Jean Sotte and (the sometimes present) Jean L'Esprit seems to be an anomaly among variants of all of the regions concerned in this study. The fact that there is mention of a character named Jean L'Esprit provides evidence of a certain vestige of the European tradition, although his apparition and function are radically different from the French oral tradition. Finally, by uncrowning the king and assuming the role as leader, Jean Sotte incites a carnivalesque reversal of the traditional power structure. The resolution of this tale corresponds precisely to Bakhtin's notion of carnivalesque dethroning: "For the fool, all of the royal attributes are reversed, inverted, up is down: the buffoon is king of the 'upside down world.'"[59]

Jean Sotte's transformation and the carnivalesque reversal of power represent a fundamental difference from the Jean Sot variants collected in White Francophone communities. Moreover, it seems to be the only variant found in the major Louisiana collections in which Jean Sotte (or Jean Sot) exhibits this fundamental change and becomes king. Although the appearance of Jean Sotte appears to be limited in the Black Creole oral tradition, this variant suggests that the appropriation of the character was dependent on a dramatic shift in the character's role in the narrative. A marginalized figure of lower social status would have been perceived differently in groups that were oppressed by slavery. Jean Sotte may have been an ideal vehicle to satisfy their psychic needs by depicting a hero capable of not only compensating for his lack of social or economic power by his cleverness but also concealing his intelligence until an opportune moment.

⁓

On one hand, comparing Jean le Sot variants from western France, Acadia, and Louisiana shows a clear delineation from the French oral tradition. The high degree of preservation can be seen in motifs J2460 *Literal obedience* and J2259*(p) *Fool's action based on pun* as well as specific tale types such as ATU

1696 *What Should I Have Said (or Done)?* and 1291B *Filling Cracks with Butter.* Another discernible similarity is the repetitive structure of bungled errands that I have identified as [L + LL + L + Consequence] through Dundes's motifemic system. On the other hand, we have seen that a much larger and more varied repertoire of Jean le Sot tales exists in France and that his role as a fool (or hero) is more nuanced. In a considerable number of these tales, Jean le Sot exudes positive character traits and is portrayed as a hero; he even marries a princess in some tales.

The tales from the Louisiana corpus generally attribute none of these heroic qualities to Jean Sot. This is not to say, however, that the tale types themselves have not survived in Louisiana. *The Land and Water Ship*, for example, was well known in Louisiana but as a Jean l'Ours tale. Heroic traits appear to be relegated to Ti-Jean, or other versions of the name Jean, but not Jean le Sot. Through prisming and false reiterability, the depiction of the fool as a hero became culturally obsolete in the Louisiana context. The cultural trauma experienced by Louisiana's Francophone children following the 1921 state constitution, along with wider linguistic and cultural stigmatization, would have made the fool an unlikely and undesirable narrative vehicle for any kind of heroic qualities. Moreover, a character that in so many variants is associated with the wasting of food and the death of farm animals would have been considered a threat to the community considering the difficult conditions of rural French-speaking Louisiana leading up to the mid-twentieth century. These tales presented a black humor in the context of rural French Louisiana, and it is likely that the Jean Sot tales would have taken on a didactic purpose for a young audience to warn them about the consequences of careless actions.

As mentioned, the one exception to the character's generally negative portrayal in the Louisiana repertoire is "Jean Sotte" found in Alcée Fortier's 1895 collection of Black Creole folktales. This tale's source also differs greatly from the other variants taken from White Francophone communities later on in the twentieth century. In this tale, Jean Sotte conceals his cleverness, dethrones the king through a battle of wit, and eventually becomes king. Similar to what is found in the oral tradition of the Antilles, Jean Sotte more closely resembles the hero of ATU 1525 *The Master Thief,* suggesting that the character was probably introduced into the Creole oral tradition of the Caribbean before arriving in Louisiana.

In all Jean le Sot tales, the character straddles the boundary between commonness and marginality. While a name as popular as Jean makes him seem relatable, one or more traits always distinguish him from the rest of his community; this could be a physical mark, a misplaced display of empathy, or an inability to comprehend words or phrases beyond their literal meanings. In sum, Jean's representations are many and diverse, at times appearing alone in the narrative, at other times alongside one or two presumably cleverer brothers. In the larger context of Francophone folklore, it could be said that Jean le Sot inhabits the space between outcast and outlaw hero, or between the ordinary and extraordinary. While he is a marginalized figure that succeeds either with difficulty or not at all, he is never a complete outsider to the community.

CHAPTER 4

Un Sacré Conte

Anticlerical Humor in Louisiana Folklore

South Louisiana distinguishes itself as one of a number of Roman Catholic enclaves in the United States. Even a quick overview of the major waves of immigration into Louisiana during the eighteenth through twentieth centuries reveals that many of these groups claimed Roman Catholicism as their dominant religious denomination. The French (including the Acadians), Spanish, Irish, Italians, and others were all predominantly Catholic. In fact, the Catholic faith of the Acadians was a major factor in the decision of the colonial Spanish government of Louisiana to assist the Acadians in settling in the region beginning in 1764. Although the Acadiana region may be more diverse today, data from the early twentieth century show that about 60 percent of the state was Catholic, while the United States as a whole counted under 3 percent of the population as Catholic.[1] The influence of Catholicism extends well beyond the practice of attending mass on Sunday. The church calendar and rituals punctuate the lives of Cajuns and Creoles throughout the year, from the reckless abandon of Mardi Gras to the solemn painting of tombstones on All Saints' Day, as well as other hallmarks of religious tradition lesser-known elsewhere, such as the May crowning of the Virgin Mary and St. Joseph's altars.

While it is tempting to view the Catholic Church in retrospect as an integral part of the French and Creole culture of Louisiana from the outset of the colonial period, this relationship is much more ambivalent than it is often portrayed. The historical relationship between the Catholic Church and the Acadians alone offers a glimpse into the complexity of this dynamic: "From the outset of Acadian settlement in Louisiana, Cajuns have been recognized—both by their detractors and their apologists—as a devoutly religious people. [. . .] Yet, Acadian piety has been matched by equally intense anticlericalism. This religious paradox is the legacy of the Catholic church's role in the early development of the Acadian society."[2]

To further obfuscate its role in Louisiana in the wake of the Louisiana Purchase of 1803, the Catholic Church found itself tending to an increasingly multiethnic flock while contemporaneously being both severed from the powerful monarchies of Europe and also newly annexed to a majority Protestant nation.[3] While it is true that the Catholic faith is and was generally shared by Acadians, White Creoles, Creoles of color, and even pockets of German, Italian, and Spanish immigrants who assimilated into the predominantly French-speaking area, the church never explicitly or implicitly asserted itself in the preservation of the French language in Louisiana. Francophones, in turn, did not necessarily see the church as a guardian of their culture nor as a representative of any particular ethnic identity. The church's role in Louisiana with regard to the French language stands in strong contrast to its position in French Canada, especially in Quebec. There the church operated as the sole institutional power for Francophones in English-dominant Canada. The many abuses of that power, in part, led to the *Révolution tranquille,* or Quiet Revolution, of the 1960s that saw intense sociopolitical change and secularization. Louisiana is perhaps the only region in North America where the Catholic Church assumed such a decidedly detached role vis-à-vis the preservation of the French language. Barry Ancelet has coined this phenomenon as *l'exception louisianaise* (the Louisiana exception) in French-speaking North America. Elsewhere, in Quebec and the Acadian communities of the eastern maritime provinces of Canada, members of the clergy such as Lionel Groulx and Anselme Chiasson were at the forefront of French-language education initiatives, not to mention their ardent fieldwork and cataloging of much of the oral tradition in their respective regions.

In Louisiana, the Catholic Church showed little interest in developing such an institutional infrastructure in French.[4] Even within the limited context of folklore studies, clergymen were often de facto ethnologists and oral historians in Francophone communities of Canada, particularly in the maritime provinces. In contrast, nearly all of the researchers who worked to document, catalog, and promote the languages and culture of South Louisiana—including Alcée Fortier, Corinne Saucier, Alan Lomax, and Ralph Rinzler—had no ties to the church. There were a select few, such as Jean-Marie Jammes (a Jesuit priest) and Catherine Jolicoeur (a Filles de Marie-de-l'Assomption sister), who took an active interest in the French language in Louisiana, but they were, as Ancelet points out, the exception and not the rule.[5] It is also noteworthy that Jammes and Jolicoeur were not from Louisiana, but from France and Canada respectively.

Only of late can one find masses celebrated in French in the Acadiana region, most often early in the morning, twice a month in Breaux Bridge and at local events like Festivals Acadiens et Créoles and Festival International de Louisiane. In 2015 began the Fête-Dieu, organized by Father Michael Champagne, now a quasi-annual event consisting of a French mass, rosaries in English and French, and a boat procession representing the 121 church parishes of the Diocese of Lafayette traveling the Teche or Vermilion River. Although many see this rise of the French language within official church practices and ceremonies in South Louisiana as a kind of return to the ways of the past, it is actually quite a new phenomenon. Historically speaking, masses in French were never prevalent in Louisiana because the liturgy was recited in Latin until the Second Vatican Council (1962–65) opted to celebrate mass in the vernacular language. In the early twentieth century, homilies were given with roughly equal frequency in either French or English or a mixture of the two. However, by the mid-1960s, it is unlikely that French speakers, many of whom were not literate in the language, would have expected (or even preferred) the standard French of missals from France to be used as the new "vernacular" per the Vatican's reform.

Both Acadians and Louisiana Cajuns have historically been portrayed and thought of as devoutly Catholic, and popular representations such as Henry Wadsworth Longfellow's *Evangeline* have no doubt been very influential in reinforcing that image. However, recent scholarship has sought to add nuance to this depiction given the history of tensions with the clergy and a current of anticlerical humor.[6] Whether or not one qualifies the majority of French and Creole Louisiana as "devout," the church's influence on everyday life is undeniable. Marcia Gaudet contends that in southern Louisiana, *"cultural*

Catholicism" more aptly describes this dynamic as it "avoids the possibly marginalizing connotations of 'folk'" and "signifies the pervasive influence of non-official Catholicism" in the region.[7]

I argue here that the confusion between these two opposing representations of religiosity among Cajuns and Creoles is largely due to a conflation of *apathy* and *anticlericalism*. In other words, the tension between the French- and Creole-speaking communities and the Catholic Church was generally focused on individual priests and church officials, not the church or system of beliefs as a whole. Ancelet observes that Cajuns and Creoles have historically been anticlerical despite being otherwise very devout, tracing this anticlerical sentiment in French Louisiana directly to the Acadians.[8] Ancelet's historical reasoning is based on Carl Brasseaux's extensive research into the church's relationship with Acadians both before and after their deportation from Acadia, or the *Grand dérangement*. Brasseaux describes the early interactions between the Acadians and the clergy on the frontier: "For many if not most late seventeenth- and eighteenth-century Acadians, Catholic missionaries were shadowy figures who provided the settlers minimal contact with the church hierarchy. Forced to fend for themselves, even to the point of conducting paraliturgical services, the immigrants ultimately came to divorce religion from the area's traditionally dominant religious institution. Priests consequently became little more than petty religious administrators, stripped of their cloak of religious invincibility and vulnerable to personal criticism."[9]

This colonial view of priests as "petty religious administrators" was a dramatic departure from their demigod-like status under the European monarchies of the Old World. In this new territory, they often were seen, at best, as itinerant "moral police" prodding colonists to construct churches in their newly inhabited land or, at worst, as bureaucrats. This historical perspective serves to underscore further the distinction between apathy and anticlericalism and how recognizing the human faults of their leaders did not necessarily make Louisiana Francophones less devout. However, contrary to the quasi-total rejection of religion that occurred in France during the French Revolution and much later in Quebec during the *Révolution tranquille*, anticlerical humor in Louisiana has tended to target only the clergy and not the church or religion as a whole. This can undoubtedly be traced back to the questionable morality of many colonial priests and to the local inhabitants' disdain for their goal to "civilize" a people perceived as backward. A natural reaction to this was "a demystification of the frock and spirit of rebellion among the flock."[10]

It seems that the friction between Louisiana's priests and their congregations had less to do with religion than that they were simply perceived as symbols of authority. This mistrust in figures of authority has been a constant in the Acadians' existence since they originated primarily from the French peasantry.[11] This tension was especially acute when priests' views and actions strayed too far from their church obligations. Residents in the small town of Cecilia still recall tales of the French priest Father Perronet, who often interdicted parishioners from dancing or playing cards as penance. Such encumbrances were interpreted as arbitrary and unnecessary, and similar stories seem especially common when referring to priests from France.

Undoubtedly, one major factor that served to further alienate priests from the parishioners is that a considerable number of clergymen came from elsewhere; even up until 1970, the "majority of parish priests in Louisiana were French, Belgian, French Canadian or Irish missionaries."[12] Even in the following decades, Francophone priests from other countries remained quite prevalent in South Louisiana. Most of these priests were native French speakers, could minister to local Francophone communities, and had the institutional knowledge of record keeping that came with being from areas where French had an official status. The result of the high numbers of foreign missionaries, coupled with remarkably few local men entering the priesthood,[13] was that Louisianians rarely viewed their priests as one of the proverbial flock. Their assumed "outsider" status made them all the more susceptible to scrutiny and mockery in both real-life interactions and the oral tradition, ranging from incisive humor to simple tongue twisters such as "Sept plats pleins de crêpes sur la tête d'un prêtre" (Seven plates full of crepes on a priest's head).[14]

My aim here is to establish the priest as a kind of folklore figure or type with specific traits and a distinct place in the folklore of French and Creole Louisiana.[15] There are, as noted, historical reasons for the development of the priest as such a figure, and his actions and treatment within the region's oral tradition support his existence as a well-defined character type. Priests are portrayed as self-indulgent, haughty, and even deceitful. These characteristics are displayed in common Louisiana French phrases as well, as in the expression "T'as jamais vu un prêtre maigre?" (Have you ever seen a thin priest?). Or in response to the question "Comment ça va?" (How is it going?), a common response is "Mieux que ça et les prêtres seraient jaloux" (Any better and the priests would be jealous).[16] This brand of anticlericalism has roots in the folklore of France, and it can be found in similar forms in the Acadian maritime provinces of Canada. Far from a new-world invention, anticlericalism in the oral tradition and oral performance is part of a long-standing tradition in the Francophone world dating back to the fifteenth century, when the *sermons joyeux* were performed as theatrical parodies of the liturgy in churches until they were outlawed and henceforth relegated to the *Fêtes des fous* (Feast of Fools).[17] In Louisiana, anticlericalism manifests itself in the oral tradition in a fashion that is as delicate as it is incisive. While often lighthearted, it is difficult to ignore the prevalence of anticlerical humor in French Louisiana folklore.

One particularly salient tactic for popular expression and upsetting order in the French and Creole cultures of Louisiana is engaging in the carnivalesque. Most are familiar with the rituals of carnival season, or at least Mardi Gras, which represents the last day before Lent, when Catholics begin a period of forty days of fasting and penance in anticipation of the Easter season. Going back to its most ancient roots, Mardi Gras and carnival are about subversion, mockery, and disturbing the status quo. The etymology of *carnival* can be traced to its older Italian form *carnelevarle*, meaning "to remove meat," a reference to the impending fast that follows the feast and revelry of the season. Even today, rural Mardi Gras *courirs* in areas such as St. Landry, Acadia, and Evangeline Parishes feature revelers dressed in a wide variety of costumes and often wearing hats such as cone-shaped *capuchons*, miters, and mortarboards (an irreverent nod to the attire worn by noblewomen, the clergy, and scholars respectively). Participants poke fun at authority and experiment with embodying their polar opposites; White men dressed as Black women and intoxicated young men disguised as pious old clergymen are all par for the course. This reversal of roles and power structures is similar to Mikhail Bakhtin's notion of carnivalesque dethronement, in which up is down and the buffoon is king.[18] In the performance of carnival, these examples of mockery and subversion are visible, even obnoxiously so. However, in literature and storytelling, the carnivalesque is a subtler stylistic tool by which the narrative or story itself achieves a similar temporary destabilization of power structures, just as one finds in the physical performance of carnival.

An intriguing example of the carnivalesque can be found in Jean Arceneaux's "Le Trou dans le mur" (The Hole in the Wall) in the eponymous collections of jokes and tales, dubbed "Cajun fabliaux," taken from the oral tradition.[19] This narrative is based on a tale collected in 1977, in the rural community of Pierre Part at the Rainbow Inn bar.[20] Unbeknownst to Ancelet at the time he heard this story, the tale is strikingly similar to a medieval French fabliau.

The fabliau *Le Prestre ki abevete* is attributed to the poet Garin and is also known by the title *Du Prestre qui fouti la dame au vilain*. Despite the vast temporal and geographic differences, medieval fabliaux and folktales share several important traits as well as common motifs and themes. One of these similarities is brevity; as a result, characters often lack depth (and even names). Moreover, they can often be identified by common types or stock figures; the peasant is opposed to the priest, the lover to the husband, the wife to the husband.[21] Such dichotomies and typecasting are not unlike the trickster-dupe dynamic in the tales of Bouki and Lapin.

The fabliau and the folktale both tell of a village priest enamored with a villager's wife. In the fabliau, it is suspected that the husband may be responsible for having not yet consummated the marriage: "She would have willingly told the priest of the life she was made to lead by he who does not know how to please a woman" (ll. 28–30: "au prestre volentiers desist quel vie ses maris li mainne, que nul deduit de femme n'aimme").[22] The woman and the priest arrange to see each other without the husband's knowledge. When the priest arrives at the couple's house, he peers through a hole in the wall and sees them dining at the kitchen table. The priest angrily accuses them of having sex in front of him, a doubly ridiculous claim since they are presumably in the privacy of their own home. The husband assures the priest from inside that he is gravely mistaken; they are merely eating their evening meal. Determined to get inside the house and near the woman, the priest convinces the man to trade places with him so that the husband can see what the priest sees. When the husband steps out of the house to peek inside through the hole in the wall, the priest and the woman begin to actually fornicate on the kitchen table, as had been their plan all along. Demonstrating just how gullible the husband is, the man calls out to the priest, who is now fully engaged in sexual intercourse with the woman, that he was indeed correct; when looking through the hole in the wall, it *does* look just like they are making love instead of eating supper. Fearing that others might think ill of them, the husband fills in the hole in the wall and returns inside to find that his wife and the priest have just "finished eating."[23]

The two narratives share a principal motif: the "mirage érotique" present in *The Enchanted Pear Tree* (ATU 1423) and found elsewhere in the oral tradition. In the ATU index, the scenario is described as follows: "With her husband nearby, a wife climbs up a tree ostensibly to pick fruit but really to meet her lover."[24] One significant difference in our two examples here is the absence of magic; the mystical setting of the enchanted pear tree is replaced with the banality of a kitchen table in a villager's mundane home.[25] The lack of context and surrounding details, such as decor or a rapport between characters, is equally absent in each text, which suggests a common theme and scenario that would be sufficiently familiar to a listener to forgo any clarification. In other words, the notion that a priest would be sneaking into a parishioner's home for adulterous reasons needs no lengthy explanation.

Both stories end in a distinctly uneventful way; the perpetrator is not punished, and the unwitting husband never even realizes that he has been betrayed. While this might be expected in French Louisiana folklore, it is exceptionally uncommon for a medieval *fabliau*. Eichmann concludes that Garin takes "a tolerant attitude toward his outrageous priest" and that "the fabliaux are generally much less tolerant of lasciviousness in priests than in members of any other class and are much less likely to award priests with a happy ending": "The tale ends with the status quo, the balance has not been violently tilted, the marriage remains intact. No tragic action has occurred, no particular sympathy has been aroused for one character or another; in spite of the reprehensible adulterous act, the audience can laugh without afterthoughts."[26]

Like French Louisiana folktales in general, the fabliaux are noted for their anticlericalism, which is often played out slyly or overtly through sexuality. Eichmann notes that a "clear and ever-present danger to marital equilibrium is the lover or suitor, who is often successful if he is a knight or clerk. If the seducer is a priest, he will arouse audience antipathy."[27] While I do not mean to trace the continuous transmission of this tale from thirteenth-century

France to twentieth-century South Louisiana, one cannot dispute that the plot structures of the two texts are almost identical. How do these two narratives, indistinguishable from one another in Todorov's sense of *histoire* (plot structure), differ significantly in terms of their *discours* (discourse), and can such distinctions be representative of cultural experience?

Fabliaux contain many motifs that lingered on in the French oral tradition in the form of fables, *contes*, and popular jokes. Moreover, thirteenth-century France and rural Francophone Louisiana were both highly oral cultures, and French folklore has heavily influenced the oral tradition of Louisiana. If "Le Trou dans le mur" is indeed related to some variant of *Le Prestre ki abevete*, it would make sense that certain discursive or even structural modifications have taken place.[28]

One striking difference between these two narratives is found in the importance of class distinction (and lack thereof). In Garin's *Le Prestre ki abevete*, the difference of social status is at the forefront of the story. This peasant-nobility distinction is evident at the very opening of the text. The characters are not referred to by name but rather by their socioeconomic roles (*vilain, dame, prestre*). According to Luciana Rossi, the author "prefers to take the opposite stance of courtly literature, adding to his *contrafacta* a shrewd satire of manners, where the contrast between the 'nobility' (most often embodied by the female characters) and the peasantry of the nouveau riche is at the heart of the author's vision."[29] The difference in social status between the male *vilain* and the noblewoman, a typical feature of the fabliaux, would likely have held little relevance in the considerably more horizontal societal structure of rural French Louisiana. In Arceneaux's telling of the story, the man is not denoted as *vilain* or *paysan* (even though this would have almost surely been the case); rather, he is consistently referred to as *le mari*, reinforcing the importance of familial relations in Catholic rural Louisiana and calling attention to the marital bonds that will soon be transgressed.

In both narratives, there is an implicit, yet rather obvious, complicity between the woman and the priest, although there is a marked difference in the representation of the woman's sexuality. In Garin's fabliau, the female character does not speak for herself. Instead, her willingness to pursue (or to be pursued by) the priest is conveyed by the narrator:

au prestre volentiers desist
quel vie ses maris li mainne,
que nul deduit de femme n'aimme.

She would have willingly told the priest
of the life she was made to lead
by he who does not know how to please a woman.

(lines 28–30)

This part is told in a past subjunctive tense, which in Old French functions as a conditional tense, softening even more the female character's agency in the text. In the Louisiana tale, the woman has a decidedly more active role both before the opening scene and during the priest's visit. The narrator, also using the conditional, says, "She also found him to be to her liking and would have liked to try to meet up with him for a little while."[30] She is in communication beforehand with the priest, who instructs her to simply prepare a meal and allow him to devise the rest of the plan. She is also vocal during the sexual act, assuring her husband, who is outside looking in.[31]

Although the woman may not say a word in Garin's fabliau, the element of sexuality is illustrated by an abundant description of the priest's actions toward her, something that is not at all the case in Arceneaux's text.

maintenant le prent par le teste,
si l'a desous lui enversee,
la roube li a souslevee,
si li a fait icele cose
que femme aimme sor toute cose:
le vit li a ou con bouté,
puis a tant feru et hurté
que il fist che que il queroit.

He caught her head,
Tripped her up and laid her down.
Up to her chest he pulled her gown

And did of all good deeds the one
That women everywhere want done.
He bumped and battered with such force
The peasant's wife had no recourse
But let him get what he was seeking.

(lines 54–61)

The signifiers for the intercourse between the woman and priest are also very different. In "Le Trou dans le mur," *faire l'amour* (to make love) is the only term used, whereas Garin uses the coarser, more vulgar verb *foutre* and includes a graphic description of what transpired. As is typical in Cajun humor, sexuality and infidelity are commonplace, although the comedic value is often more implicit than explicit, leaving more to the imagination of the listener. Furthermore, the effect of the punch line is directly related to the length and intricacy of narrative buildup, often featuring gratuitous repetition and extraneous details. In "Le Trou dans le mur," the narrator explains the priest's overly elaborate plan to spy on the couple. The manner in which sexuality is represented is telling of the cultural context from whence it originates. It could be argued that the history of sexuality and the history of literature, in the end, are mutually illuminating.[32]

Both texts function with the duality of inside and outside. In such a carnivalesque scenario, what one sees (or rather what one is told to see) is not at all the interior reality. After all, the cuckolded husband's error is that he believes what he is told and not his own eyes.[33] *Mengier* (eating) seen from the outside equals *foutre* (fucking) in the interior. Once on the other side of the wall, the priest gains access to the house and, by extension, to the woman as well. For Garin, the momentary upheaval and role reversal between the peasant and the priest is an extrapolation of the already absurd notion that a *vilain* should be married to a noblewoman. When the priest subverts his role as a cleric, the peasant takes his place in the physical sense, thus adding a layer of irony to the title (The Priest Who Peeked) because, in actuality, the husband acts as the voyeur, not the priest.

Surely the element of criticism of the clergy is present in both texts. However, in Garin's fabliau the main target of the criticism is the peasant. The introduction draws our attention immediately to the fact that he is a peasant and that she is a noblewoman. The moral at the end of the fabliau reinforces this difference:

> Ensi fu li vilains gabés
> et decheüs et encantés
> et par le prestre et par son sans
> qu'il n'i ot paine ne ahans.
> Et pour ce que li vis fu tius,
> dist on encore: "Maint fol paist Dius!"[34]

> And thus the peasant was tricked
> by the priest and by his ruse
> without suffering or pain
> as if he had been enchanted
> enchanted, so was the door! and it is why
> they say: God keeps alive many a fool.

The priest's nefarious demeanor is underlined by the absurdity of the priest's accusation. Why should a married couple be ashamed of having sexual relations in the privacy of their own home? The man's unwillingness to question the priest's moral authority becomes his downfall. Despite sharing a mostly identical plot structure, these two texts are expressed through different discourses, each indicative of their sociocultural context and period. What for Garin is a short, sexually explicit tale in which cleverness triumphs over foolishness is an understated yet potent illustration of the Louisiana Francophones' complex attitude toward priests and religious authority.

What is most noteworthy about *Le Prestre ki abevete* is that the priest is successful in his act of adultery. Among Garin's tales featuring the theme of priests seducing women, only five of seventeen show the priest having succeeded.[35] Those who fail are murdered, castrated, or severely beaten. In contrast, the knights, squires, bourgeois, and clerks of Garin's 's fabliaux all succeed in their lewd acts, without one single exception.[36] The fabliaux *Le Prêtre crucifié* (The Crucified Priest) and *Le Prêtre teint* (The Painted Priest) both tell of priests who have been frequenting the wife of a crucifix carver. In each of these two similar fabliaux, the husband is aware of his wife's infidelity.

When he returns home one day, startling the woman and her lover, the priest quickly poses along the wall of the man's workshop, imitating a crucifix. In the first example, the man pretends to notice that he has carved a penis on the statue, unbefitting of a holy object, and means to remove it immediately. In the latter example, he notices that the "crucifix" has not been lacquered; he remedies this at once, leaving the priest to cure by the fire while the couple eats supper. *Le Prestre ki abevete* thus presents a sharp contrast from the more typical, albeit gruesome, treatments of nefarious priests in the fabliaux. A survey of the fabliaux indicates that only four out of fifty-six priests could be said to be positively portrayed in their respective narratives. Other ecclesiastics, both male and female (namely, abbots, abbesses, nuns, and monks) receive an even worse fate: in each of fifty-seven examples, they are treated unfavorably.[37] This has an important implication for the Louisiana tale collected by Ancelet because it shows that the similarity is found within *the exception among the exceptions.* In other words, it does not seem that the fabliaux themselves, neither their general form nor themes, had any obvious impact on the folklore of Louisiana, but this particular type of anticlerical humor (as rare as it appears to be) shows a remarkable degree of overlap.

There is some debate among scholars about whether the fabliaux truly embody anticlericalism or whether they were merely conceived to please an apathetic or even heretical audience.[38] Gabrielle Hutton, for instance, observes two strategies exhibited by fabliau characters: *avoir* (having) and *savoir* (knowing). The first relates to the character's social status or innate qualities, while the second refers to acquired skills or cunning.[39] The few examples of priests who do not face severe punishment, as in *Le Prestre ki abevete,* tend to be clever and do not rely on their superior positions as figures of authority. In thinking of French Louisiana as "culturally Catholic," it is worth asking the same question about Louisiana folklore and how it compares to other Francophone oral traditions.

Based on Brasseaux's account of early colonial relations between Acadians and representatives of the Catholic Church, it is unsurprising that anticlerical humor should be prevalent to this day in Acadian communities of maritime Canada. The Centre d'études acadiennes Anselme Chiasson (CEAAC) at the Université de Moncton in New Brunswick houses a considerable number of examples. Several contain instances of physical revenge or beating of priests (for example, jealous husbands who discover the infidelity of their wives). The storyteller Réginald Brideau of St. Irinée, New Brunswick, tells a lengthy and elaborate variant of ATU 1360C (Old Hildebrand) in which a woman feigns an illness each week so that her husband will depart to retrieve water from a particular fountain to cure her. As is typical in this tale type, the husband teams up with his neighbor, who disguises himself as a beggar while the husband hides in a basket in order to catch the woman by surprise. This complicated ruse allows the man to enter the home while the priest-lover is present but also adds a humorous complexity as he presumably has a key and could have simply walked in. "Le Mari trompé" (The Cheated Husband) ends with the husband jumping out of the basket and attacking the priest. The presence of physical violence against the priest is unlike otherwise similar stories in the Louisiana repertoire. This intricate tale, complete with several sung stanzas from each character, is indicative of the rich storytelling techniques and memorization skills of Acadian *conteurs* that contrast with the shorter, more to-the-point style of Louisiana storytellers.

In more contemporary folklore of France, a survey of jokes and tales concerning adulterous priests from western France—specifically from the Poitou and Charentes regions, from which many Acadian and non-Acadian French departed for New France and Louisiana—reveals a considerable amount of similarity with the Louisiana repertoire, including several tale types in common. In the main catalog alone of the CERDO archives in Parthenay, France, thirty-nine of the fifty-four tales feature corrupt or adulterous clergymen. Some real-life priests have carved out a place as a fixture in regional folklore, such as Joseph Gabriel Guérin, known as the *petit curé rouge de Champigniers* (the little redheaded priest of Champigniers) in the Poitou region. Thought by some to be a sorcerer or magician, one can find a whole cycle of tales about him.[40] In addition, tales from the Poitou region include more brutal handlings of priests not unlike Beach and Eichmann's assessment of the medieval fabliaux. Adulterous priests are sometimes beaten, humiliated, or otherwise punished, a trait that is noticeably absent from the Louisiana folktales.

An interesting counterexample to "Le Trou dans le mur" and *Le Prestre ki abevete* can be found in the Charente-Maritime region of France.[41] A blacksmith who suspects his wife is having an affair with the priest waits for the opportune time to catch them in the act by spying through a hole in the wall.

When he bursts into the house yelling "Fire! Fire!" the priest hides in the armoire and replies, "Save the furniture! Save the furniture!" The representation of the priest here is congruent with his common characterization as a coward as well as his association with luxuries and finer ornaments.

Another theme shared by the Louisiana and Poitou repertoires is the correlation between corruption and hierarchy among the clergy; in other words, the higher a clergyman climbs in the church hierarchy, the more corrupt he must be. Ancelet collected a variant of ATU 1738C (*Chalk Marks on Heaven's Stairs*) from a Francophone priest in the Lafayette area, Father Calais. In this tale, a recently deceased priest arrives at the Pearly Gates and is told that he must atone for his sins by climbing a ladder and marking each rung with a piece of chalk. As he begins to wonder how long this will go on, he is relieved to see his former monsignor descending the same ladder; however, he is soon disappointed to learn that he is only returning to the bottom to fetch more chalk.[42]

In a similar vein, the CERDO archives contain several variants of a tale from the Vienne region of France in which a young priest is invited to his monsignor's home for supper. The monsignor notices the young priest admiring his attractive housekeeper and assures him that their relationship is strictly professional. A week later, the housekeeper encourages the monsignor to write the young priest to inquire about the silver ladle that has mysteriously gone missing since his visit. The young priest writes back promising his monsignor that had he been sleeping in his own bed for the past week, the ladle would not be "missing."[43]

There are, however, instances in French folklore in which malicious and trickster-like priests seem to avoid any violent consequences, thus resembling their Louisiana counterparts. One example that can be found both in the Louisiana repertoire as well as in the Poitou region deals with an adulterous priest. Ernest Rivière recounts this version of ATU 1777A *"I Can't Hear You"* in one of Ancelet's field recordings.[44] In the first, the village priest grows suspicious when he notices the sacramental wine missing so consistently. He suspects that the usher, who has a reputation for being a hard drinker, is to blame. When the priest confronts the usher, asking, "Who drank the priest's wine?" the usher pretends to be hard of hearing, answering "What? What?" The usher then responds with another question: "Who's messing around with the usher's wife?" The two men reach a tacit, unspoken agreement to ignore each other's misdeeds and move on. This exchange reveals that the usher had been aware of the priest's activities with his wife but was willing to avoid confrontation as long as he had access to the wine. In any event, this tale provides a stark contrast to the kind of corporal revenge unleashed upon priests by cheated husbands in the folktales from France.

The second tale told by Ernest Rivière hinges on the interplay between two homophones in French, *têt* (coop) and *tête* (head). When a husband leaves his young, pregnant wife for an extended period of time for work, the priest notices that the man had not built the chicken coop (*têt à poules*). The priest shrewdly offers to build the coop and "anything else that the husband usually does." Upon the man's return, the wife recounts what the priest told her, and the husband decides to exact justice by crossing over the priest's fence and chopping off the heads of all his chickens (*têtes de poules*). The very next Sunday, the priest expresses his anger about what has happened. The husband cleverly responds, "Vous qui êtes si bien metteur de têts, pourquoi vous avez pas remis les têts?" (You're so good at putting up chicken coops [*têts*], why didn't you just put the heads [*têtes*] back on?).[45]

This tale serves as an illuminating counterexample to the kind of blunders that Jean Sotte causes through literal or phonetic interpretations of words and includes the same "black humor" resulting from the death of farm animals, a real threat to the livelihood of rural families.[46] Instead of Jean Sotte unwittingly killing animals because of a misunderstanding (as in motifs J2460 *Literal obedience* and J2259*[p] *Fool's action based on pun*), the homophone acts as an inspiration for the man's vengeful actions. Even here, in what is likely the most violent example of anticlerical humor from the Louisiana repertoire, the violence is not focused directly toward the priest. Despite the clear anticlerical sentiments and mistrust of priests, the French Louisiana folktales are unquestionably nonviolent with regard to the priests.

Jude Chatelain, a White Creole from Avoyelles Parish and native speaker of Louisiana French, offers an interesting tale in his book of stories and adaptations of folktales, *Graines de parasol* (2012). "L'Évêque et le corbeau" (The Bishop and the Crow) preys upon the long-winded and lackluster sermons of the bishop while at the same time demonstrating the disengagement of the congregation, with the exception of Madame Draguée Parfait (Miss Perfect), who seems to be the only one who appreciates the tiresome homilies. Chatelain chooses to place this story in the sixteenth century, a highly unusual choice.[47]

The tale describes a congregation long since dulled by the homilies of the bishop. The only creature bold enough to protest the bishop is the crow, who has nested under his miter. The crow's squawking causes mass chaos in the church, and the congregation thinks it is the devil; immediately, everyone begins to blame "the devil's" arrival for their individual problems—why the baker's bread has not been rising, why the farmer's hens have not been laying eggs, and so forth. While the bishop tries to continue his sermon outside on the steps of the cathedral, the crow's shrill noise eventually forces the parishioners to return to their homes.

This tale is yet another example of anticlerical humor charged with carnivalesque imagery. The crow—a "low" animal often associated with carrion or being a scavenger—forces the respectable members of the church, clearly denoted by their names (Miss Perfect and Mr. Tata) outside of the cathedral, thus from the sacred inside to the profane outside.[48] The following week, the crow flies away with the bishop's miter and, to add insult to injury, his toupee along with it, resulting in a veritable *carnivalesque uncrowning*. Since the tale ends with the permanent closure of the cathedral under lock and key, the crow has succeeded in silencing the bishop and altering daily life in the village. This carnivalesque imagery accomplishes the kind of revolution that Bakhtin describes as celebrating "the destruction of the old and the birth of the new world."[49] In this sense, the symbolism of the crow is not to be discounted, as it represents not only the bringer of truth in Native American traditions but also the revolution of ideas or life, much like Bakhtin's notion of *negation* through carnival imagery.

While Ancelet, Brasseaux, and Carroll have approached anticlericalism in Francophone Louisiana as a specifically Acadian trait or suggest that, at the very least, it is rooted in the Acadian experience, a wider consideration of the region's French- and Creole-speaking communities suggests that negative sentiments toward the clergy were not unique to the Acadians. Brasseaux notes the moral friction between the church and the early colonial population of Louisiana, stating that without a strong presence of moral structure from the church, a "frontier morality developed as successive waves of Canadian and French soldiers and settlers deviated at will from traditional values."[50] Moreover, the remarkable degree of overlap between the anticlerical folklore of Louisiana and the Poitou region of France indicates a continuity with the French tradition as a much more likely source of anticlerical humor. While the Acadians' early colonial experiences with church officials in Acadie could have certainly reinforced the interest in anticlerical humor, I argue that they are unlikely to be the primary source of this distinct variety of humor.

For instance, Jude Chatelain hails from Avoyelles Parish, home to historically high concentrations of French speakers in communities like Marksville, Mansura, and Hessmer but minimal settlement by Francophones of Acadian descent. Likewise, the two following tales were collected in Mamou, located in Evangeline Parish, primarily settled by White French Creoles. In his 1986 study, "How Acadian Is Acadiana?" Glenn Conrad accumulated data from the most French-speaking pockets of the twenty-two-parish region designated as Acadiana by the state. His findings place the Mamou area of (ironically named) Evangeline Parish at the very bottom of the list, with only 6.2 percent of residents possessing Acadian surnames.[51]

As a place of cultural fusion, Louisiana's French folklore includes examples of a Catholic and Protestant relationship. Unsurprisingly, this is not a prevalent theme in France, for example, where Catholicism has historically been the dominant religion. One tale told by Burke Guillory features a Catholic priest and a Protestant preacher who are friends.[52] The preacher asks the priest if he wants to go fishing on Saturday, but the priest explains that he must be present at the church to hear confessions. The preacher, in turn, suggests that he share the work by using the second confessional, allowing them to form two lines and finish in half the time. Although they could presumably be at odds and the preacher should certainly not be hearing the confessions of Catholics, this scenario implies complicity between the men whose equal status as men in power gives the illusion of a kind of cabal of "holy men" regardless of their particular denomination. Unseen inside the confessional, the preacher hears the confession of a woman who has committed adultery. The preacher recognizes the seriousness of the offense and instructs her to place a one-hundred-dollar bill in the collection box as a penance. Surprised, the woman exclaims that just last week the "other priest" required only a ten-dollar bill of her. "Oh! Well, he didn't know what that kind of sin is worth!" bellows the preacher.

This tale offers a parody of the arbitrariness and irrationality of establishing an exact correlation between the gravity of a specific sin and an exact monetary amount that might redeem a certain wrongdoing. Moreover, it is not customary or generally accepted for priests to give a monetary penance to parishioners. A deeper meaning of this joke would indicate that the preacher (or perhaps Protestants in general) is more conscious of money or at least readier to capitalize on the shortcomings of his congregation. After all, in the Catholic tradition, poverty can be considered a moral virtue, but the church also has a history of abusing the practice of indulgences. However, this kind of mockery can be seen in another way. Following this tale is another from Guillory wherein he describes a priest who comes across a young boy playing in cow manure along the side of the road.[53] When the puzzled priest asks the boy what he is doing, he replies that he is fashioning a Baptist preacher out of the manure. Somewhat offended, the priest inquired why he has chosen a preacher and not a Catholic priest as his subject. "Parce que j'ai pas assez de merde" (Because I don't have enough shit), answers the youngster.

Guillory's tale provides an exemplary illustration of the Rabelaisian humor and carnivalesque irreverence with which the clergy are treated in much of the French oral tradition of Louisiana. This kind of humor harks back to early modern Europe, known for its "copious and ubiquitous scatological rhetoric."[54] The tale features all of the hallmarks of Bakhtin's carnivalesque, most notably the juxtaposition between the popular (a young boy) and official (a priest), the high and the low (crouching versus standing), and the "creation" of man who is no less than the earthly representative of God—fashioned not of earth or mud, as in the book of Genesis, but of bovine excrement. All of these components combine to achieve the *debasement* and *negation* of official culture explored by Bakhtin in *Rabelais and His World*. An essential element of this phenomenon is the downward motion drawing the official world into the underworld, otherwise represented in "popular-festive merriment" by the reversal of the upper stratum (the cerebral, the official, or a physical crown) and the lower stratum (the anus, the unofficial, a crowned fool). The same kind of downward movement is visible in many kinds of popular-festive merriment. Whether they be literal (that is, physical) or metaphorical, downward, inside-out, and upside-down movements symbolize the disruption and subversion of official power structures.[55]

Despite the mundane and crude nature of this scatological humor, its symbolism is not to be discounted. In popular-festive imagery, negation is never abstract; it is invariably the obvious and tangible that reconfigures the object's image, modifying its own position in space, as well that of its parts.[56] Here the preacher is brought down in terms of space and reconstructed by a child using fecal matter from an animal. The fact that the amount of excrement is insufficient to construct a Catholic priest is an audacious testament to the lack of regard for the clergy and the fearless lucidity of the child, who does not feel threatened by repercussions from a moral authority.

Given the presence of anticlerical humor in the larger context of Francophone folklore, it is worth noting that this theme seems to be largely absent from Creole of color communities. Alcée Fortier's collection of late-nineteenth-century Black Creole folktales, the earliest and most extensive study of its kind, includes no stories of priests at all. That said, it is possible that Fortier may have chosen to omit them, favoring tales dealing with the more exotic vernacular beliefs (for example, "The Devil's Marriage" and "An Old Zombie"). Moreover, the White Creole elite of nineteenth-century New Orleans were not immune to harsh criticism from the Catholic Church, as was experienced by Fortier's contemporary Alfred Mercier for his 1877 work *La Fille du prêtre* (The Priest's Daughter). Furthermore, this would not be surprising because enslaved individuals typically had significantly less direct contact with the clergy, and it was not uncommon for priests to perform mass sacraments, such as baptism, on large groups of enslaved people.

Slave communities certainly did not see individual priests or the Catholic Church as an institution as any kind of assistance or moral advocate against slavery. The post-Revolution climate in France, characterized by strong anticlericalism, caused many French priests to adopt an ultramontane stance in terms of political authority. This reinforced the conservative ideals from before the Revolution that did not necessarily oppose slavery.[57] Although some clergy recognized the injustice of slavery and offered public support of the abolitionist movement, this was by no means the general posture of the church. Even before Bishop Louis William DuBourg, who maintained slaves in his household, many French and Spanish priests contributed to the sustainability of a slaveholding society along the Mississippi River and throughout the Gulf Coast during the colonial period. This practice was reflected in the church's lack of a strong stance against slavery within the Catholic Church and made it the largest slaveholding entity in the Louisiana Territory.[58] Within the context of the "frontier morality" described by Brasseaux, missionary priests were often unwilling or unable to take sides in social issues like slavery:

> The physical hardship of rural life, the lack of an institutional infrastructure, and lay opposition to Catholic moral teachings produced reluctance among many missionaries to criticize social ills already present in the missions. Therefore, missionaries tried to legitimate themselves as a source of religious authority *within* slave societies of the South and *within* a church that understood slavery to be morally acceptable; they tried to apply the sacramental and catechetical prescriptions of Catholicism to what they perceived to be the given social and ecclesiastical orders. As they began to engage the system of slavery, however, missionaries found great frustration in the difficult implementation of canon law in slave societies.[59]

Considering the precarious state in which slaves or former slaves found themselves in Louisiana, the near total absence of anticlerical folktales is not surprising. One must also keep in mind that few folklorists were fluent in Louisiana Creole, and the nature of recording informants' accounts (often while requesting details such as names, age, and place of birth) would have naturally discouraged Creoles of color from sharing such potentially offensive narratives for fear of retribution. There are nevertheless a few instances that provide insight into this question.

One example can be found in Adam Shelby Holmes Trappey's 1916 study, one of a considerable number of studies directed by James Broussard in the early to mid-twentieth-century at Louisiana State University. Trappey presents fourteen songs and fourteen folktales (*contes*) in phonetic transcription. The second tale in this master's thesis is entitled "Confession d'ein vié esclave" (Confession of an Old Slave).[60] Were it not for the humorous ending, this first-person narrative would read much more like a slave narrative or oral history account than a folktale.

From the beginning of the tale, the cultural distance between the slave and the priest as well as the compulsory nature of confession are evident: "Vié maîtresse té dit moin fallait mo cou confesser. Mo couri trouvé prête-là dans confessional. Mo dit, 'Père, qui fo mo dit vous?' Li dit moin ça mo té fait mal. Mo dit, 'Mo pas fait mal personne'" (My old mistress told me that I had to go to confession. I went to find the priest in the confessional. I said, "Father, what am I supposed to say to you?" He said, whatever I had done wrong. I said, "I've done nothing wrong to anyone"). The explicit use of *fallait* (had to go) suggests that this was an order, not an act of the slave's own volition. Moreover, it is clear that the slave does not even know why he is there and insists that he is innocent of each of the crimes that the priest suspects him of: stealing a bull, hens, a cow, pigeons. Exhausted from a series of accusations and denials, the priest finally concedes: "Toi c'est ein saint; to capab couri" (Well, you're a saint! You can go now).[61] Having deflected each of the priest's suspicions, the slave enters the house and crosses the mistress in the stairwell. She asks him how it went, and he nonchalantly replies that the priest never asked about the duck, which he actually stole. She angrily responds: "Maudit, couri brilé dans difé lenfer" (Damn you! Go burn in the fires of hell!). The defiant slave ends the narrative, saying, "Mo pas couri, et mo là toujou" (I didn't run, and I'm still here).[62]

While it would have been rare that a priest should be present to hear the confession of slaves,[63] the experience of confession has little to do with the slave's spiritual salvation. Rather, the process seems to be more of a mandatory interrogation that the woman is requiring. In the end, the slave is victorious, in a sense, by using his cleverness and defying their pressure. Perhaps he is aware that he is needed on the plantation, and stealing a duck is far from being a sufficient reason to send him away.

Unfortunately, it cannot be ascertained with any degree of certitude whether anticlerical humor or tales of priests are exceedingly rare among Creoles of color because of a lack of interest among storytellers and listeners or because of societal pressures and a lack of folklore field research in these communities. Perhaps it is their scarcity in this particular community that has, in turn, accentuated anticlerical tales' presence among Cajun *conteurs* and therefore their interpretation as a specifically Acadian trait.

While Ancelet and Brasseaux are correct in recognizing the early inter-actions between the Catholic Church and the Acadians (both pre- and post-deportation) in the development of an overriding attitude of anticlericalism still present in Louisiana today, it is clear that it is not the only cause; this is borne out by an exceptionally high level of congruency with the folklore repertoire of western France as well as in regions of Louisiana with particularly low concentrations of Acadian settlers. Although much of South Louisiana remains very much "culturally Catholic," an animosity toward figures of authority within the church prevails insofar as clergymen wield the power to discipline or reprimand. This is the case despite a strong adherence to the faith as a whole. Acknowledging this shared repertoire of humor casts doubt on the singularity of Louisiana among other predominantly Catholic predominantly Latin cultures, in which "cultural Catholicism" is practiced.

What is most distinct about anticlerical humor in the oral tradition of French and Creole Louisiana is the treatment of the priests, which can generally be characterized as comical and innocuous despite the biting social critiques subtly conveyed through the tales. This trait is in sharp contrast to the examples from the oral tradition of France and Acadia that quite often feature violent retaliations in response to priests' transgressions. The dissimilarity in how the immorality of priests is handled is illustrative of a general disinterest in (and even mistrust of) the organized official structure of religion, coupled with a much broader affinity for the trickster figure. To return to Hutton's assessment of anticlericalism in the medieval fabliaux, the overriding strategy adopted by the priests in Louisiana French and Creole folklore is that of *savoir* (knowing). For while they abuse their position of authority (*avoir*), they are not merely gluttonous or grotesque caricatures; their clever, albeit malicious, deeds and quick-wittedness suggest precisely how they might have arrived to their positions of power. Much like Lapin, the priest figure in Louisiana folklore does not generally suffer consequences for his trickster-like behavior, for despite his loathsome characteristics, he is nevertheless a trickster. And anticlericalism aside, the trickster, even though at times mocked, must be respected.

CHAPTER 5

Bayou Belles

The Fairy Tales of French and Creole Louisiana

For many, especially those outside of the rather confined world of folklore studies, fairy tales like *Cinderella, Snow White,* and *Goldilocks* exemplify the quintessence of folklore. Not only do these tales capture the imagination with magical motifs and familiar narrative structures, but they have also been put on a pedestal in popular culture. As far back as the seventeenth century in France, Charles Perrault's *Histoires, ou contes du temps passé* (1697) became a sensation in courtly society and left an indelible mark on our conception of classic fairy tales. In the early nineteenth century, Jacob and Wilhelm Grimm demonstrated the folktale's ability to form a national folk repertoire and popularized many of the stories that have since been adapted countless times in film, books, and visual art. The influence of Perrault and the brothers Grimm can still be seen today in Disney's productions and elsewhere in popular culture.

Our modern-day notion of fairy tales is heavily predicated by the popular media representations of little more than a handful of characters (for example, Cinderella and Snow White), which are in turn influenced by specific *literary* renderings of narratives from the oral tradition. The most notable authors of this genre, the literary folktale, are Giambattista Basile, Charles Perrault, and Jacob and Wilhelm Grimm. Critical to our understanding of the fairy tale, however, is the fact that the literary fairy tale, relative to the oral wonder tale, is a rather recent phenomenon made possible by key historical and cultural developments in the early modern period, including the standardization of vernacular languages (creating a larger readership) and of course the development of the printing press.

Given its complex history of adaptation and interaction between different media, the fairy tale genre today problematizes more than any other the complicated relationship between orality and literature.[1] However, the perviousness between oral tradition and literature does not imply an equivalency between oral narratives collected by folklorists and the literary fairy tale. Ruth Bottigheimer explains:

> The term "literary fairy tale" has come to be understood as a reworking of orally composed and transmitted tales. In this context, "reworking" is understood to have been carried out by literate, and literary, authors like Giovan Francesco Straparola, Giambattista Basile, Marie-Catherine d'Aulnoy, Charles Perrault, Jacob and Wilhelm Grimm, and by many other writers [. . .]. In the case of the Grimms, it was long—and erroneously—believed that they had made great efforts to preserve existing, but nearly extinct, folk versions of the tales published in their collection, whereas in fact their fifty years of editing can be fairly characterized as having turned widely available tales from literary sources into carefully crafted reflections of contemporary folk grammatical usage and contemporary bourgeois beliefs about folk social values.[2]

There is also some ambiguity surrounding the terminology of certain tale genres. While the term *fairy tale* conjures specific elements such as magic, giants, or princesses, folklore scholars do not completely agree on the specific criteria for designating a narrative as such. The creators of the Aarne-Thompson-Uther classification system do not even use the term as a category, opting instead to group tale types 300–749 as "Magic Tales." It seems logical, however, to distinguish between a "folktale" and a fairy tale. A folktale typically involves a shorter, more direct plot and characters that are familiar to the tale's audience. On the other hand, the "fairy tale" exhibits a narrative trajectory that is "a fundamentally defining part of their very being" combined with conventional elements associated with the genre (motifs, structure, or happy ending).[3]

Literary fairy tales' long-standing popularity obscures the separation between the oral tradition and written culture. Furthermore, the cultural weight and prestige of the literary fairy tale likely played a large part in nineteenth-century folklorists' obsession with finding vestiges of a "pure" European oral tradition in the New World. Unfortunately, less attention was paid to the fuller, more complex set repertoire that had developed in situ, and, as Ancelet bemoans, "scholars found only what they were looking for."[4] Indeed, a preoccupation with clearly identifiable tale type remained an essential part of much folklore scholarship through the mid-twentieth century.

In Louisiana, the situation is more nuanced in this regard because there simply is not a plethora of folktales in general. While folklorists of the early twentieth century are sometimes criticized today for only seeking out fairy tales in Louisiana, they nevertheless collected a rather modest number of them. Moreover, the works of Corinne Saucier, Elizabeth Brandon, Lafayette Jarreau (1931), Lahaye (1946), and others actually approach the study of "folklore" with a more holistic perspective, exploring tales in addition to superstitions, proverbs, and vernacular medicine. It is true that the tales collected by Ancelet in the 1970s from Lafayette and surrounding parishes include relatively few fairy tales or tales of magic; however, these genres were quite prevalent in prior fieldwork conducted through the 1950s. Saucier, in the introduction to her book of Avoyelles Parish folktales, asserts that her collection represents "proof that fairy tales are the favorite type [in French Louisiana], because they outnumber the other types" in her collection."[5] Calvin Claudel's doctoral thesis, "A Study of Louisiana French Folktales in Avoyelles Parish" (1947), likewise includes a significant number of fairy tales.[6]

The notion that the oral repertoire of Francophone Avoyelles Parish would differ somewhat from that of the southern parishes of "Cajun country" is plausible because this region is distinct in several significant ways. Geographically, the region's settlement patterns have been closely tied to the Red River and several elevated areas. The various ethnic and cultural groups that came to the area also differ from the parishes immediately to its south. The name of the parish (and the Poste des Avoyelles that preceded it) finds its origin in the autonym of the first indigenous inhabitants, the Avoyelles tribe. In the late eighteenth century, French settlers established themselves near what is now the town of Mansura.[7] Around the turn of the century, however, many more immigrants came directly from France and other European countries, most notably Italy, Spain, and Germany. Only a few Acadian families, including the Roy and Tassin families, settled in Avoyelles Parish by way of the Atchafalaya.[8] However, the surnames most closely associated with Avoyelles Parish are those of descendants of immigrants who came directly from France, such as Grémillon, Bordelon, Ducoté, and Lemoine.

Because much of the French spoken in this area derives from the language spoken by nineteenth-century European immigrants, the French of Avoyelles Parish is also distinct from the dialects spoken elsewhere in the state. The distinction between *savoir* (to know a fact) and *connaître* (to be acquainted with), the use of *attendre* meaning "to wait" (as in standard French) rather than *espérer* as is more common in Louisiana, as well as a more frequent use of both the subjunctive form and simple future tense all defy distinctive features of "Cajun," or Louisiana Regional French, that contemporary linguists consider to be hallmarks of a regional language variety. Given these discernible differences in geography, demographics, and language from the more southern parishes, it is not surprising that the folktale repertoire of Avoyelles Parish should also be distinct.

Finally, it should be noted that in the early nineteenth century, residents of Avoyelles Parish seem to have benefited from a higher socioeconomic status than their southern neighbors, which allowed for an earlier development of educational institutions. While these institutions were, for the most part, bilingual until the end of the nineteenth century, the shift toward the new dominant language of English by 1910–15 likewise predated a similar move to Americanization that truly took hold after World War II in Lafayette and the surrounding parishes.[9] The combination of a relative advantage with regard to education and social status along with a greater cultural proximity with European culture would certainly have played an important role in the characterization and morality of folktales. Specifically, in the fairy tale genre, in which wealth and social status are closely tied to morality, it is worth noting these differences in cultural context that contrast with other parishes where a stronger Acadian presence and a largely subsistence farming lifestyle would have been more influential.

THE REPRESENTATION OF WOMEN IN FAIRY TALES

Another important aspect of fairy tales in the larger context of French and Creole Louisiana's oral tradition is that it is the only genre in which women play a primary role as protagonist, which is striking when one considers the significant number of female storytellers represented in Louisiana's Franco-phone folklore.[10] The portrayals of heroines in fairy tales have rightfully been the target of criticism in contemporary readings—perhaps most famously by Marcia Lieberman, who asserts that "good" female protagonists are invariably docile, beautiful, and well-tempered. On the other hand, female villains are ugly, cruel, and bad-tempered.[11] With regard to the problematic correlation between physical beauty and moral goodness, the fairy tales of French and Creole Louisiana are no less deserving of such criticism; however, there exist a number of counterexamples featuring more active heroines that should give us pause concerning the overall characterization of women in the fairy tales of South Louisiana. For example, we find several tales about women who fall prey to (and eventually overcome) monstrous husbands. Tales such as *Barbe bleue* (Bluebeard), ATU 312, and *La Belle et la bête* (Beauty and the Beast), ATU 425, are also among the most well-known fairy tales in the Western world. Fortier's 1895 collection includes an intriguing tale, "Mariaze Djabe" (The Devil's Wedding), which features a young woman who unwittingly marries the devil but escapes using some magic and her quick wits.[12] There are also two variants, one in Saucier's collection and another recorded by Ancelet, of ATU 883A, sometimes known as "Sainte Geneviève" or "Geneviève de Brabant."[13] Supposedly based on a medieval legend, these are perhaps the longest narra-tives recorded from the French and Creole oral tradition of Louisiana.[14]

Similar to their counterparts in other European and North American oral traditions, these tales and others like them tend to emphasize the physical attractiveness of their heroines and often depict marriage as a means of reso-lution of the narrative. Nevertheless, there are a number of examples in which female protagonists are accorded considerable agency and are admired for their cleverness as much as their male equivalents. This may be because a ma-jority of the storytellers recorded in the repertoire available to us are women. By comparison, the realm of literary fairy tales has historically been very much dominated by male writers, such as Perrault, Grimm, and Lang.

CENDRILLON

Cinderella is one of the oldest known folk narratives found in the oral tra-dition. The oldest tale that corresponds to this tale type is *Yeh-hsien*, a story that dates back to at least 850 CE in southern China. Earlier forms of the tale in eastern Asia likely predate *Yeh-hsien,* but this early Chinese influence is thought to be at the root of an otherwise peculiar aesthetic link—at least for Western audiences—between female beauty and the heroine's extraordinarily small feet, a physical trait that comes to play an important role in the narrative when the prince must find the owner of the shoe left behind at the ball. While the tale's genesis likely occurred in China or elsewhere in East Asia, its arrival in Greece was key in its dissemination and the solidifying of the association of the protagonist's name with ashes.[15] From Greece, the tale was translated into other languages and included in Giambattista Basile's 1634 volume of *Pentamerone (Tale of Tales)* as "la Gatta Cenerentolla" (Cat Cinderella), a reference to a popular expression of the time. An "ash kitten" referred to a woman who mostly stayed at home. Other forms retained the association with ashes, symbolic of the character's low status in the household and obligation to toil away at menial chores. The first written attestation of the French "Cendrillon" is attributed to Charles Perrault's iconic *conte* "Cendrillon, ou la petite pantoufle de verre," almost certainly influenced by the popular Italian version of Basile.[16]

In the Aarne-Thompson-Uther classification, ATU 510 refers to a cycle of related tales that can be divided into two basic subsets: 510A (*Cinderella*) and 510B (*Peau d'Âne,* or Donkey Skin). Because of the extraordinary prevalence of *Cinderella,* many motifs prove to be interchangeable across regions. In the Francophone oral tradition, the most typical name of *Cendrillon* appears in several common variations, including *Cendrillonne, Cendrouse,* and *Cendrillouse.* Variants of the tale can be found in practically every French-speaking part of the world, and they are particularly prevalent in Acadie.[17]

Because of the sheer popularity of Perrault's "Cendrillon," many believe the tale to be steeped in aristocratic ideology for, in this version, Cinderella's father is a widowed nobleman (*gentilhomme*). Whereas his first wife was "amazingly sweet-natured" and "the most charming person," his second wife was haughty and controlling.[18] The implicit friction is found in the contrast of a harmonious marriage between nobles and a second, "unnatural" marital bond between a nobleman and the nouveau riche. Frequently, a reviled stepmother represents the lower class, fraught with jealousy and a lack of good taste. The wicked stepmother thus "impinges on the sanctity of the noble household" and "embodies the forces of luxury which were blamed for undermining the society of orders by obscuring the distinctions of rank."[19]

While class distinctions in Europe certainly played a role in the origins and development of fairy tales, *Cinderella* is generally considered to be a "rise tale"; Bottigheimer coins this term to mean "tales begin with a dirt-poor girl or boy who suffers the effects of grinding poverty and whose story continues with tests, tasks, and trials until magic brings about a marriage to royalty and a happy accession to great wealth."[20] In contrast, restoration fairy tales "begin with a royal personage [. . .] who is driven away from home and heritage. Out in the world, the royals face adventures, undertake tasks, and suffer hardships and trials. With magic assistance they succeed in carrying out their assigned tasks, overcoming their imposed hardships, and enduring their character-testing trials, after which they marry royally and are restored to a throne that returns them to their just social, economic, and political position."[21] It would be hazardous to consider Perrault's version as particularly representative of the French oral tradition, as Perrault indicated no specific sources of his tales and it is clear that he wrote primarily for a courtly audience.[22] Again, the literary fairy tale and folk narrative are not one and the same.[23] Outside of France, versions of ATU 510A display even greater variation.

For example, no Francophone Louisiana variants of ATU 510A make any mention of Cinderella's social status or poverty. This detail's absence stands in sharp contrast to what we have seen in the previous chapter concerning the poverty of the Master Thief's family, which is often at the forefront of the narrative precisely because it justifies the character's subsequent immoral actions. In French and Creole Louisiana, however, it would seem that poverty plays no role in Cinderella's situation or the tale's overall moral. One element that is constant in the variants of Louisiana is motif K2212.1 *Treacherous step-sisters;* however, the protagonist's mistreatment by her family members is not necessarily predicated by the death of her father.

Saucier includes in her doctoral dissertation a tale titled "Cendrillone" told by Eunice Bordelon Lacour in 1949.[24] Saucier's notes indicate that the story-teller learned the tale from her mother. In many ways, this variant is quite typical, containing all of the hallmarks of ATU 510A, including Cendrillone's mistreatment at the hands of her stepsisters, magical aid to attend the ball, and the prince's quest to find the woman to whom a missing slipper belongs.

The family dynamics at play in this variant are quite different from more typical examples involving an abusive relationship between the female characters following the father's death. "'Ne fois i n'avait 'ne femme qui s'est r'mariée pour la seconde fois. A l'avait deux filles et son mari avait 'ne fille il appelait Cendrillone dans la cendre parce qu'a restait dans l'coin d'la cend'e. Ils vouliont jamais l'amener nulle part. Alors al était tout l'temps laissée seule. Et a passé [sic] son temps à jouer dans la cend'e" (There once was a woman who remarried for the second time. She had two daughters and her husband had one daughter whom he called Cendrillone in the ashes because she stayed in the corner in the ashes. They never wanted to take her anywhere. So, she was always left alone. And she spent her time playing in the ashes).[25]

These details present a strikingly different familial setting; the storyteller emphasizes the second wife who has remarried, rather than lamenting the death of the father's first wife. Furthermore, there is not even any mention of the father's death. And rather than Cendrillone's mistreatment being initiated by the stepdaughters, it is actually the *father* who had already given the heroine her unflattering nickname of Cendrillone. Therefore, what the storyteller describes is not as much a tragic turn of events brought on by untimely death and class distinctions but rather a tale of a marginalized and solitary young woman.

Likewise, the supernatural aid who comes to Cendrillone's rescue is not a fairy godmother but a *magicien*. After asking if Cendrillone would like to attend the ball, he taps a wand against the fireplace in order to make a coach, horses, and a coachman appear. However, the magician warns to be home before eleven o'clock or she will lose the coach and be transported back to the ashes.

The next morning, Cendrillone's sisters recall their amazement at the ravishing young "princess" present at the ball: "'Cendrillone, si t'aurais vu la belle princesse, i n'avait. La plus belle t'a déjà vue!' A dit: 'Ben, al était pas plus belle que mon.' 'Ben,' ils disent, 'Cendrillone, tu devrais avoir honte.' 'Mais non,' a dit, 'elle était pas plus belle que mon'" ("Cendrillone, if you had only seen the beautiful princess who was there. The most beautiful you've ever seen!" She says: "Well, she wasn't more beautiful than me." "But," they said, "Cendrillone, you should be ashamed of yourself." "But no," she said, "she was not more beautiful than me").[26] While such quips do not necessarily make her a trickster figure, the consistency with which it appears in the Louisiana repertoire and its general absence from variants from elsewhere suggest a tendency on the part of the storytellers to hint at a mischievous side to the otherwise saintly heroine, a character trait for which she refuses to be ashamed.[27] Furthermore, the tale's resolution contributes an ambivalent tinge to the overall moral of the story; rather than focusing on her impending marriage and future happiness—or as in Perrault's version, Cendrillone graciously inviting her cruel family to live with her in the castle—it is the stepsisters' jealousy of her that is emphasized.[28]

In three variants of UTA 510A collected by Calvin Claudel, each entitled "Cendrillone," the family dynamic is also effaced or problematized. In the first variant, storyteller Mrs. A. E. Claudel only speaks of *trois orphelines* (three orphans) but makes no mention of any remarriage or conflict between their biological parents; and in the second and third variants, told by Roberta Roy and Marie Louise Couvillon, respectively, we are simply told of *trois sœurs* (three sisters) with no mention whatsoever of the parents, be they alive or deceased. Only in the first variant of his collection is the death of her parents a recurring motif. Just as Cendrillone taps a magic wand thrice to make her gown and carriage appear, she must repeat this action to return to her usual state.[29] Each time upon doing so, her enchanted gifts transform into white pigeons that fly away to alight on her parents' graves.[30] This motif offers the memory of her parents as a kind of allegory foreshadowing justice that will be served later on in the narrative.

Although these tales from Claudel's collection are, like many examples of fairy tales, somewhat timeless, there is nevertheless a surprising degree of localization. For example, each of the Avoyelles Parish variants collected by Claudel describes the social ball not as a rare and grand event but as a weekly celebration occurring every Saturday, clearly corresponding to the traditional *bals de maison,* or houses dances, common throughout rural French and Creole Louisiana. Similar to the events described in these tales from Avoyelles Parish, *les bals de maison* were family affairs that typically took place on Saturday nights. Neighborhood participants would partake in drinks and live entertainment from local amateur musicians and would often share a large collective meal such as a gumbo.[31]

The setting of Cendrillone's home is also highly representative of primarily rural Avoyelles Parish in the early twentieth century. She is simultaneously homebound and ostracized as her sisters force her to stay in the bread oven behind the house. There her only company is her best friend, a small dog that lives in the furnace with her. Near the end of the narrative, when the prince is poised to leave, the dog comes to her aid by drawing his attention to the bread oven.[32] Her complicity with the dog and their shared marginalization from the household suggest a closeness with nature not unlike that of Jean Sotte.

Bettelheim, basing his interpretation of Cinderella primarily on the literary versions of Perrault and Basile, argues that the tale is overtly about sibling rivalry; however, the parents are actually at the source of what is known as "sibling rivalry." Feeling incompetent relative to an older brother or sister only causes mild or temporary feelings of jealousy. On the other hand, a lack of attention or feeling of rejection by the parents is truly hurtful to children.[33] However, Bettelheim's reading of Cinderella is problematized by these Avoyelles Parish variants because, as I have pointed out, there is little or no mention at all of the parents. The resulting dynamic could be interpreted as either truly a scenario of sibling rivalry or a story of defiance and individuality.[34] In the latter case, let us consider the subtle indications given by the storyteller that help us to understand the heroine's personality. Together the Avoyelles Parish variants examined here portray a Cendrillone quite unlike the typically meek protagonist to whom most are accustomed. In Couvillon's version, for example, the *fée bonheur* endows Cendrillone with a whip, rather than a magic wand, that she must crack three times in order to make her dress and carriage appear. The whip as a magical object characterizes the heroine as a young woman with considerably more physical strength and agency than in typical European or Acadian variants from Canada. The difficult conditions of early settlers in rural Louisiana would have certainly created a context where strength and tenacity would be seen as necessary traits for survival.

She also displays a determined and even brazen quality, which is exceedingly rare in the *Cinderella* repertoire. The fact that the balls are hebdomadal affords Cendrillone the chance to repeatedly taunt her stepsisters the following morning, saying how the mysterious maiden was "not more beautiful than her."[35] This sly and gratuitous remark in each of the variants of "Cendrillone" collected by Claudel shows a rebellious character in Cendrillone. At the end of the tale, after the prince has found Cendrillone and asks for her hand in marriage, she does not agree to leave with him right away. Instead, she goes into the house alone and conjures her magic dress again expressly to annoy her sisters and incite their intense jealousy of her before leaving. The prince, presuming that she is now ready to depart, invites her to embark in his coach with him. However, Cendrillone refuses; she calls upon her magic carriage, enraging her sisters once more, and accompanies the prince to the castle in her own coach. Her comportment here evokes the "surface humility" of a character who accepts her lowly place in the household temporarily but who is keenly aware of her superiority. As Bettelheim notes, her conviction is supported by the tale's ending, "which assures every 'Cinderella' that eventually she will be discovered by her prince."[36] Only the Cendrillone of Avoyelles Parish is sure to accept her life with the prince on her own terms—and in her own carriage.

The Avoyelles Parish variants demonstrate a remarkable degree of homogeneity and represent some of the very few recorded examples ATU 510A in the state's Francophone oral tradition. The only outlier is a 1953 recording from Elizabeth Brandon's collection of Vermilion Parish folklore told by one of her most prolific informants, Lucille Saltzman, born in 1885 in Abbeville. Like the aforementioned variants, the tale includes no comment on the social status or poverty of Cendrillon's family, only that her two older sisters are the daughters of her stepmother. Again in this variant, the father is not deceased.

Saltzman tells this tale in Louisiana French, explaining how Cendrillon was "la négresse de la maison." However, with the exception of these few elements, Saltzman's rendition of this tale exhibits an extraordinary resemblance with Charles Perrault's *conte*. As in Perrault's text, the heroine's supernatural aid is a fairy godmother who instructs her to go into the garden and find a large pumpkin, eight mice, two rats, and one lizard, which she magically transforms into a coach, eight horses, two coachmen, and a valet.[37] Saltzman even states that after the prince finds Cendrillone and proposes to her, she invites her family to come stay in the castle with her and the royal family.[38]

Such congruency with Perrault's literary fairy tale seems difficult to comprehend. However, this anomaly could be explained by the fact that Mrs. Saltzman could very well have simply been reciting from her own memory of Perrault's "Cendrillon." This would be entirely possible as Brandon indicates in her notes that the storyteller had attained a master's degree and was teaching French and English at Gueydan High school in Vermilion Parish.[39]

Beyond the confines of AT 510A, the name Cendrillon(e) is also found in unrelated tale types. In 1977, Barry Ancelet recorded Martin Latiolais of Catahoula, Louisiana, telling a version of ATU 565 (*The Magic Mill*).[40] Latiolais recounts a tale of two starving orphans. While in the woods one day, they see *une vieille petite Cendrillonne* (a little old Cinderella). The old woman gives to the children a magic pot and two sticks. At the first strike, the empty pot will begin filling with pudding (*bouillie*), and at the second strike, it will stop. However, when the formula is forgotten, the pot overflows and fills the street with pudding.

David Lanclos, a prolific storyteller from Pecanière, Louisiana, offers another tale that is unrelated to ATU 510A called "Une Cendrillone acadienne."[41] In this tale, the protagonist finds herself before her ailing grandfather, who no longer sees a point in living because he has nothing new to learn. Cendrillone aids her grandfather in lighting his pipe from cold ashes found outside and embers taken from the fireplace. The grandfather, having never seen this technique before, declares that he must surely have much more in life to learn and decides to continue living.

SNOW BELLA

Aside from *Cinderella* and the various iterations and translations of ATU 510A found throughout the oral tradition, one of the most recognizable fairy tales is ATU 709. Commonly known as *Snow White* in English, versions of this narrative have circulated practically throughout the world. In the European tradition, the most notable literary examples are found in Basile's *Pentamerone* (1634–36) and Jacob and Wilhelm Grimms' *Kinder- und Hausmärchen* (1812–15).[42] Given the remarkable number of geographical regions where the tale has been attested,[43] the considerable extent of cross-regional variation is not surprising. However, a number of features remain relatively constant: origin, jealousy, expulsion, adoption, renewed jealousy, death, exposition of the heroine's body, revival, and resolution (revenge).[44]

Claudel's collection of Avoyelles Parish tales includes an intriguing variant of ATU 709, told by Mrs. A. E. Claudel, which casts a young girl named Snow Bella in the eponymous tale.[45] The heroine's name suggests a fusion of Anglo-American, German, and Italian elements, which is consistent with the considerable German and Italian immigration to Avoyelles Parish and its complex identity as both part of French-speaking Louisiana and the predominantly Anglophone American South.[46]

This Avoyelles Parish variant begins like many typical examples of ATU 709. On a snowy winter day, a woman sits at her window sewing and accidentally pricks her finger. Differing considerably from the more popular version by the brothers Grimm, the woman places her finger in the snow. This tale exhibits a high degree of localization. It therefore may seem surprising that the element of snow has remained constant given the subtropical climate of Louisiana. This might be explained by the crucial role that snow plays in the narrative, the temporal proximity with a European tradition brought by a later migration to Louisiana, or the fact that the during the late nineteenth century and early twentieth century, snowfall was moderately heavier and more regular in Louisiana.[47] However, the stable status of snow as a narrative element is more likely due to its fixed relationship with a tricolor motif of red, white, and black dating back centuries.

This part of the narrative is deeply rooted in Germanic oral tradition and Norse mythology. In the Germanic legend Perceval, Arthur's falcon attacks one of three geese flying over the hero's head. Three drops of blood fall on the snow, and he is immediately transfixed and can think only of his beloved Condwiramurs. Jacob Grimm famously referred to this combination as "die drei Farben der Poesie" (the three colors of poetry).[48] These three colors form one of the most distinctive features of ATU 709, identified as motif Z65.1.1 *Red as blood, white as snow, (and black as a raven)*. Each of these colors corresponds to essential images in the tale—blood, snow, hair—and these symbols are echoed later in the narrative. Furthermore, the colors are each imbued with their own connotations that are themselves subject to specific cultural references.

Red, for example, was the first color admired and mastered by humankind, and its early predominance remains apparent in certain languages in which "colored" and "red" are expressed by the same word, such as in classical Latin (*coloratus*) and modern Castilian (*colorado*).[49] Red remained the color par excellence until the end of the Middle Ages and to this day is profoundly associated with women's beauty, as cosmetic products for cheeks and lips are often composed of various nuances of red. In contemporary Western societies, red is also associated with passion, fire, and love (*eros*). White, on the other hand is emblematic of purity, innocence, and virginity. In juxtaposition, black evokes the heroine's raven hair and provides contrast against white, thus heightening its affect while at the same time hinting at the foreboding prospect of death.

"Snow Bella" begins in a fashion similar to many other variants of ATU 709: a woman is sewing by the window during winter. However, unlike many other instances of the blood-on-snow motif, here the woman chooses to place her finger into the pure white snow, presumably to stop the bleeding. In this case, it is not the striking chromatic contrast that incites her to wish for a child with skin as white as snow and cheeks as red as blood.[50] Rather, she is taken by the shade of pink resulting from the mixture of her blood and the snow: "Elle a touché son doigt dans la neige; le sang et la neige étaient ensemble. Ça faisait beaucoup une jolie couleur."[51] In awe of such a sublime shade of pink, she wishes for a daughter who might have cheeks of the same hue.

The fact that motif Z65.1 within the ATU 709 tale type survived in Louisiana is remarkable; however, the mixture of the red and white represents a quite singular variation on this quasi-archetypal motif. The subversion of conventional blood-on-snow imagery is intensified by the exceeding rarity of the color pink in the folklore repertoire. The color that we know as "pink" today possesses a complex history as it was generally undefined in antiquity. In the early modern period in France, the mixture of red and white was generally considered to be *jaune* (yellow). In fact, the Académie française did not enter *rose* (meaning the color pink) until the sixth edition of its *Dictionnaire,* in 1835. For other languages as well, such as Spanish (*rosa*) and German (*Rosa*), this contemporary usage as an adjective referring to the color pink only dates back to the mid-nineteenth century.[52] Given the color's relatively short history, it is no surprise, then, that the *Motif-index of folk-literature* only contains one motif featuring the color pink. In contrast, there are nearly two hundred motifs that include the color red and roughly the same amount for black. The color white figures in well over six hundred motifs. Does the substitution of pink for red attenuate the more passionate side of her affection, or is it simply more realistic? Or still, might this mixture suggest a Creole aesthetic more in tune with the standards of beauty in the storyteller's social milieu?

Upon uttering her wish, a fairy appears before the woman and offers to grant her a daughter with rosy red cheeks but also warns her that such a beautiful girl might bring her grief. Not even a decade later,[53] the mother passes away and the father chooses to remarry. Much like the typical *Cinderella* story, the stepmother is haughty, arrogant, and increasingly jealous of Snow Bella's beauty. Again, similar to many versions of ATU 510A, the father dies soon thereafter, leaving the young girl alone with her treacherous stepmother.[54] The stepmother plots to enlist the family's longtime servant to lead Snow Bella out into the woods under the pretext of collecting flowers for a *soirée* that evening.[55] To prove to her that Snow Bella is indeed dead, he must return with her heart and her tongue. They take along Snow Bella's beloved dog. Like Cendrillone, Snow Bella repeatedly displays an affinity with nature and an innate complicity with animals. The servant cannot bear to kill Snow Bella and offers her his apologies along with the idea of sacrificing the dog in order to return its tongue and heart, thus deceiving the stepmother.[56] Snow Bella walks until almost nightfall, when she comes upon an empty house (*auberge*). She later discovers that the house belongs to seven dwarves, who welcome her to stay in their home.[57] In accepting her duties and household chores, Snow Bella accepts responsibilities that mark her transition into a grown woman and somewhat of a mother figure for the dwarves.

Some time later, the servant who aided Snow Bella in escaping dies, and the widow believes her secret will remain hidden forever. But one day, while the widow is sitting on the porch in her rocking chair, a traveling salesman approaches and entices her into buying a magical mirror that will tell her any secret she wishes to know.[58] Falling prey to her own vanity, she purchases the mirror. Believing that Snow Bella is dead, she asks the mirror:

'Tit miroir, 'tit miroir,
Dites-moi qui c'est qu'est
La plus jolie fille
Et la plus jolie femme
Dans tous les effets
Du canton?

C'est votre belle-fille
Qui reste chez les 'tits nains
À la bordure de l'auberge.[59]

Little mirror, little mirror,
Tell me who is
The most beautiful girl
And the most beautiful woman
In all of the quarters
Of the canton?

It is your stepdaughter
Who lives with the little dwarves
At the edge of the woods.

This tale provides several illustrations of localization. Because all traces of a royal or monarchical hierarchy have been removed in the sociocultural context of Louisiana, the stepmother is consistently referred to as "la veuve" (the widow), rather than "the queen." Moreover, the indications given suggest an abode that is far from what one might consider a castle; she lives in a house that is representative of Creole architecture, including a walkway leading up to a front porch, where she is seated in her rocking chair. Whereas in the Grimms' "Schneewittchen," the queen is in possession of the magic mirror from the beginning of the narrative, Claudel's "Snow Bella" features a traveling salesman who approaches *la veuve* on her porch. This corresponds to a method of commerce that was commonplace in rural Louisiana through the mid-twentieth century whereby customers depended on itinerant merchants for clothing and dry goods.

When the widow learns that Snow Bella is still alive, she disguises herself ("elle s'est attriquée") with a *garde-soleil*, a traditional sunbonnet. She then walks to the dwarves' house, where Snow Bella is alone, and offers to sell her a necklace. Immediately upon placing it around her neck, Snow Bella falls to the ground and dies. Fortunately, the dwarves return in time to remove the necklace and are able to revive Snow Bella. The tale follows the conventional triple repetition of attempts on the heroine's life found in the Grimms' version and many others. The stepmother learns from the mirror that Snow Bella is not dead, as she believed, and so must return to sell her combs for her ebony hair. Again, Snow Bella falls dead after putting the comb in her hair (motif S111.3

Murder with poisoned comb), and again the dwarves are able to resuscitate her by removing the comb. Finally, the widow returns with a poisoned apple.[60]

Each of these attempts to kill Snow Bella subtly reiterates the tricolor schema introduced at the heroine's origin. This series of poisoned or cursed objects closely resembles what we find in the Grimms' "Schneewitchen" with the exception of the first visit, in which the evil queen uses lace, rather than a necklace. The presumably pearl necklace (or lace) represents white; the comb used for Snow Bella's ebony hair evokes black; and finally, the red apple symbolizes the culmination of the stepmother's passion and rage.

The apple is particularly salient here because it highlights the abutment of the (poisoned) red skin and the (pure) white flesh. In the Grimms' tale, the queen proposes to Schneewittchen: "You eat the red cheek and I eat the white."[61] This highly evocative scenario offers a metaphor for an exchange of roles;[62] Schneewittchen succumbs to the aggression and passion represented by red, while the queen gains access to the beauty of the Ideal by consuming the apple's white flesh and, by extension, the heroine's innocent nature. Meanwhile, in the Avoyelles Parish variant, the stepmother only convinces Snow Bella to make a slight crack in the door in order for her to roll the apple into the house.[63] The poisoned apple acts as an agent of the evil stepmother that is able to transgress the liminal space of the doorstep and infiltrate the home. In doing so, Snow Bella contributes to her own demise by picking up the apple and eating it.

When the dwarves return home and find Snow Bella lifeless on the floor, they are unable to resuscitate her and must place her in a coffin and bring her to a cemetery.[64] The storyteller emphasizes the brutal path to the graveyard, highlighting the many precipices, ridges, and ditches. Once they finally arrive, the oldest dwarf wishes to say farewell one last time, and the others agree to open the coffin. To their surprise, Snow Bella bats her eyes and begins to awaken. They notice that her dress is covered in vomit from the bumpy voyage. However, regurgitating the apple allowed her to regain consciousness and come back to life.

At this point, Snow Bella recounts all of the stepmother's wicked deeds, and they decide to exact revenge on her. Meanwhile, the widow seeks to reassure herself of Snow Bella's death and questions the mirror one last time. The mirror responds:

La plus jolie fille,
La plus jolie femme
Dans tous les effets
Du canton
C'est Snow Bella
Votre belle-fille
Qu'est sur votre escalier
Asteur là
Est venue pour vous tuer![65]

The prettiest girl,
The prettiest woman
In all the quarters
Of the canton
Is Snow Bella
Your stepdaughter
Who is at your steps
Right now
She has come to kill you!

In a fit of rage, the widow throws the mirror to the ground, breaking it. When she rushes outside, Snow Bella and the dwarves meet her. At that moment, the eldest dwarf aims his rifle at the woman and kills her. He and Snow Bella marry, reclaim the family home, and live on happily.

The ending of Snow Bella represents a departure from more typical variants of ATU 709 in several significant ways. Perhaps most obvious is the absence of a prince figure responsible for resuscitating the heroine. In a way, that role is filled by one of the dwarves, but her revival is described as having more to do with chance and the rough condition of the path to the cemetery. The tale's resolution for the most part hinges on revenge against the stepmother. There is nothing mysterious or magical about this scene. On the contrary, this scenario more closely resembles a kind of folk justice enacted by Snow Bella and the dwarves. In the Grimms' "Schneewittchen," for instance, the queen begrudgingly decides to attend the new royal couple's wedding, where she is met with a pair of red-hot iron shoes and is forced to put them on and dance until she drops dead.[66] The motif echoes the Grimms' *drei Farben der Poesie* present at the heroine's origin and (near) death. The black iron shoes are heated until red and then placed with tongs onto the queen's white feet, thus linking the notion of ideal beauty with a final sense of poetic justice.

While this rendition of ATU 709 might seem quite typical to the contemporary listener on a superficial level, a number of crucial elements indicate dramatic differences with the Grimms' variant. For instance, there is a complete effacement of any references to royalty or upper-class social status, save the fact that the family has employed a servant for many years. Most notably, the prince who in many versions awakens the heroine and later marries her is completely absent from the narrative. Whereas in many variants, the queen pricks her finger at the beginning of the narrative, here we are simply told of a *mère* (mother). At the end of the tale, Snow Bella and the eldest dwarf inherit the *maison* (house) of her late father; it could by no means be described as a castle.

In reading the brothers Grimm's tale, it is difficult to fathom such a tale being removed from the old-world hierarchy of kings and queens. And yet to the listener who is attuned to such a version, it is easy to transpose this setting on the Avoyelles Parish version, so subtle are the narrative techniques of localization employed. Let us consider, for example, how the narrative remains coherent without the arrival (or presence) of a prince, who in the Grimms' version initiates her awakening. In their version, Schneewittchen regurgitates the apple and is thus freed from the queen's spell while the prince is taking her away from the cemetery to bring her to the castle, where he wishes to keep her body. However, in Claudel's "Snow Bella," it is *on the way* to the cemetery that the dwarves encounter rough terrain that causes the heroine to regurgitate the apple. This simple deviation renders the prince—at least from a narratological standpoint—unnecessary.

In addition to Claudel's "Snow Bella," a Black Creole tale also warrants investigation. While it cannot truly be categorized as a version of ATU 709, "Lé Roi Pan" (King Peacock) in Alcée Fortier's 1895 collection exhibits several key elements of the tale type.[67] In this peculiar tale, an exceedingly handsome young lady gives birth to a baby girl. As the girl grows older and more beautiful, her mother is overcome with jealousy and locks the girl away at the opposite end of the house with only the nurse to tend to her. One day, she spies through an open door a magnificent peacock in the yard and tells her nurse that if she is ever able to marry, she wishes to marry the king of the peacocks. The mother, fearing that her daughter is becoming more beautiful than her, instructs the nurse to kill her daughter. Sympathetic to the mistreated young girl, the nurse gives the daughter three magical seeds. She must eat one and throw the other two into a nearby well before jumping into the well herself. After failing at this task, she escapes into the woods and comes upon a house, where a woman welcomes her inside. However, the woman warns her that her husband is an ogre and will surely attempt to eat her. Already dismayed by the fact that her mother wishes her to die, she resigns to simply await her death. The ogre, however, is so taken by her beauty that he wishes to keep her alive. Nevertheless, she later decides to take her own life and swallows one of the remaining seeds. Upon finding her body, the ogre procures a golden coffin, puts her in it, and places it into the river. By chance, the king of the peacocks is standing on the levee, sees the floating coffin, and sends his courtiers to retrieve it. King Peacock finds a seed stuck in her front teeth and removes it, thus bringing her back to life.

Animal tales tend to remain distinct and limited to a cast of only animal characters in the European and African traditions. However, in a number of tales from Fortier's collection, the fusion of a cast of animal and human characters demonstrates the creolization of the oral tradition repertoire in Louisiana at the turn of the twentieth century. Furthermore, the similarities with ATU 709 are most likely of more direct African lineage as opposed to borrowing of a European-sourced repertoire. In "Lé Roi Pan," the antagonist is the heroine's own mother (as opposed to her stepmother), which is the case in nearly all of the attested African variants. One of the most distinctive motifs of ATU 709 within the European oral tradition, motif Z65.1, seems to be completely unknown in the African repertoire, which is unsurprising, as the image of "skin white as snow" and "cheeks as red as blood" are based on European aesthetics of the early modern period. Also lacking in this Creole variant is motif D1311.2, borne out by a survey of African variants, which shows only six instances of the magic mirror motif.[68] Another strong indicator of African influence is the presence of the nurse whom the mother orders to guard her daughter; Héli Chatelain recorded a nearly identical scenario in a tale named "Ngana Fenda Maria" from Angola during the same period.[69]

One commonality between European and African variants is the unusual role of the hero helper. The prince who discovers Snow White is unlike typical active fairy tale heroes who win their bride through exemplary courage, a series of challenges, or a bold quest. On the contrary, the heroine's resuscitation is unintended and not even of his own doing. The same tendency is present in the African versions. Minor characters not formerly mentioned appear unexpectedly to save the heroine and bring about the final resolution.[70] If any aspect of "Lé Roi Pan" could be identified as a specifically European influence, it would be the postponement of the girl's death and her resuscitation. As Schmidt notes, the motif of three attempts to kill the heroine with poisoned objects (for example, a necklace, a comb, and an apple) is unknown in the African oral tradition. In almost all cases, the mother succeeds in killing her daughter the first time.[71]

～

The fairy tales of Louisiana examined in this chapter suggest that the social and hierarchical constructs associated with a monarchy have persisted to some extent, as in a tale such as "Lé Roi Pan," which displays a strong resemblance to West African variants of ATU 709. However, this social hierarchy is less prevalent than in the Master Thief tales and even notably absent in numerous variants. While this may be expected, as it is precisely the kind of defunct social reference that, according to Zumthor, should recede from the oral repertoire, this does not seem to be the case elsewhere in the Francophone world. From Acadian communities of Canada to the Caribbean, fairy tales continue(d) to feature kings, queens, and princesses despite being far removed from this social reality. For example, in "Blanche Neige," a variant of ATU 709 collected in Guadeloupe, the servant deceives the stepmother by delivering an elephant heart. And yet the stepmother is described as *Pwincesse* (princess), and Blanche Neige marries the *woi* (king) at the end of the tale.[72] Furthermore, other tale types in the French and Creole Louisiana oral repertoire also include elements of monarchical structure to a lesser degree. Perhaps the most familiar is the tale of "Jean l'Ours et la fille du roi," which was later adapted to the stage by the theater troupe Nous Autres (and later Théâtre Cadien).[73] Still other tale types consistently feature a tyrannical king pitted against a trickster-like underdog protagonist, as we have seen with Roquelaure in the

Master Thief tales (ATU 1525). This dynamic is also prevalent in the *Jean* tale cycle (for example, 'Tit Jean, Jean-sans-peur).

Where these old-world social structures' staying power do manifest themselves in the oral tradition of Louisiana, their importance is considerably truncated. "Snow Bella" proves how the narrative structure of ATU 709 remains perfectly coherent even in dispensing of the parents' and stepmother's status as king and queen. In the Louisiana repertoire, kings and queens are often depicted as symbols of injustice that will be overthrown or disrupted by the hero(ine) later in the tale. These cases are not "rise tales," in which, for example, a peasant girl marries a prince; royal status is not the goal of the protagonist. There is also a purely performative use for these old-world structures as a locative device. Elements such as castles and royalty act as a signifier much like opening formulas such as "Once upon a time" or "Il était une fois," which is why, as in "La Beauté," a variant of ATU 410 (*Sleeping Beauty*) from Avoyelles Parish, the storyteller describes a castle hidden by bamboo in a seemingly subtropical landscape like that of South Louisiana. Here the castle indicates a timeless narrative space that persists despite a high level of localization.

While in much of the European tradition, fairy tale heroines are passive characters whose narrative journeys seem to invariably lead to marriage (often to a prince), several of the Louisiana variants examined here—particularly those from Avoyelles Parish—depict female protagonists with more agency. Snow Bella's triumph over her stepmother is only truly achieved after she recruits the dwarves to murder her. While in most versions, Cinderella has perfect virtue, the variants from Claudel's collection depict a heroine who actually realizes her self-worth, although it is not linked to any notion of class distinction or nobility. As we have seen, she is not afraid to taunt her sisters, to act in spite by reentering the house to don her fancy gown before leaving with the prince, or to assert herself before the prince by insisting on traveling to her new home in her own *carrosse* (coach).

A significant counterexample is "'Tit Chapilon Rouge" from Avoyelles Parish, a variant of ATU 333, commonly known as *Little Red Riding Hood*.[74] The tale is quite typical except for the ending: when 'Tit Chapilon Rouge is duped into believing that the bear is her grandmother, the bear devours her.[75] In most popular versions of ATU 333, a hunter or passerby finds the wolf in the grandmother's house, cuts him open, and rescues the grandmother and Little Red Riding Hood alive. The morbid conclusion of this Avoyelles Parish variant offers a harsh lesson: do not be gullible or else you will die. As we have seen, the French and Creole folklore of Louisiana generally affords an increased level of prestige to the trickster or other clever figures. By the same token, characters that are clumsy, gullible, or lacking in common sense suffer grave consequences.[76]

THE FUTURE OF FAIRY TALES

In examining the folklore collections of French and Creole tales from Louisiana, it would seem that fairy tales are fading from the repertoire or have already done so. However, folklorists have been lamenting the demise of fairy tales in the oral tradition for many years. As far back as 1697, Perrault chose to name his collection of literary fairy tales *Histoires, ou contes du temps passé* (stories, or tales of times past). In Louisiana, Fortier proclaimed storytelling a dying tradition as early as the late nineteenth century. And yet we have seen that a robust oral tradition persisted much longer, as evidenced by the collections of Saucier, Claudel, Brandon, Ancelet, and others. Today, however, it is clear that language loss and dramatic changes in our contemporary lifestyles have caused the French- and Creole-language fairy tales to go all but extinct.

Another factor is that fairy tales remain very much in the lives of young Louisianians today, but the source of these stories is more likely to be large commercial productions, rather than a parent or grandparent. South Louisiana even finds itself in such productions as Disney's *The Princess and the Frog* (2009), which features Tiana, a young Creole girl from New Orleans.[77] The film presents an adaptation of a familiar narrative while drawing on various stereotypes: an alligator sidekick (Louis), a Cajun firefly named Raymond who sings "Ma belle Evangeline," a voodoo priestess who lives in the bayou, and so on.

But if the everyday practice of storytelling at home has been in steep decline for years, some Louisiana authors have turned to literature as a way to retain a regional identity in fairy tales. *Cajun Folktales* (1997) by Celia Soper offers an illustrated collection of Bouki and Lapin tales and others; a French translation has also been published. Numerous adaptations of familiar fairy tales by Abbeville native Sheila Hébert-Collins include *Jolie Blonde and the Three Héberts* (1999), *'T Pousette et 'T Poulette: A Cajun Hansel and Gretel* (2001), and *Blanchette et les Sept Petits Cajuns: A Cajun Snow White* (2002). These tales are written in a heavily affected English with many words borrowed from Louisiana French. Still others, like Barry Ancelet (*Jean le chasseur et ses chiens* [2016]) and Susan Spillman (*Compère Lapin Voyageur,* 2013), continue to write children's literature exclusively in Louisiana French. In this way, Louisiana can hope to maintain its own specificity within some of the tales that make up the *canevas commun* of the oral tradition.

CHAPTER 6

Mystery, Magic, and Curses

Considering Louisiana's mysterious and exoticized portrayal in popular media, it may be surprising that the oral tradition of French and Creole Louisiana is not quite as fantastical as one might imagine. As the previous chapters have served to illustrate, the most significant element in the region's folklore is arguably everyday life and how to navigate it. Nevertheless, numerous magical and spritely figures inhabit the imagination of the region, and some of these are among the most well known to Louisianans. However, this does not necessarily mean that they are the most prevalent in the repertoire according to the archival and documentary record. This is in part because certain figures do not possess a specific tale type, or types, with which to identify them. While this certainly does not delegitimize them in the folklore repertoire, it has made them less desirable for inclusion in published collections. Moreover, several of these figures, such as the *lutin* and *loup-garou*, are especially representative of the French-speaking communities of southeastern Louisiana and are shared by Cajun communities and the Houma nation. These tales, as well as others, illustrate perhaps more than any other genre the complex changes and adaptations of narrative resulting from cultural contact. For this reason, they particularly warrant our attention here.

THE (MIS)USES OF ENCHANTMENT

In providing a closer look at some of the magical and fantastical figures of French and Creole folklore in Louisiana, I focus here on two main axes. On one hand, I discuss how folklore figures are often used as a motivating factor to influence "good" behavior among children. Generally speaking, this implicitly means following societal and cultural norms. One could say as much of practically any culture that uses folklore as a didactic tool. Bruno Bettelheim most notably explored folklore's capacity to act as a vehicle for subtle moral and cultural lessons in his study on the "uses of enchantment." At a basic level, certain characters exist to frighten children into returning home before dark or to kindly encourage them to behave well and so forth. Louisiana is no exception; such figures abound in the repertoire and include a diverse set of figures, including Pa Janvier, Madame Grands Doigts, the *loup-garou* (or *rougarou*), and others. On the other hand, I will examine—in a complementary fashion—how children directly and indirectly become actors in the repertoire itself. Whether as listeners or future initiated members of the community, children find themselves at stake in a number of ways. The superstitions surrounding the fate of unbaptized children are a striking example of how folklore functions not only to teach children but also to bring them fully into the culture. As in the previous chapters, my analyses draw on archival research and a comparative approach to shed light on numerous sources and adaptations in the development of these figures in the Louisiana repertoire.

FOLKLORE AS A CHILDREN'S GENRE

Folklore is often portrayed, although reductively so, primarily as a children's genre. Even much of the scholarship on the subject has focused on the folktale's place in education and the psychological underpinnings of the morals found in folktales, from Bettelheim to the sinister and thinly veiled endorsement of the patriarchy in Marcia Lieberman's "Some Day My Prince Will Come."[1] Certainly, this rather limited view of folklore is due in part to the conflation of the typical fairy tale (*Märchen*) genre and a broader understanding of oral tradition. In addition, children are generally considered to be the largest and most enduring audience for folktales. One need only observe the countless books and films conceived from iconic folktales by media giants like Disney.

The folklorists who spoke French and who most competently collected folktales in their original French focused their efforts on the central Acadiana region, generally speaking the parishes surrounding Lafayette, which also served as the cultural hub of the French language movement of the 1970s through the 1990s. While some folklorists collected tales from the parishes of southeastern Louisiana, they were generally not able to do so in French, and the question of linguistic specificity is generally absent from their accounts. Coincidentally, several of the folklore figures examined in this chapter, most notably the *lutin* and *rougarou,* are particularly indicative of southeastern Louisiana. Possibly the largest collection of recordings and transcriptions of *loup-garou* tales, compiled by Cheryl Cannon, was lost or discarded before scholars were able to access it.[2] Unfortunately, the folklore of this part of the state has long been under-studied. This shortcoming in the recorded repertoire presents challenges for analysis, not only in the number of tales available to us but also in the tales' unavailability in their original French.

The oral tradition of the Houma Indians is one of the most significant lacunae of folkloristic scholarship in this portion of the state.[3] As we will see, several folklore figures of southeastern Louisiana are intertwined in the oral traditions of the Houma and Cajuns.

THE *LUTIN*

One of the most popular folklore figures of southeastern Louisiana is the *lutin,* a spritely little being found in the forest.[4] In French, *lutin* simply translates to "elf" and naturally has many applications, including Santa Claus's helpers and spritely figures in the oral tradition of many cultures. Creatures called *lutins* can be found in the oral tradition throughout France and the Francophone world, although similar legends can be found practically worldwide but by different names and with slight variations. In France alone, several names for these magical little people exist depending on geographic region: *korrigans, cornandons, korils,* and *teus* in Brittany, *gobelins* in Normandy, *fadets* in Berry, *sortrets* in Lorraine, *dracs* in Provence, and the list goes on.[5] In French-speaking Canada, one finds the most similarity with the *lutin* of South Louisiana; however, they are by no means identical. Their basic characteristics— small in stature, mischievous, and mysterious—are generally all that they share across regions.

The *lutin* found in Houma folklore is portrayed as a trickster figure. *Lutins* are described as small, human-like creatures about the size of a small child, sometimes with attractive faces or long beards. While most of their mischievous deeds could be seen as largely innocuous, they nevertheless incur significant inconveniences when one considers the difficulties of everyday life in the rural southeastern parishes of Louisiana. It is said that one can repel them by placing mustard grains in a cup placed on the table because they find the odor repulsive. Or, if one suspects the presence of *lutins* in the home, spreading flour on the floor will serve to detect their little footprints. A common belief is that the *lutins* ride horses during the night, and when one finds horses exhausted first thing in the morning, sometimes wet or with their mane braided, it is a sign that a *lutin* is the culprit. Chasing chickens and hiding in barrels are not exceedingly menacing acts, but other accounts of the *lutins* are more disturbing.[6] One informant portrays them as an almost vampire-like creature: "When little babies would wake up with sore chests, and they were crying and had a little trouble breathing, people said that it was because the loutains [*sic*] came at night and sucked on the babies' breasts. The way to stop them from doing that is to place a pair of scissors underneath the pillow of the baby in the form of a cross. The loutains would stay away after that."[7]

Because the Houma Indians have adopted the French language and certain customs of the early colonizers and Acadian settlers, it can be difficult to discern between cultural elements that have been borrowed from the French and those that predate the arrival of the Europeans and their descendants. The *lutin* provides an excellent illustration of this problem. Although the word *lutin* is unquestionably French, its characteristics more closely resemble the *bohpoli* or *kowi anukasha* of the Choctaw. The Choctaw use these two terms interchangeably. *Bohpoli* roughly translates to "thrower" as he "often playfully throws sticks and stones at the people."[8] *Kowi anukasha*, true to the Houma's description of the *lutin*, means "forest dweller." These creatures are also called *les hommes des bois* by the Houma. Likewise, the *hashok okwa hui'ga*, according to the popular Choctaw belief, is a mysterious light that leads people astray at night, much like the *feu follet*.

The similarities between these Choctaw folklore figures and the *lutins* and *feux follets* of the Houma appear to have gone unnoticed by folklore scholars, even though they differ only in the language used to describe them, Choctaw or French. Houma writer and historian T. Mayheart Dardar notes, "The stories are very similar, but over the years the anthropologists have failed to make connections, or if they did, they chose not to record them as such," perhaps because they just "didn't sound *Indian* enough."[9] Moreover, the presence of such clear resemblances between the oral traditions of the Houma and Choctaw are consistent with a plethora of shared aspects of culture as members of the Muskogean language group.[10] Yet for all of its commonalities with the *bohpoli,* a couple of traits distinguish the *lutin* from its Choctaw counterpart. For the Choctaw, the *bohpoli* are not seen by most; they make themselves seen and heard only to the medicine men and women.[11] The *bohpoli* is also said to be a shape-shifter, sometimes manifesting itself as a bright light in the dark forest.[12] The *bohpoli* and the *lutin* both occupy a significant place in their respective oral traditions; tales and accounts of the *bohpoli* or *kowi anukasha* are still recounted, and the *lutin* seems to be equally known to the Houma's Cajun neighbors in Terrebonne and Lafourche Parishes.[13]

While it is not one of the most prevalent folklore figures in the oral tradition of French Canada, it is helpful to consider the *lutin* among the Acadians of New Brunswick and Nova Scotia. The *lutin* repertoire in Acadian communities in contemporary maritime Canada seems to be limited to the *lutin des granges* (barnyard elf), although earlier attestations of the *lutin des maisons* (house elf) exist.[14] Catherine Jolicoeur's collection includes eleven Acadian *lutin* tales that display a remarkable level of similarity not only to each other but also to some of the southeastern Louisiana variants. Nearly all of these Acadian tales include the braiding of horses' manes, sometimes used as stirrups by *lutins,* who were short in stature. Popular Acadian belief included several methods to prevent *lutins* from entering or staying in one's barn. One could place holy water, a medal of Saint Benedict or a blessed palm, or scatter flaxseed on the ground, as it is said that they are unable to count beyond a certain number and will become distracted. This motif (J2030 *Absurd inability to count*) is among the most common for dispensing of supernatural intruders.[15]

A major difference revealed by this comparison between the Acadian and Houma variants is the age of the tales' audience. To take Jolicoeur's collection as a primary example, in almost every one of the eleven *lutin* tales of Acadie, the informants frame their narratives as either personal childhood memories or legends shared by a parent or grandparent when they were children. Coincidentally, Bruce Duthu's collection of Houma folklore also includes eleven *lutin* tales;[16] however, in contrast, only one informant recalls hearing of the *lutins* riding their horses all night as a child. The other first-person testimonies seem to be clearly framed as experiences from adult life. Moreover, certain methods of repelling *lutins*—(for example, protecting infants or spreading flour on the floor—would only have been performed by adults.[17] In this sense, the status of the Houma *lutin* more closely resembles that of the Choctaw *bohpoli;* while its appearance is unusual, it is not entirely relegated to superstition or child's play but is, rather, integrated into a larger belief system.[18]

In the absence of written documentation of the *lutin* repertoire imported by the Acadians who sought to resettle in southeastern Louisiana, any attempt to distinguish the exact degree to which the *lutin* is "Acadian" or "Houma" remains a futile, if not misguided, task. It is impossible to ascertain whether at some point the French term *lutin* may have replaced a Houma word in the eighteenth century as the tribe gradually adopted French as its primary language or if a vestige of Acadian folklore may have fused with a preexisting Houma belief that in turn reinforced it among the White Francophone population. Certainly, multiple traits of the *lutin,* despite its French name, are of Native American origin and predate the arrival of European settlers in the region. Yet for all these similarities with the Choctaw *bohpoli,* the *lutin* of southeastern Louisiana is likely the result of a confluence of Native American and Acadian oral traditions. Such a level of fusion between these two traditions would have been made possible by the proximity of the two groups and their relative social isolation from others.[19]

THE *LOUP-GAROU*

The *loup-garou,* or *rougarou,* is arguably the most well-known folklore figure of Louisiana, specifically in the southeastern parishes of Lafourche and Terrebonne. It is widely thought of as a fixture of "Cajun folklore," although the *loup-garou* is equally integral to the folklore repertoire of the Houma. For many Louisianans, their knowledge of the *rougarou* is quite shallow. Parents tell young children, perhaps in half-jest, that the *rougarou* will catch them if they do not behave, return home before dark, or follow other such advice. On the other hand, the first-person narratives found in archives and written collections are almost entirely from adults. The *rougarou* differs considerably, then, from other magical figures like Santa Claus or the Easter Bunny, whereby parents encourage their children to believe something they know to be fictitious. Children and adults perpetuate *rougarou* legends equally.

Accounts and superstitions surrounding werewolves and lycanthropy go back many centuries and are found throughout Europe and the Americas. If one simply approaches the *loup-garou* of Louisiana as one regional iteration among an immense repertoire of werewolf folklore and superstitions, it would seem logical to begin our analysis here with a discussion of the werewolf's history dating back to medieval Europe. After all, the word *rougarou* is incontestably derived from the French *loup-garou,* and the Francophone influence on the region can hardly be overstated. Nevertheless, it must be stressed from the outset that the *rougarou* of southeastern Louisiana bears little resemblance to the *loup-garou* of French folklore, that is, beyond its most basic attributes as a nocturnal shape-shifter. Much previous scholarship has emphasized the European origin of the *loup-garou,* probably because of the obvious origin of its name; however, this "genealogical" approach inadvertently serves to obscure the connections between the Louisiana *rougarou* and the Native American oral tradition. For this reason, we must proceed with caution in attempting to trace the figure's development in a linear fashion as an outgrowth of European folklore.

In European legends dating back to the Middle Ages, the wolf has been portrayed as the "quintessential carnivore," embodying the wilderness and chaos.[20] As a nocturnal creature, the wolf is shrouded in ambivalence, resembling its domesticated counterpart, *canis familiaris,* known as "man's best friend." The wolf maintained an ambiguous aura throughout the medieval and early modern period in Europe, ranging from Dante's gluttonous she-wolf to the dim-witted Isengrim in the *Roman de Renart.*[21] Attempts to understand the wolf's place in the popular imagination in Louisiana are rendered even more hazardous due to the fact that the *rougarou* of Louisiana is generally not portrayed as a wolf at all but, rather, as a variety of different animals or ambiguous creatures.[22]

While there is certainly an abundance of werewolf lore and superstition in France, these legends bear hardly any strong resemblance to the *rougarou* of Louisiana. One aspect, however, deserves mention here:

In the Middle Ages [in France] it was often believed that if any person had been denounced from the altar and remained impenitent, refusing to make restitution and confess, the curse of the werewolf fell upon him. In

Normandy any man who was excommunicated became a werewolf for a term of three or seven years. In Basse-Bretagne any person who had not been shriven for ten years nor used holy water could become a werewolf. This belief was still current in the middle of the eighteenth century. In La Vendée the man who was excommunicated became a werewolf for seven years, during which he was obliged to haunt certain ill-omened and accursed spots.[23]

The notion of becoming a werewolf as a form of punishment for one's sins—particularly failing to fulfill one's obligations as a parishioner—seems to be especially prevalent in Louisiana. Such tales are similar to the condemned hunter (motif E.501), who forgoes attending mass in favor of hunting.[24] However, metamorphosis into a dog, bird, or wolf can also be found in the folklore of France and French-speaking Canada. A tale from Cap-Rouge in Quebec specifies that men become werewolves after neglecting Easter festivities for seven consecutive years.[25] The repertoire of *rougarou* tales in Louisiana contain a wide range of reasons why one might be transformed as a form of punishment, from swearing too much to marrying outside of one's own race.

Yet for all of its popularity in the Louisiana folklore pantheon, primary sources and first-person attestations of *loup-garou* tales are surprisingly scarce compared to other lesser-known folklore figures. The attestations that exist today, be they in written form or sound recordings, generally fall into one of two categories: personal accounts and mere descriptions of the creature's traits and characteristics. Unlike other figures such as Jean Sotte or Bouki and Lapin, there are no common cycles of motifs or specific tale types associated with the *rougarou* in South Louisiana.

One could even argue that the *loup-garou* of Louisiana has enjoyed more notoriety in literature and popular culture than it has had in more traditional veins of folklore. This is not surprising, as the character evokes the dark and exotic side of the South Louisiana marshes, yet it is readily understood and recognized by those unfamiliar with the region. Chris Segura's *Bayou* (1984) popularized George Rodrigue's now famous "Blue Dog."[26] While southern gothic novels abound, there are also lesser-known works like Berthe Amoss's *Loup Garou* (1979), which frames the legend within a simplistic retelling of the Acadian deportation.[27] The *loup-garou* was also a prevailing symbol of the

French-language poetic movement of the 1980s and 1990s led by Louisiana Francophone writers such as Jean Arceneaux (*Suite du loup*), Deborah Clifton (*À cette heure, la louve*), and David Cheramie (*Lait à mère*).[28]

Perhaps the earliest written description of the *loup-garou* in Louisiana is found in *Gumbo Ya-Ya*, a large book of folklore and superstitions compiled by workers of the Works Progress Administration first published in 1945. Excerpts in the book accredited to Cajuns do not include informants' names and are written in a probably exaggerated dialect of English, including traits and grammatical errors atypical of Louisiana French speakers. While the contents of the book are to be interpreted with some reserve, it is nevertheless interesting to compare this description to other, more recent field recordings. An anonymous "Cajun" describes the *loup-garou* as "them people what wants to do bad work, and changes themselves into wolves. They got plenty of them, yes. And you sure know them when you see them. They got big red eyes, pointed noses and everything just like a wolf has, even hair all over, and long pointed nails. They rub themselves with some voodoo grease and come out just like wolves is. You keep away you see any of them things, hein? They make you one of the them, yes, quick like hell. They hold balls on Bayou Goula all the time, mens and womens, both together."[29]

This description differs considerably from most others available to us. Moreover, the popularity and visibility of this collection seems to have had significant reach, as one can find reprintings or nearly identical descriptions in newspapers throughout the United States from the 1950s onward.[30] Despite this description's dubious reproduction of Cajun speech and its incongruence with other *loup-garou* accounts, it does contain the element of contagion prevalent elsewhere. Again, most accounts or descriptions of the *loup-garou* in Louisiana do not refer to wolves at all because wolves are so uncommon in South Louisiana. The confusion of the liquid consonants *l* and *r*, what linguists would consider a rhotacism or assimilation, further demonstrates the disassociation between the folklore figure and the wolf. This same linguistic phenomenon has occurred, seemingly independently, elsewhere in Francophone North America and is common in the Laurentides of Quebec and among the Métis in Manitoba.[31]

Loup-garous often transform others by biting them, in some cases relieving themselves of the curse, thus becoming once again normal humans. In many

Rougarou (Loup-garou). Digital illustration. Jonathan Mayers, 2020.

accounts, *loup-garous* are surprisingly difficult to detect, especially once they have temporarily regained their human form. The most common form of the *rougarou* in southeastern Louisiana is a dog; however, other variations include the owl. Typically, a human is imprisoned in the body of the dog and seeks to be freed. To do this, he must entice someone to draw blood from him. The *rougarou* will thus pester his prey to incite them to stab or prick him. Once blood is drawn, the *rougarou* will regain human form.[32] This motif (D712.4 *Disenchantment by drawing blood*) is not unique to South Louisiana, but it is definitely more prevalent than in other areas of the French-speaking world, including Missouri and Quebec. If one is to discover the identity of the *rougarou*, it must be kept a secret for either a year and a day or one hundred and one days, lest that person becomes a *rougarou* him- or herself.[33]

Those who claim to have witnessed a *rougarou* often describe where on its body they inflicted the wound and purport to see someone in town the next day with the same injury. Sometimes it is only by such a physical sign that they will identify them. In some tales that diverge considerably from the more typical narratives, the *loup-garou* is much less menacing. Loulan Pitre of Cut Off, for example, tells of a recurring appearance of the *loup-garou* who would cull oysters while Pitre and his companions were resting at night. Sometimes the *loup-garou*'s appearance was welcome because it would accomplish part of their task for the next day, but other times the men would find half of the oysters already eaten. On one occasion, the storyteller explains that he tried to sneak up behind the shadowy creature and strike him over the head. It then disappeared and never returned.[34]

The *loup-garou* stands out from the majority of folklore figures of French and Creole Louisiana in several ways. First of all, considering the *rougarou*'s supernatural aura, it is remarkable that so many tales are first-person accounts that pertain to individuals known by the informant. The figure also presents an interesting case of moral ambivalence. The *rougarou* does not choose to take on its animal form; he is compelled to do so either by contagion from another or as punishment for prior misgivings. Often such sins as missing mass are not seen as objectively harmful to others but rather pertain to church dogma or practice. Given the strong anticlerical sentiment found in much of South Louisiana's folk repertoire, as explored in chapter 4, the *rougarou*'s fate may also provoke a certain amount of sympathy. Moreover, the *loup-garou* in Louisiana is decidedly less menacing than its counterparts elsewhere in the French-speaking world and in Europe. In Louisiana, one does not die as a result of encountering a *loup-garou*, and they are not typically portrayed as being innately evil. The *loup-garou* represents a mysterious creature that is to be avoided if possible, but perhaps even more so, it represents the moral gray area found between man and beast that is both contagious and nearly universal in folklore.

SPIRITS AND THE SOULS OF UNBAPTIZED CHILDREN

For centuries, adults have evoked folklore figures in an effort to push children to behave in a way that meets specific cultural and societal norms. This practice is a testament to the oral tradition's place in maintaining the cohesion of a larger familial and cultural framework. Particularly because children are quite literally the future of the community, their inclusion (or exclusion) finds itself at stake in the very legends that are shared with them. The most prevalent example of this phenomenon in South Louisiana is a stock of superstitions associated with the souls of unbaptized children. The most well-known example is undoubtedly the *feu follet;* however, there are several other similar legends in Louisiana and a multitude of similar folk beliefs elsewhere in the world.

Baptism in the rural South is generally revered as a Christian ritual, and in the Roman Catholic enclave that is French and Creole Louisiana, it is one of the seven sacraments. At its core, however, the concept of baptism is a rite of passage into a community, and this concept is by no means limited to the Christian faith. The notion of an initiation ceremony for infants is common in many northern European cultures and even predates the Christian baptismal rite. Like many Christian customs and holidays, the church superimposed practices upon existing pre-Christian rituals. The deep bewilderment of infant death or stillborn babies is rooted in a dual sense of loss; the child is unable to join the community of the living and that of the dead, since the rite of initiation acts as the key to the afterlife. Substantial attestations from western Europe, the Americas, and Australasia demonstrate the folk belief that those born "without status" in the natural world will remain so in the next.[35]

In Catholicism, the harsh reality of infant mortality was at odds with the church's teachings on the necessity of baptism to attain eternal salvation. What fate awaited the souls of the unborn, and why should the innocent be denied from heaven? The problem of unbaptized children's souls therefore presented a problem to early theologians. Limbo, at first a rather loosely defined concept with roots in Greek mythology, was offered as a likely final destination for the souls of the unbaptized. It was believed that two types of limbo existed: *limbo partum,* where the souls of the Old Testament saints awaited liberation by Christ's descent into hell; and *limbo puerorum,* where the souls of unbaptized children remained. The reasoning was that these children had not committed worldly sin, but they had not been absolved of original sin and thus could not enter heaven. They were denied the pleasure of heaven but nevertheless received eternal life and were not condemned to punishment. More definitive views were proposed and developed by the church in the Middle Ages and most notably during the Council of Trent.[36]

The implicit understanding was that only a soul in limbo, neither in heaven nor in hell, would be considered able (or inclined) to haunt those in the physical realm. This was also because, St. Thomas Aquinas theorized, limbo was an eternal state that differed from purgatory, which is believed to be only a temporary space where souls are eventually purified before entering heaven. In several folk traditions, including Ireland and parts of France, the unbaptized souls return among the living because they seek baptism.

The existence of limbo, although not explicitly promoted in Roman Catholic dogma, was generally accepted and supported by Catholics from at least the sixteenth century through the mid- to late twentieth century. Today limbo is no longer part of the church's teaching, but this change is relatively recent; limbo was only removed from the catechism in 1992. Therefore, this change would not be at all reflected in Louisiana's folklore tradition. As late as 2004, Pope John Paul II created a commission to examine the merits of limbo; however, the committee's findings released in 2007 stated that limbo offers an excessively "restrictive view of salvation" and that it should be hoped that unbaptized souls would enter heaven.[37] Because the belief in limbo remained pervasive and unchecked for so long, it makes sense that several natural phenomena, similar folklore figures presumed to be the souls of unbaptized children, are also found in Irish folklore and Scandinavian folklore.[38] The *feu follet*'s presence in the folklore of France is due to a continuity of Celtic tradition in Breton legends and folk beliefs. The extraordinary level of similarity between Irish and French legends regarding the souls of unbaptized children as part of a shared Celtic tradition was reinforced by the cross-fertilization of ideas and writings between Ireland and France in the post-Tridentine Counter-Reformation period.[39]

In French and Creole Louisiana, as in most predominantly Catholic cultures, the fear of a child dying without receiving the sacrament of baptism was significant enough that the practice of *ondoiement* was quite common and remains in practice today. Derived from the Latin *unda*, meaning "running water," *ondoiement* corresponds to a simplified lay baptism that is performed when a child is stillborn or if death is thought to be imminent. While this ritual may seem to border on folk or vernacular religion, it is actually supported by the Catholic Church and described in the official catechism: "In case of necessity, anyone, even a non-baptized person, with the required intention, can baptize by using the Trinitarian baptismal formula. The intention required is to will to do what the Church does when she baptizes."[40] In Louisiana, a simple blessing would have been offered to the child while pouring water over the forehead: "Je te baptise au nom du Père et du Fils et du Saint-Esprit." Typically, a family member or even a nurse, depending on the urgency of the situation, would have performed this simplified version of the sacrament.

The ritual itself is relatively simple when compared to a traditional Catholic baptism, which is planned in advance, performed by a priest, and includes the presence of a godmother and a godfather. In one testimony from Vermilion Parish found in Elizabeth Brandon's recordings, when asked if *ondoiement* is equivalent to baptism, Henry Saltzman, one of her most prolific informants, states:

Mais, non! C'est pas exactement ça. C'est une manière, il y a une certaine petite cérémonie que quelqu'un fait, une prière ou quelque chose. Et c'est un enfant généralement qui est malade ou qui devient pas bien et ils croient ils vont le faire ondoyer et puis ils le promettent à un saint ou une sainte. Eh bien, cet enfant-là, il va porter du linge bleu pour tant de temps, ou du linge blanc, juste du linge blanc. Et généralement ils ont un cordon de l'ondoiement et cet enfant le porte. Il commence à porter ça quand il a six mois et il va porter ça jusqu'à il a six ans. Vous savez? Avant qu'il change ce linge-là. S'il a des bas, les bas sont bleus. Et les souliers généralement, c'est des souliers bleus. Tout le linge est bleu. Le cap est bleu itou.

Oh, no! It's not exactly the same thing. In a way, there's a certain kind of short ceremony that someone does, a prayer or something. And it's generally a child that is sick or is not well and they believe that they must *ondoyer* the child, promising it to a saint. Well, that child must wear blue clothing for a certain period of time, or white clothing. And generally, there is a baptismal cord that the child wears. It starts to wear it at six months and will wear it until six years of age. You know? Before it changes clothes. If it has stockings, the stockings are blue. And the shoes generally, are blue shoes. All the clothing is blue. The cap is blue, too.[41]

Saltzman's description of *ondoiement* is charged with Catholic religious symbolism wherein the number six is associated with imperfection and (human or imperfect) creation. The prevailing notion in Catholic numerology is that six is not quite seven, which corresponds to divine creation and the number of days needed by God to create the world. Blue not only represents health and new hope in the Catholic Church, but it is also the traditional color of the Virgin Mary, who is evoked in Saltzman's account of the blue baptismal cord that symbolizes devotion to Mary.

But for those children or stillborn babies who did not have the good fortune of receiving a lay baptism, it was believed that their souls wandered in the natural world in various forms, particularly near water or marshes, suggesting a yearning to attain the peace of baptism. Their fate beyond the physical realm was also reflected in very real terms in church practice; unbaptized children could not be buried on holy ground, and no priest was allowed to officiate any kind of funeral service. Such souls were truly treated as being, as Anne O'Connor contends, "without status" and condemned to restlessly roam and haunt the living.

THE *LÉTICHE*

One example of the souls of children appearing as revenants, although by no means the most well known, is the *létiche*. Like the *feu follet,* the *létiche* is also said to be the soul of an unbaptized child, sometimes described as a nearly imperceptible animal or a white, shapeless aura. The origin of the *létiche* seems to be clear; all accounts point to the region of Normandy in France. In earlier dialects of the region, several variants were said to be common, including *laitisse* or *létice,* which is said to predate its present pronunciation.[42] Its name certainly evokes the whiteness of *lait,* "milk," which is echoed in a number of studies.[43] One account describes the being as "an animal whose form is scarcely defined, of dazzling whiteness, which is only seen in the night-time, and disappears the moment any one attempts to touch it."[44]

Like many other magical apparitions, what the viewer perceives can be explained in rather simple, physical terms. In this case, the white ermine that dwell in the marshes of Normandy typically move in small groups and are nocturnal creatures. It is clear that the association between the animal and the soul of unbaptized children was well anchored in the popular beliefs of Normandy before the folklore figure was introduced to Louisiana. In addition to accounts of local Norman folklore, an 1851 novel by Émile Souvestre, *Les Derniers paysans,* includes a stirring passage confirming the *létiche*'s place in the popular imagination of the time: "About twenty small shapes, white and graceful, after climbing up on the marsh, suddenly grew, taking on the appearance of a bluish flame and began to dance atop the reeds. 'You see, the létiches are spirits, he said to Étienne, we are here in their kingdom.'"[45] In this same work Souvestre includes another superstition associated with this animal, which is that they are the incarnation of the souls of priests guilty of adultery during their earthly life.

Both Souvestre's novel and a brief entry in *Omens and Superstitions* were published shortly after another better-known work exploded on the English-speaking literary scene, Henry Wadsworth Longfellow's *Evangeline: A Tale of Acadie,* first published in 1847. The narrator describes the children's affection for the village notary, blessed with an impeccable memory and large stock of stories that fascinate the town's children: "Ripe in wisdom was he, but patient, and simple, and childlike, He was beloved by all, and most of all by the children; For he told them tales of the Loup-garou in the forest, And of the goblin that came in the night to water the horses, And of the white Létiche, the ghost of a child who unchristened, Died, and was doomed to haunt unseen the chambers of children."[46]

Longfellow's choice to include the *létiche* among the folklore repertoire of the Acadians is deceptive in terms of the figure's origins. In writing *Evangeline,* Longfellow is known to have conducted very limited research in developing his description of the Acadian people and their land and customs. Perhaps conflating Acadie with the inhabitants of what would become Quebec, Longfellow overemphasized the importance of the region of Normandy, and this misconception persisted in the historical discourse of the Acadians for some time.[47] In truth, there is no evidence that the Acadians in maritime Canada ever knew of the *létiche.* Its absence seems logical when one considers the actual geographical locations from where the early Acadian settlers originated.

Given the origin of the significant majority of the core of Acadian settlers, there is no reason to believe that such a popular superstition surrounding an animal like the *létiche,* found only in Normandy and parts of Brittany, would have been known, much less popular enough to have been transported to the New World when Acadia was founded. No evidence of the *létiche* can be found in any of the folklore archives or written sources on Acadian folklore; the figure seems, by all accounts, to have never existed in the maritime provinces of Canada. Well over half of Acadia's seventeenth-century immigrants hailed from the Centre-Ouest provinces (Poitou, Aunis, Angoumois, and Saintonge or Anjou Province), which formed the core of the early Acadian population and resulted in linguistic and cultural continuity in their new homeland.[48]

This realization makes Longfellow's reference to the *létiche* in *Evangeline* an anomaly. While, in theory, it is possible that he may have found or heard of some association between the Acadians and this obscure folklore figure that has since been lost, it is extremely unlikely, especially given the amount of scholarship on Longfellow's reading records at the time.[49] Longfellow would have likely learned of the *létiche* through his readings on the folk traditions of Normandy and one of the region's great writers, François-René de Chateaubriand, a native of the Norman port city of Saint-Malo. The erroneous inclusion of the *létiche* joins an extensive list of glaring oversights and misrepresentations of the Acadians in *Evangeline*. To his credit, Longfellow never claimed to be an expert on Acadian history or culture; however, the extraordinary reception of *Evangeline*, which spoke of a people previously unheard of by most Americans, resulted in an assumed credibility of the work and its author that even resulted in the widespread misconception that Acadians were primarily of Norman descent.[50] These distortions apply to the people's characteristics as well as the geographical and natural realities of Louisiana and Nova Scotia. Brasseaux surmises:

> Longfellow, however, possessed a very limited knowledge of Acadian history [. . .]. Never having encountered the Acadians residing in his native Maine or in the neighboring Canadian Maritime Provinces, he was unaware of the rich, but untapped, vein of dispersal lore, which survived in the exile communities. [. . .] His initial efforts were hampered by his ignorance of Acadian and Louisiana history and geography. To correct this deficiency, Longfellow turned to the scanty information available in the Harvard Uni-

versity Library. Particularly significant in shaping his conception of predispersal Acadian society, the Acadian diaspora, and the ultimate disposition of the Acadian exiles was Haliburton's *An Historical and Statistical Account of Nova Scotia,* a work seriously flawed, for it incorporated uncritically extensive sections of Abbé Guillaume Raynal's fanciful description of the early Acadians.[51]

However, this still leaves unanswered the question of how the *létiche* arrived in Louisiana. The most likely possibility is that the Acadians learned of the *létiche* after the deportation. Many of the exiles were sent to France, where two cities served as the primary points of entry: La Rochelle in Charente-Maritime and Saint-Malo in Normandy. Many of these Acadians, or their children, eventually made their way to Louisiana. Given the relative isolation of this folk belief (and the habitat of the animal itself), it would be reasonable to assume that only a significant immigration to Louisiana from Normandy and/or Brittany, like that of the Acadian exiles, would explain its presence in Louisiana.

The earliest attestation of the *létiche* in Louisiana dates back to early 1940s. The authors of *Gumbo Ya-Ya* described it as "the soul of an unbaptized infant" said to haunt children in their beds at night as they try to go to sleep.[52] While the essence of the *létiche* is the same, the fact that it appears in children's rooms implies a dramatic shift in its manifestation in Louisiana. Rather than appearing in the marshes or the near the ocean, the *létiche* of Louisiana's oral tradition seems to have already changed to resemble a more ghostlike creature, presumably capable of penetrating walls. This phantomlike characteristic, combined with its affinity to frighten and disrupt sleep, correspond to another folklore figure of Louisiana, the *cauchemar.*

Another account from 1974 curiously attributes the *létiche* to Black Creoles. Jos Bill Thériot of Breaux Bridge states: "The older Black folk with their voodoo used to talk about létiches. A baby that died before being baptized, that's a létiche."[53] While it may seem far-fetched to link this Normand legend to voodoo, there are a number of examples in which this kind of mutability of terminology has taken place, particularly when the literal meaning of a word becomes lost and appropriated.[54] On the other hand, this account could indicate a certain prejudice in attributing an unfamiliar practice to the other even though doing so seems illogical. Black Creoles were, presumably like the speaker, overwhelmingly Catholic in St. Martin Parish.

THE *FEU FOLLET*

Many in South Louisiana are familiar, at least by name, with the *feu follet*, or will-o'-the-wisp. There are streets and even a musical group named after the spirit; however, folk superstitions related to the *feu follet* are not unique to South Louisiana. After all, this very phenomenon corresponds to the origin of the jack-o'-lantern, the pumpkin being added later on. The French name common in Louisiana, Canada, and France is a quite literal translation of the Latin *ignis fatuus,* which can be found in earlier folklore studies. The etymology indicates the "folly" of those duped into following it. Roughly translated as "fool's fire," the *feu follet* has generated a remarkable number of accounts and tales, particularly in areas in or near marshes and bayous. Wetlands specialists have since identified this mystifying display as the result of the decomposition and movement of several gases, including methane and hydrogen sulphide. Like the *létiche, feux follets* appear especially in marshy areas, and the fact that the regions of Normandy, Poitou, maritime Canada, and Louisiana all feature marshland as an integral part of their topography has undoubtedly contributed to the *feu follet*'s enduring presence in the oral tradition.

The overwhelming majority of *feu follet* accounts in Louisiana correspond to motif F491.1 *Will-o'-the-Wisp leads people astray.* While they are not usually aggressive or malevolent in the Louisiana folk repertoire, they can be mischievous enough to cause people to become lost in the swamp, often until daylight. Remedies for resisting the *feu follet* often include shiny and/or sharp objects. Inez Catalon, a prolific storyteller from Kaplan, Louisiana, offers this explanation: "Mais ils disont si jamais le monde, ça voyait un feu follet et qu'il avait un couteau de poche, fallait il ouvre le couteau, et tu le plantes sur un poteau. [. . .] Et là, cette petite lumière reste. Elle joue avec ce couteau. Là, ça te laisse tranquille" (But they say that if ever you saw a *feu follet* and had a pocketknife, you had to open your knife, and stick it on a fence post. [. . .] And then, that little light will stay. It plays with the knife. Then it leaves you alone).[55]

Variations on this motif (F491.3.2 *Power of Will-o'-the-Wisp over person neu-*

tralized if person sticks his knife into the ground) are exceedingly common in the French and Creole repertoire of Louisiana, although they can be found in a number of European traditions as well. This motif is so widespread in folk traditions that it suggests there might be some physical explanation for its prevalence. Perhaps disturbing or penetrating the ground in some marshy areas may have been sufficient to disturb the emissions of gas causing the light to dissipate. Regardless of the motif's genesis, accounts from the oral tradition of France, Louisiana, Ireland, and other areas in northern Europe include motif F491.3.2 in a way that is similar to its mention by Inez Catalon, that is, one must distract the *feu follet* as one would a small child with a shiny toy. Numerous variations of motif F491.3.3 *Steel protects person from Will-o'- the-Wisp* support the subtle depiction of *feux follets* not only as the souls of children but also as spirits who maintain a childlike playfulness.

Nearly all descriptions of the *feu follet* found in the Louisiana repertoire describe the being as the soul of an unbaptized child; however, there exist considerable regional discrepancies with regard to its visual manifestation. While most accounts from Lafayette and the surrounding parishes—including that of Inez Catalon of Kaplan in Vermilion Parish, who describes the *feu follet* as "pas beaucoup plus grosse qu'une chandelle" (not much bigger than a candle)[56]—portrayals from members of the Houma community describe a much larger and more menacing presence.

John Verret, a member of the Native American Houma tribe described in 1989 the *feu follet* as a "bad angel," purportedly as large as an owl, intent on distracting those who pass nearby and causing them to become lost. Verret recalls: "One of my uncles was brave. Brave enough. They said you put a needle up like this, and that thing goes through that needle and comes out sparking on the other side, flies, fire flies."[57] The use of a steel object, in this case a needle, is corroborated by two more recent accounts of two Houma men, Jimmy and Felicien Verret, recorded in 2001. Having seen *feux follets* often while hunting nutria whenever the moon was full, they suggest sticking a needle into the side of one's pirogue. The *feu follet* should come to the boat and rest upon the boat. This account is exceptional in that it is the only testimony with instructions on how to attract, rather than repel, the spirit. Verret also describes the light as "une boule de feu rouge" that evokes motif E742.2 *Soul as will-o-the-wisp. Appears as a ball or fire or a figure in a fiery garment.*[58]

Bruce Duthu, a member of the Houma community who collected folktales from thirty-five individuals in 1978, recalls his informants' descriptions of the *feu follets* as "strange balls of fire floating through the sky at night, and their purpose was only to misguide people and render them lost. [. . .] One woman spoke of a burning tree that people called a feu follet, only because upon inspection the tree was found to be unharmed."[59] Unlike the description of a small, candle-like light in the distance as provided by Inez Catalon, most Houma accounts depict a large and even aggressive red ball of light. One informant relates: "Then, I saw this shining red light coming at me, it seemed. It came as far as the tree, the top of it. It circled, and then suddenly went away. A while later, it came again. This time, it looked like it was really coming at me, but it got to the tree and circled it three or four times, and then left again." Another account from Duthu's collection describes a *feu follet* of similar color and size: "You see them in lakes. You see them like lights. And you head towards that light. And you ride and ride. The light will always stay in front of you, and you find that you have not been moving at all. They'll come on board with you. What causes them is beyond me. But to get rid of them, you take a needle. You make it pass through the eye of the needle. It's like a ball of fire."[60]

While the notion of the *feu follet* being the soul of an unbaptized child seems to be shared by all of the French- and Creole-speaking communities of Louisiana, there is a marked difference in the size, color, and general demeanor of the spirit in the Houma community. It is possible that this difference is the vestige of an older Native American belief that has since fused with the French term *feu follet,* in a similar way that the *bohpoli* became known as *lutins.* However, the remarkable homogeneity of the Houma accounts of the *feu follet* from various time periods suggest that this marked difference could be better explained by a physical phenomenon related to the combination of gases found in the area, since it is known that this can affect its color.

One important similarity with the *feu follet* tales collected in southwestern Louisiana is that the lights are only found near or on still or stagnant water. Of course, this can be explained scientifically given the types of gases needed to produce the will-o'-the-wisp's luminous effect; however, other legends, particularly in France, include explicit references to the cries of the *feux follets* begging passersby to anoint them with the nearby water. Sometimes referred to as *brandons* or *illayés* in southeastern France, *culards, feu follet,* or *loumerotte* are found in northern France.[61] They are otherwise similar to the Louisiana variants, even including the motif of distracting the *feux follets* with a pocketknife. Sébillot's 1905 *Folk-lore de France* includes an account of children coming out of limbo each night and competing for the attention of a passerby: "Ce n'est pas ton parrain, c'est le mien!" (That's not your godfather, he's mine!).[62] In the Creuse and Poitou regions, the souls of unbaptized children are associated with the *chasse-galerie,* or Wild Hunt, as they emit cries to be saved from limbo. It is possible that the idea of the *feu follet* or child's soul pleading to be baptized might have existed in Louisiana at some time, but no attestations seem to exist. It is also odd that Louisiana has preserved a version of the *chasse-galerie,* but it is unassociated with the souls of children.[63]

THE *FIFOLÉ* OF POINTE COUPÉE

While the most common description of the *feu follet* seems to be that of the soul of an unbaptized child, numerous accounts of Louisiana Creoles of color give a very different justification. Several examples from the early twentieth century can be found in the linguistics fieldwork on Louisiana Creole conducted by graduate students of Louisiana State University under the direction of Joseph Broussard.[64] Several such examples warrant our attention, for although they differ greatly from the accounts already examined here, they demonstrate significant similarities with one another, suggesting a relatively stable and consequential subset of the *feu follet* repertoire.

Lafayette Jarreau (1907–78), a scholar and native speaker of Louisiana Creole, collected just over thirty folktales, all from elderly Black Creoles. One tale, entitled "Fifolé," is recounted from the perspective of a slave, making reference to "nègres" and a "maître" (master).[65] The storyteller describes an old Black man (*ein vié nègre*) who possesses the ability to become a *fifolé.*[66] At night, the old man would remove his skin, roll it up, and place it in the corner of the barn. He would then take the form of a ball of fire and disappear, frightening everyone else on the plantation. The master took note of his absence and decided to stand watch one night, peering through the crack in the side of the barn. Realizing that the man would shed his skin before disappearing, he placed salt and hot pepper inside the skin. Upon placing the skin back on his body later on that night when he regained human form, the man had no choice but to jump into water, which cured him of this supernatural affliction.

In strong contrast with the previous descriptions of the will-o'-the-wisp figure, this tale contains characteristics and motifs that are more indicative of a werewolf or shape-shifter than the typical *feu follet*. Nevertheless, the importance of water is also key here, although its role is likely more rooted in the African tradition as a cleansing power, rather than the Catholic rite of baptism. The end result, however, is the same; water relieves the *fifolé* from its curse.

Another account, listed among "superstitions," describes a similar kind of metamorphosis, here a woman: "Ein jou quand mo té couri Chemin Neuf mo wa ein gros boule di fé dans chemin. Quand mo couri pou ramasser li pou

Fifolé de la Pointe Coupée. Digital illustration. Jonathan Mayers, 2020.

limmin mo cigarette mo wa ein faume avec la flame dans so jambe yé et li volé dans l'air en traver la Fosse Rivière, c'était ein fifolé" (One day, when I went to New Roads I saw a great ball of fire in the road. When I approached it to pick it up and light my cigarette, I saw a woman with flames in her legs. She flew away in the air across the False River. It was a *fifolé).*[67]

Another Creole variant from Pointe Coupée includes motifs reminiscent of *loup-garou* tales in that it describes the possibility of an individual being transformed into a *fifolé.* Magio Etienne, a resident of Morganza, related the following tale in 1930, at the age of sixty-five. When a woman gives birth, an old woman hears of this and decides to *jouer fifolé* (to "play" or to become a *feu follet)* and suck the blood of the newborn baby. She aims to do so at night when everyone is asleep. The father suspects that there might be a *fifolé* about and takes the precaution of placing two needles in the form of a cross and many mustard seeds at the door.[68] Upon arriving, the *fifolé* is compelled to count the mustard seeds until sunrise, at which point she flies away from the house.[69]

This account contains an interesting confluence of Catholic symbolism and Afro-Caribbean motifs. Of course, in the three preceding Creole tales of the *fifolé,* the creature is not a *feu follet* at all in the usual sense of the term. The transforming figure more closely resembles a ghost or werewolf creature than a will-o'-the-wisp or jack-o'-lantern. The needle, already evoking the afore-mentioned tales of needles being used to ward off (or attract) the *feu follet,* comes into play again here.[70] Two needles form the sign of the Christian cross (motif D1181 *Magic needle)* and serve to protect the household. Furthermore, the mustard seed is a powerful symbol of Christian faith, although in this instance, it serves to confuse the *fifolé;*[71] the same motif of counting objects (for example, the holes in a sieve) to cause confusion is prevalent in Louisiana tales of the *rougarou* and *lutin.* While the presence of Christian symbolism may seem at odds with the magical elements in the tale, this is quite common in African American folklore of the South: "The relationship between Conjure and African American religion—in particular, Christianity—is somewhat ambiguous. Conjure is usually associated with magical practices, unlike Christianity, which is seen as a 'religion,' a dichotomy that suggests that they are in conflict with one another. Yet from slavery days to the present, many African Americans have readily moved between Christianity, Conjure, and other forms of supernaturalism with little concern for their purported incompatibility."[72]

Motif G229.1.1. *Witch who is out of skin is prevented from reentering it when person salts or peppers skin* can also be found in another tale collected by Remi Lavergne in 1930. In "Ein fifolé" (A Feu Follet), a sixty-five-year-old Black Creole named Frank Terrance tells of an elderly man and woman who decide to marry.[73] On their wedding night, the woman retires to the bedroom early. When the husband enters the room, he notices that she looks different; she has removed her hair and her teeth. Later he notices that she has disappeared, leaving behind her skin. At this point, he is convinced that his new wife is a *fifolé* and puts salt and pepper into her skin. When the woman puts the skin back on, it burns her unbearably. As she contorts in pain, she cries, "Skini, skini! Don't you know me?" before vanishing, never to return again.[74]

This incantation, in particular, suggests that the *fifolé* of Pointe Coupée shows more resemblance to African American folklore in the rest of the Gulf South than with the French oral tradition, despite its French-derived name.

African Americans portrayed witches as otherworldly beings dwelling liminally between the realm of human persons and the wilderness. Impetuous and wicked, they slipped through keyholes and windows, mounting "nightmares," their dream horses, the unfortunate individuals whose sore muscles and tangled hair remained the sole evidence of their victimization when they awoke. Such accounts were told and retold, with slight variation, among black Americans for generations. African American witch stories, or witch tales, were distinguished by several consistent themes. The motif of the skinless witch was one of the most popular accounts in the slavery era and persists to the present day.[75]

Another tale from Lavergne's 1930 fieldwork in False River incorporates elements of the vampire-like *fifolé* described by Magio Etienne as well as the incantation featured at the end of Terrance's tale. Louise Gasserand of False River recounted the following tale:

Y navait ein vié fome qui té ginyin ein tas l'argent et tous les soirs li té conin a clef so la maison pour pecher fifolé yé volé so l'argent. Ein soir ein vié fifolé vini pou volé l'argent; li oté so la peau pi li passé dans ein ti trou la clef; pis li rentré dans la maison [. . .]. Quand li té dans la maison li wa ein ti bébé, li commencé sisé so di sang pis la li fout so quand [*sic*] (camp). Lendemain papa ti bébé la trouvé so pitit té tout pale. Ça fait li té conin fifolé té vini sisé li. Ça fait soir la li prend graine maïs li mette dans so fisil et li gété pou fifolé la, li cassé derrière barriere mais [. . .] pas voir fifolé la quand li vini li tend ein train, ça fait li gardé et li voi fifolé té apé rentrer dans la maison; ça fait c'était trop tard pou tirer. Li attend ein ti moment pis la li voi so la peau li prend di sel et di poive et li sallé la peau la. Quand fifolé la vini pou pati encore li mette so la peau li commencé totiller. Ça brilé li et li dit, "Mais Skini, Skini, Don't you know me?" Li té pas ca diré so la peau; ça fait li oté li et la nhomme la trapé vié fome la pis li réconin li pis la li tchué li.[76]

There was an old woman who had a lot of money and every evening she would lock up her house to keep the *fifolés* from stealing her money. One evening, an old *fifolé* came to steal her money. It took off its skin and slipped through the keyhole.[77] Then, it entered the house [. . .]. When it was inside the house it saw a little baby and started to suck its blood and then vanished. The next day, the baby's father found his child all pale. He then knew that a *fifolé* had been there and sucked the child's blood. So, that night he took kernels of corn, loaded them into his rifle and stood watch. It broke through the back gate, but [. . .] he did not see the *fifolé* when it entered. It made a noise, so he looked and saw the *fifolé* entering the house and it was too late to shoot. He waited a moment and then saw its skin. He took some salt and pepper and salted the skin. When the *fifolé* moved to leave again, it put on the skin and began to twist and turn. It burned it and it said, "But Skinny, Skinny! Don't you know me?" It was unable to stand the burning skin and removed it. The man caught the old woman and recognized her. Then, he killed her.[78]

The reoccurrence of the haunting formula, the only words pronounced in English by both Creole-speaking storytellers, poses several questions. Why is this one sentence in English? Why is it identical in each tale? Why is this False River *fifolé* so radically different from the will-o'-the-wisp tales found everywhere else?

It is important to note that this incantation and the skin motif are not unique to the oral tradition of French and Creole Louisiana. In fact, there are a number of attestations in the African American folklore of the South. Variations have been attested in Georgia, Missouri, Virginia, and North Carolina.[79] Newbell Puckett wrote in 1929: "The belief is too widespread to be an independent development; to the best of my knowledge it is not found in Europe; but in West Africa there is the widespread idea that the witch leaves her skin behind on going out, and among the Vais it is thought that salt and pepper sprinkled in the room will prevent her from getting back into her hide."[80] Evidence of similar witch tales from Louisiana told in English also exists. The Louisiana Writers' Project collection *Gumbo Ya-Ya* contains a variant told by Rebecca Fletcher in the section on "Slave tales": "My Grandma told me about a witch what went into a good woman's house when that woman was in bed. [. . .] Ole witch went out and lef' her skin layin' on the floor, and the woman jumped out of bed and sprinkled it wit' salt and pepper. Ole witch come back put on her skin. She start hollerin' and jumpin' up and down like she was crazy. She yelled and yelled. She yelled, 'I can't stand it! [. . .] Skin, don't you know me?' She said this three times, but the salt and pepper keeping bitin'."[81]

Given the wide swaths of the American South where similar tales have been attested, we can establish that this witchlike figure known as the *fifolé* in Pointe Coupée as well as its accompanying motifs are not indigenous to Louisiana. Rather, they are a vestige of West African folk belief and Afro-Caribbean oral tradition. While this assertion may seem evident on the surface, I aim to illustrate more specifically here that the significant discrepancy between more typical will-o'-the-wisp tales and the *fifolé* found in Pointe Coupée is due to a transposition of the Afro-Caribbean folklore figure *soucouyant* (or *sukuyan*) onto the preexisting term of *feu follet* in French Louisiana. The *soucouyant* is found in the oral tradition in numerous islands of the Antilles. Its primary characteristics are identical to that of the *fifolé* of False River, Louisiana. In Caribbean folklore, the *soucouyant*'s true form is that of a ball of fire; however, it can disguise itself as an old woman during the day, donning an exterior skin that can be removed when roaming at night seeking a victim. This allows the *soucouyant* unnatural abilities of metamorphosis, enabling it to penetrate keyholes or slip under doorways.[82]

Elsie Clews Parsons includes several variants in her 1941 collection *Folklore of the Antilles, French and English,* including one told by sixteen-year-old

Ernest Allenby of Dominica. In the young man's account, he tells of a child whose mother is suspected of being a *soucouyant*. He explains: "If you meet de skin, an' put salt on it, de skin can not go back on de *soucouyant*."[83] Other variants from Dominica include the motif of blood sucking and the practice of placing grains of sand at the doorstep in order to confuse the *soucouyant*, whose compulsive nature compels her to count each grain.[84]

An essential element of the *soucouyant* that in and of itself distinguishes the figure from the conventional parasitic vampire is its strong association with the female gender. This detail significantly alters how the figure and motifs are interpreted because of the subversion of certain gender norms. The *fifolé* of Pointe Coupée, which we have established is congruent with the *soucouyant* of Caribbean folklore, occupies a marginal space both literally and figuratively. She penetrates her victims in several ways, including entering the home through keyholes or under doorways, and even piercing the skin of her victims to extract blood. Moreover, several behavioral traits challenge societal gender norms for women. Like the *soucouyant*, she is not only childless but preys on the young; rather than remaining at home, she roams at night. She destabilizes the notion of outward appearance by shedding her skin, and "she accentuates her flouting of the acceptable spaces for women to inhabit: she travels outside the domestic sphere as well as the physical landscape occupied by ordinary humans."[85] Both figures are at odds with male figures in the narrative; the *fifolé* or *soucouyant* often target a baby boy, and it is typically a man or a group of men who succeed in killing or banishing her.

> The anxieties engendered by the soucouyant figure in cases from all around the African diaspora can be attributed to numerous sources: discomfort with those who are advanced in age and perceived to be on the brink of death; the thought of an unwelcome visitor entering the private property of one's home; this uninvited figure breaching the sanctity of the sleeping quarters, where one is often in an exposed state of undress or in intimate apparel; being caught completely unaware and defenseless, in the vulnerable state of slumber; having one's body penetrated, whether by physical fangs or intangible powers; not knowing whether part of oneself—the blood or "life-blood," ostensibly the soul—has been stolen by another person. The notion of transgressed borders—whether those are the boundaries

of one's property or of one's physical, corporeal body when its fluids are drained—seems to be one of the key factors in the distress caused by the folktales about vampiric characters.[86]

The *fifolé* found in Pointe Coupée thus bears little resemblance, if any, to the will-o'-the-wisp. Likewise, the anxieties expressed through these narratives are very different. While the Creole *fifolé* depicts the fear of bodily harm and the invasion of one's home and security, the *feu follet* tales demonstrate fear for the souls of unbaptized children who are unable to join the spiritual and physical community. This preoccupation would have been even more acute given the scarcity of priests available to perform the sacrament, as we have seen in chapter 4.

THE *CAUCHEMAR*

Another common spirit in Louisiana's folklore is the *cauchemar,* sometimes spelled *kooshma* or *koushma* in Louisiana Creole.[87] In the contemporary sense of the word, *cauchemar* (nightmare) typically refers to a frightening or un-pleasant dream. The term is also associated with the spirit that supposedly causes sleep paralysis in its victims at night. Sleep paralysis can be defined as "the experience of either falling asleep or waking up and finding oneself unable to move. With the exception of the eyes, no other voluntary muscle movements are possible during this state except for respiration."[88] In many cultures throughout the Americas, Europe, and Asia, supernatural phenomena related to incubi, like the Old Hag or Night Hag, provided a way of under-standing the physical effects of sleep paralysis.[89] No fewer than 118 terms from various cultures around the world have been documented.[90] In South Louisiana, *cauchemar* is still relatively known, especially among Creoles of color. Folk knowledge surrounding the experience of sleep paralysis and a handful of popular culture references, including a regional hit song by Joe K K and Zydeco Force, "Kush-Mal," have helped this folklore figure to maintain a slight foothold in the popular imagination.[91]

The supernatural explanation of the physical experience of sleep paralysis is in fact at the etymological root of the word *cauchemar.* In an earlier form, *cauquemare* was formed from Picard *cauquer* (to press or hold) and the Dutch

Koushma (Cauchemar). Digital illustration. Jonathan Mayers, 2020.

mare (phantom).[92] Now an archaic albeit valid use of the word, its earliest attestation from 1375 describes an experience that corresponds precisely to the condition that physicians today recognize as sleep paralysis.[93] The broader sense of *cauchemar* as simply an "unpleasant dream" is thus relatively recent, likely dating from after the primary waves of Francophone immigration to Louisiana. As a result, this present-day definition is rarely used by or even known by native speakers of Louisiana French, as most speakers would translate "nightmare" as *mauvais rêve* or *pesant*.[94] *Pesant* (heaviness) illustrates quite viscerally the connection between a frightening dream and the weight of the spirit associated with sleep paralysis on one's chest.[95] The importance of weight or pressing is also apparent in the medieval French *appesart* as well as in other cultures and languages, including *hexendrücken* (witch pressing) in German and the Spanish *pesadela*.[96]

It would appear that three factors contribute to the range of symptoms generally recognized as sleep paralysis: the neurological basis for the experience; the social and cultural myths or explanations that accompany the phenomenon in one's milieu; and personal beliefs, feelings, or daily experiences.[97] It is this second contribution that offers a potential for understanding the *cauchemar*'s place in the collective imaginary of French and Creole Louisiana because it pertains to the set of beliefs—religious, personal, or cultural—that form the understanding of this phenomenon for members of the community. As a deeply Catholic culture, nearly all accounts of Louisiana Creoles describe religious tactics to repel the *cauchemar*. Praying, attending church regularly, and placing crosses and holy water near one's bed are common techniques.[98] Placing a rosary under the pillow and even drinking holy water have been said to be effective.[99]

The importance of such a belief within the oral tradition could conceivably create sufficient anxiety, especially among young children and adolescents, that would in turn incite the experience more frequently. While this connection is not made explicit in Patricia Rickel's study, the informant Cotton Mather's account provides an illustration of this causality. After his grandfather, a gifted storyteller, tells a harrowing tale to him and a group of neighborhood children about the "witch" in a black dress, he experiences intense visions of a physical battle with the witch for two consecutive nights.[100]

It bears mentioning that early studies like those of Rickels, Bourque, and Brown draw overwhelmingly from accounts given by two groups: adolescents (or young adults recounting experiences from their teenage years) and the elderly. Scientists have since established that sleep paralysis disproportionately affects adolescents and those over the age of sixty, as demonstrated by a Chinese study of the "ghost oppression."[101] Because stress has clearly been identified as a negative factor in sleep hygiene, the fact that adolescents experience sleep paralysis at higher rates is not surprising given the dramatic social and sexual changes associated with puberty.[102] Furthermore, the age gap in these two most affected groups could reasonably create a kind of narrative loop whereby older family members who are themselves experiencing *cauchemar*-like episodes would more readily provide a supernatural explanation to the children and adolescents when they begin to experience sleep paralysis or nightmares.

A key component to understanding the *cauchemar* of Louisiana that distinguishes it from a number of cultures is the notion of punishment for one's sins. As Mather confirms: "Grandfather went on to say that her evil duty among others, was to sneak into the home of bad boys and girls and haunt them while they slept. [. . .] The only way to get her off your back was to pray."[103] Rickel's study includes another account from a woman whose husband was "hoodooed" by "a bad woman called Big Marie." After consistently returning home after midnight and gasping for breath in his sleep, it became clear that the *cauchemar* was punishing him for his infidelity.[104] The notion of sleep paralysis as a form of punishment for sins committed during one's waking hours is especially common in testimonies from children and adolescents who claim to have been the victim of the *cauchemar* after swearing, fighting, and disrespecting their parents.[105]

Compared to other folk beliefs, the *cauchemar* has demonstrated a remarkable resilience in the popular imagination. Surely, as research on sleep hygiene develops (namely, the relationship between sleep paralysis and possible contributors such as stress, caffeine, and alcohol), it may prove pertinent to explore the physical reasons for the *cauchemar*'s sustained presence in the region's folklore. Although the medical community has developed a better understanding of this quite common phenomenon, a variety of cultural, social, and religious explanations for this experience remain prevalent. On one hand, the *cauchemar* of French and Creole Louisiana is but one cultural manifestation of sleep paralysis among over a hundred others in the world. On the other hand, the physical experience has very clearly fused with the fears and supposed dangers of sin in a profoundly Catholic culture like that of the Louisiana Creoles.

Of course, not all attempts to influence the behavior of children are done in a negative sense. We have seen how the *rougarou* and *cauchemar* exhibit a kind of dual existence in the folk belief. Adults sincerely believe in these beings and in some cases testify to having encountered them, and yet they are used as a vehicle to cultivate fear by parents or other adults in order to influence children's comportment. However, other figures are specifically conceived for the purpose of affecting the behavior of children. Not surprisingly, several remain closely tied to the rituals of Christmas.

Contrary to the simple notion of a jovial and generous Santa Claus that dominates images of the holiday season in the United States and to an increasing degree elsewhere in the world, many European Christmas traditions were predicated on the notion that children's behavior could be equally motivated by the threat of punishment and the promise of gifts. Together, European figures such as *Weihnachtsmann* or Père Noël, Perchta, Schmutzli, and others represent a multifaceted view of influencing ideal behavior and the roles and expectations reserved for children during the Christmas season. In Louisiana, Christmas figures range from the generous little *souris de Noël* (the Christmas mouse) to the more ominous ones, such as Pa Janvier or Bonhomme Janvier.

LA CHRISTINE

One mostly benevolent figure commonly associated with Christmas or New Year's Day is La Christine. This folklore figure has hitherto garnered little attention and is completely absent from the major folklore collections of Louisiana. Furthermore, its origin and the opaque significance of the name *Christine* has largely remained a mystery. While she is not known throughout South Louisiana, in parts of St. Landry Parish, in the vicinity of Leonville, Arnaudville, and Pecanière, Cajuns and Creoles recognize her with surprising consistency. Storyteller David Lanclos, from the Arnaudville area, recalls how his grandmother and other elders described La Christine in her long flowing dress. She would magically appear, unseen by the children, and fill their shoes with candy the day after Christmas. It was generally understood that La Christine was Papa Noël's wife. According to the tradition, she was often reluctant to join her husband on his long trip around the world on Christmas Eve night; however, she would always regret staying home and decide to leave alone later on, hoping to catch up with Papa Noël. Because she was always just behind Papa Noël, children expected her to arrive the day after Christmas.[106] For children who were less deserving of such treats, La Christine reserved *coton-maïs et de la cendre* (corncobs and ashes). Lanclos's account of La Christine is quite consistent with the majority of variants found in the area, with the exception of the day of her arrival; it is generally believed that she passes on New Year's Day.

The importance of New Year's Day in Christian culture is easy to overlook today; however, in France, it was historically a far more festal day than Christmas Day itself. It was on the first of January when one exchanged gifts and held family gatherings. Children expected their stockings to be filled with presents and fruits, and families made a point of paying visits to nearby relatives.[107] In Louisiana, this custom remained in effect through the mid-twentieth century, before giving way to mainstream American practices that tended to recognize Christmas Day as the focal point of the season. While a possible connection with the German figure Christkind has been informally proposed, I aim to delve into this question here.

Das Christkind, literally "the Christ Child," can be traced back to the days of Martin Luther. Reformists disagreed with the overtly Catholic notion of Saint Nicholas bearing gifts on his feast day. Since early Protestant thought favored a more direct connection between the believer and God, it was proposed that the Christ, in child form, would bring presents to children. Protestant Germans began giving gifts on Christmas Eve, rather than on Saint Nicholas's feast day of December 6. Over time, however, Das Christkind became a mythical figure to German children and has lost the sacred nature of its original meaning—so much so that popular representations of Das Christkind resemble a tall, blond figure in white nearly always portrayed by a girl. Das Christkind's precise identity is ambivalent, resembling both an angel and fair-skinned sprite.[108] In towns such as Nuremburg, Das Christkind is still a major element of the lavish Christmas markets for which local girls vie to be elected to the coveted position in pageant fashion.

The fact that Das Christkind had already been recognized as a female figure relatively early on in Germany makes it all the more plausible that a Gallicized form, La Christine, of this Protestant Christmas tradition could have been integrated into the predominantly Catholic and Francophone Louisiana as the wife of Père Noël. However, La Christine's German origins were likely overlooked because of the original German figure's obscurity in Louisiana combined with a gradual corruption of the original pronunciation of the term. Common pronunciations include "Chrichequine," "Grichine," and of course "Christine."

Despite its significance in sheer demographic importance, German im-migration to Louisiana is often overlooked or glossed over, particularly with regard to the region's French- and Creole-speaking communities. German-speaking immigrants were indeed some of the founding groups of Louisiana. Soon after the founding of New Orleans, John Law's Compagnie des Indes encouraged as many as ten thousand individuals from both sides of the Rhine River and from Switzerland to settle in Louisiana based on grossly exaggerated claims of fertile lands and gold-laden mines.[109] However, an overwhelming majority of those who left Germany following Law's false claims died en route from disease and malnourishment; it is estimated that only some two thousand arrived in Louisiana.[110] Many of these Germans and Swiss Germans eventually settled in what is now the area of St. Charles and St. John the Baptist Parishes, which led to the region being dubbed la Côte des Allemands (the German Coast). Because the German Coast was located immediately downstream of the Mississippi River and thus adjacent to the Acadians' coasts (present-day St. James and Ascension Parishes), intermarriage between the groups began early on. The introduction of the Christkind figure, later known by other Gallicized deformations, likely dates from this earlier German settlement.

Of course, subsequent and much larger waves of German-speaking im-migrants arrived in Louisiana, notably a significant contingent from the Alsace-Lorraine from the periods of 1815–60 and 1880–1930.[111] However, the *émigrés* from Alsace-Lorraine included a considerable number of Catholics as well as Jews, who quickly dispersed and settled in multiple towns in Lou-isiana, including Shreveport, Plaquemine, and Opelousas, and in Vicksburg, Mississippi.[112] An even later and more isolated German community exists in Acadia Parish. Roberts Cove is actually near the general area where La Chris-tine is recognized; however, despite robust collections of oral history in this community, no evidence shows that Das Christkind was ever celebrated as a Christmas tradition there.[113] This, of course, would be logical given that Father Peter Thevis guided Roberts Cove's foundation and the community remained almost entirely Catholic.[114] Considering the relatively confined area where the Christine figure is found today and the fact that Das Christkind is essentially a Protestant figure, it is much more likely that this figure's introduction to Louisiana predates the arrival of these nineteenth-century immigrants and harks back to an earlier German and Swiss German immigration and the Côte des Allemands region, whose descendants would have brought the Christine tradition with them as many of those families acquired cheaper farmland in parishes west of that area.

MADAME GRANDS DOIGTS

Madame Grands Doigts (Lady Long Fingers) enjoys popularity in South Louisiana to this day among children. Yet despite her relatively large reputation among children as a folklore figure, she remains decidedly ambivalent regarding her demeanor. While in some families Madame Grands Doigts brings small gifts or fruits to good children, others portray her as a wicked woman who punishes naughty children.[115] In both instances, her unusually long fingers create a distinctive physique, whether it serves to reach down into hung stockings to deposit treats or to strike fear into the hearts of children. Louisiana Francophones who remember Madame Grands Doigts as a benevolent figure provide details of her visits with remarkable consistency. Most recall her arriving during the night of New Year's Eve. On New Year's Day, children would awaken to find pecans and fruits, most commonly citrus fruits like satsumas. Those more fortunate remember small firecrackers or simple toys. These gifts would invariably have been placed in the children's shoes, which would have been left out for Madame Grands Doigts to fill.

Some families tell tales of a Madame Grands Doigts who is completely dissociated from the Christmas season, a frightful witchlike figure who terrorizes children. It would appear that this version of the figure is invariably portrayed as a malevolent being. Often inhabiting the woods or an attic, she will attack children who come near her or sneak into children's room and pull their toes while they sleep. In the cases in which she is portrayed as malevolent, she is generally unassociated with Christmas or the holiday season. Many adults recall being told that Madame Grands Doigts lived in the attic or in a specific part of the woods or in still some other place that parents wished for their children to avoid altogether.

Lanclos provides a tragic origin story encompassing elements of these two divergent descriptions that may point to an older, more complete interpretation of the figure. Lanclos describes a beautiful young girl with exquisite hands who attracted the admiration of the young men of the village. The other girls became so jealous of her popularity that they cast a spell on her hands, making them ugly and full of warts (*poreaux*). As she grew older, her unpleasant physical appearance prevented her from finding a husband, although she greatly wanted to become a mother. After her death, it was said that her ghost haunted the attics of children's homes because she longed to be near children. However, the children, unaware of her innocent intentions, were simply frightened by the sight of her hands.[116]

The ambivalence of magical figures associated with Christmas is a defining factor of Christian traditions in many cultures of Europe and the Americas. Characters like Schwarzpeter in Germany and Schmutzli in Switzerland acted as a foil to St. Nicholas. If children were not sufficiently swayed to behave well by the promise of toys and sweets, Saint Nicholas's counterpart was there to punish those who had misbehaved during the year. What is unique about Madame Grands Doigts is that she plays, depending upon region and family, both of the roles, but never at the same time or in the same family.

This kind of duplicity in Christmas figures may simply be a vestige of an anterior set of customs related to children's behavior. As Ernest Miles has noted, both Pelzmärtte (Skin Martin) in Swabia and even St. Nicholas would reward good children with apples, nuts, and cakes and beat the bad children:

> Can it be that the ethical distinction is of comparatively recent origin, an invention perhaps for children when the customs came to be performed solely for their benefit, and that the beating and the gifts were originally shared by all alike and were of a sacramental character? [. . .] They are common enough in folk-ritual, and are not punishments, but kindly services; their purpose is to drive away evil influences, and to bring to the flogged one the life-giving virtues of the tree from which the twigs or boughs are taken. Both the flogging and the eating of fruit may, indeed, be means of contact with the vegetation-spirit, the one in an external, the other in a more internal way. Or possibly the rod and the fruit may once have been conjoined, the beating being performed with fruit-laden boughs in order to produce prosperity.[117]

La Christine, Madame Grands Doigts, la Souris de Noël, and other figures provide yet another example of the complicated relationship between religion, folklore, and family life. While religion has certainly played a significant role in creating folklore figures, often transposed on existing pagan traditions, French and Creole Louisiana provides a compelling example of how cultural contact and localized needs and customs molded traditions brought from the Old World. Surely, the dangers of the environment and mysterious natures of marshlands can explain why several prominent folklore figures like the *rougarou* and Madame Grands Doigts hinge on preventing children from transgressing specific physical boundaries. In Louisiana, as in many regions, folklore figures are not only used as a means of entertainment for children, but they also demonstrate how development and culture are intertwined.[118]

⁓

Louisiana is no exception when it comes to folklore's ability to frighten children into behaving in accordance to adults' wishes. However, Louisiana's folk repertoire demonstrates a marked tendency toward biblical overtones in that certain supernatural phenomena are expressly described as punishment for venial sins. Previous scholarship has portrayed French and Creole Louisiana folklore primarily as a confluence of European and African traditions, but this has obscured Native American aspects, namely Choctaw and Houma influences, that should be more apparent when they are taken into account. Were it not for numerous Afro-Caribbean influences, it could be said that the fantastical imaginary of French and Creole Louisiana is largely similar to that of French-speaking Canada; however, these Afro-Caribbean elements related to the characters portrayed (the *soucouyant* or *fifolé*, for example) suggest a fusion of these multiple traditions that was previously estimated to be limited to a small number of motifs. In addition, other communities such as German-speaking immigrants contributed significantly to the folklore repertoire of Louisiana.

Given folklore's capacity to provide rationalizations for mysterious natural phenomena, many of these figures offer an identifiable explanation for frightening occurrences still observable in the largely rural regions of southern Louisiana. And because specific actions or tangible materials such as praying, sticking a knife into the ground, or scattering mustard seeds are believed to ward off these supernatural beings, such folk beliefs provide psychic relief from the mysterious sights and sounds of rural South Louisiana. Figures meant to intimidate or punish naughty children are generally less brutal in Louisiana than their counterparts found elsewhere in the world. For example, the *rougarou* is, for the most part, only mischievous; he is usually either compelled or cursed into animal form. Conversely, he means primarily to frighten his victims into moral conformity. This in itself suggests a moral ambivalence among the community with regard to marginalized figures like the *rougarou, fifolé,* or *lutin.* All is not black and white; the state of liminality inhabited by figures like the *feu follet, létiche,* and *rougarou* illustrate the understanding that everyone in the community has faults. Contrary to otherwise similar folklore figures in Europe, these examples found in Louisiana are not altogether shunned or feared. They necessitate a nuanced view of right and wrong and a measured approach to moral judgment.

Epilogue

Contemporary Uses of Folklore Figures

In comparison to today's fast-paced lifestyle saturated by mass media entertainment and social media platforms, the nineteenth century may seem like the golden era for folklore and the storytelling tradition. But during that period, the brothers Grimm in Germany, Léon Pineau in France, and Alcée Fortier in Louisiana all lamented the imminent disappearance of traditional storytelling. And yet folklorists in Louisiana continued to collect a wide range of tale types and oral histories throughout the twentieth century. On one hand, we could say the forewarnings of the oral tradition's impending demise were greatly exaggerated. On the other hand, a sense of optimism does not negate the fact that the traditional place of storytelling in everyday life has been lost in much of the contemporary world.

The French- and Creole-speaking areas of Louisiana went through fundamental social and cultural changes in the twentieth century as a result of multiple natural disasters, forced linguistic assimilation, two world wars, expanded railroad access, and the advent of TV and radio. As in many parts of the world where the social contexts conducive to storytelling—extended family visits, *veillées*, or manual tasks such as net weaving, for example—have eroded, much of the oral tradition has been lost with them. So, while South Louisiana is no exception to these general trends that can be seen throughout the world, the changes in social life were compounded by a simultaneous linguistic shift toward English, making many jokes and tales that depend on wordplay obsolete. There was also an intergenerational language gap that often made it difficult or impossible for older monolingual French-speaking family members to communicate with monolingual English-speaking children.

Some elements of folklore have proven more fragile than others, such as longer narratives (as in "Geneviève de Brabant" and "Le Fin voleur") and fairy tales. Again, South Louisiana is no exception to this downward trend. In the late twentieth century, Ancelet made the case for including jokes, oral history, and tall tales in our conception of "folklore." This indeed presented a more positive outlook for an otherwise dwindling folklore repertoire at the time.[1] Today, however, one would be hard-pressed to find Louisiana French speakers capable of recounting the kinds of folk narratives collected by Ancelet in the 1970s.

One might argue that some part of an oral tradition lives on under the guise of stand-up comedy. In addition, storytelling artists such as Yannick Jaulin in France have adapted the *conte populaire* to the stage in bringing full-fledged performances, complete with lights and decor, to modern audiences. While this medium would not be considered "stand-up comedy," there are a number of performative similarities. In Acadiana, Cajun Comic Relief has enjoyed a large audience since its inception in 1992. Exclusively in English and relying on an often exaggerated Cajun accent, this brand of Cajun stand-up comedy is campy and family friendly. And while some jokes, like the vast repertoire of Boudreaux and Thibodeaux jokes, may have analogous versions elsewhere in the world and perhaps even identifiable tale types, this genre's potential status as a form of folklore is debatable at best.[2]

I do not mean to imply, however, that folklore in South Louisiana has ceased to exist. To an increasing degree, folklore is experienced outside of traditional performative contexts through various modes of recycling.[3] Most contemporary uses of folklore in Louisiana's popular culture fit into one of two categories: children's literature and marketing. In both of these distinct arenas, the repertoire of folklore figures is considerably limited in comparison to the wide array of tale types and figures historically found in the oral tradition and folklore collections.

A survey of elements of South Louisiana's oral tradition that are still visible in popular culture, be that in children's literature or in branding and marketing, reveals that only a few folklore figures have managed to persist. The *rougarou* is undeniably the most popular, as even many young people have a vague understanding of the legend. Bouki and Lapin have also maintained a certain level of popularity thanks to more recent children's literature or integration of local folklore in schools. *Cauchemar*, although perhaps to a lesser degree, has also managed to preserve a place in the popular imagination, particularly in Creole families and new fiction.

The prevalence of these particular folklore figures is remarkable considering their relative scarcity in the major folklore collections. No *rougarou* (or *loup-garou*) tales are found in any of the collections by Fortier (*Louisiana Folk-Tales*, 1895), Claudel (*Study of Louisiana French Folktales*, 1947), Ballowe (*Creole Folk Tales*, 1948), or Saucier (*Histoire et traditions de la paroisse des Avoyelles*, 1949). Ancelet records a tale entitled "Le Chien étrange" (The Strange Dog) in *Cajun and Creole Folktales* (1994), and the collection of Lindahl, Owens, and Harvison, *Swapping Stories* (1997), which includes examples from many different ethnic and cultural communities in Louisiana, contains only two *rougarou* tales. Only Bruce Duthu's collection of Houma folktales, published as a special issue *Louisiana Folklore Miscellany* in 1980, includes a considerable number of testimonies relating personal experiences with *loup-garou*.[4] Still, the *rougarou* is by far less attested than other figures such as Jean le Sot.

Tales featuring Bouki and/or Lapin were more numerous in folklore collections. The characters appear in eight out of twenty-nine animal tales in Fortier's collection, in two out of four animal tales in Saucier's, and multiple Bouki and Lapin tales can be found in the collections of Claudel, Ancelet, and *Swapping Stories*.[5] Still, they represent a minority among a much larger cast of animal characters, particularly in the collections of Fortier and Saucier, which included the elephant, the turtle, the tiger, and many others.[6]

Rather than drawing conclusions from the absence or scarcity of these figures in published folklore sources, I am more interested in their strong presence in popular culture, children's literature, and regional branding today. These are arenas, I should note, that do not feature some of the genres and figures that *are* more prevalent in the folklore collections and archives.

FOLKLORE IN CHILDREN'S LITERATURE

There are numerous examples of Louisiana folklore figures in film and literature. Independent short films like *Rougarou* (2016) and *Kooshma* (2016) show how these mysterious figures' nebulous descriptions and the lack of a definitive narrative associated with them make them easily adaptable to the horror film genre.[7] Not surprisingly, however, most contemporary folktale adaptations have been in the children's literature genre.

Folklore elements can be found in a surprising number of children's books. Some publications, such as Celia Soper's *Cajun Folktales,* consist of literary adaptations of well-known tale types like ATU 175 *The Tarbaby* and others.[8] Some authors have been able to adapt folklore narratives in new ways, as in Susan Spillman's theatrical text *Compère Lapin voyageur.*[9] Others have taken inspiration from the conceptual essence of certain folklore figures in order to create new fictional stories. One example is musician Yvette Landry's *Madame Grand Doigt* [*sic*], written in English.[10] The story tells of a young girl who tries to save her friend who is captured in the home of Madame Grands Doigts.

Still other authors have created original characters that resemble some of the iconic characters of Louisiana folklore. Eunice native Mary Alice Fontenot, for example, has authored some twenty books in her Clovis Crawfish series, some of which were translated to French under the name *Clovis écrevisse.* As mentioned in chapter 5, Sheila Hébert-Collins has written numerous literary adaptations of classic fairy tales, adapting them to the context of South Louisiana, in English peppered with French terms.

Folklore and children's literature have been used for several decades in efforts to preserve and develop the French language in Louisiana and increase cultural awareness among the younger generations. Activists and educators such as Amanda LaFleur, Barry Ancelet, Richard Guidry, and Brenda Mounier have utilized folklore in various forms to revitalize the cultural and linguistic specificity of the region. More recently, Louisiana—which has historically been lacking in options for French-language publication—has strengthened ties with Canada, where Francophone publication benefits from greater financial and institutional support. Bouton d'Or Acadie, a youth literature publisher based in Moncton, New Brunswick, has collaborated with Éditions Tintamarre in Shreveport and the University of Louisiana at Lafayette Press to produce several children's books in French, most recently a posthumously published alphabet book by the late Richard Guidry *B pour bayou* (2019).[11] *Qui est le plus fort?* (2014) by Barry Ancelet is an illustrated adaptation of the cumulative tale "Neige casse la patte de la froumi" (The Snow Breaks the Ant's Foot) told by storyteller Inez Catalon of Kaplan.[12] Ancelet's *Jean-le-Chasseur et ses chiens* (2016) is not only written in Louisiana French but employs an orthography that captures the pronunciation and orality of performed speech.[13]

FOLKLORE IN BRANDING AND MARKETING

The *rougarou*'s prominent place in contemporary South Louisiana's popular imagination is surprising when one considers its scarcity in the folklore collections. And yet one can find any number of instances of the *rougarou* in popular branding as a regional cultural symbol today. Particularly leading up to Halloween, the *rougarou* can be seen in local news stories as many people seek a kind of origin story for the creature. Because the *rougarou* already corresponds to the exotically dark and mysterious image of South Louisiana, the creature is very present in fantasy literature and popular media, but it has also appeared on national television, such as on the Discovery Channel and in an episode of *Cajun Justice*.

Within Louisiana, especially southeastern Louisiana, the *rougarou* is very much a cultural and regional symbol. The Rougarou Fest that takes place just before Halloween each year in downtown Houma is perhaps the largest manifestation of the *rougarou*'s continued popularity in South Louisiana.[14] This festival highlights Louisiana folklore with panels, parades, and conversational workshops while also raising awareness of coastal erosion.[15] In 2019, the musical lineup included New Orleans–based Francophone indie-pop band Sweet Crude, which released its new single, "Rougarou."

In marketing, the actual significance of the *rougarou* is used as a cultural marker for a wide gamut of products, from Rougarou guitar pedals created by a small company in Hammond, Louisiana, to beer and spirits. Baton Rouge–based microbrewery Tin Roof produced a now-retired imperial black ale named Rougarou, which the brewery described as a "dark, malty beast of a brew."[16] In Thibodaux, Louisiana, Donner-Peltier Distillers was known for its Rougaroux rum, which was distilled to 55.5 percent alcohol by volume—101 proof—to symbolize the number of days that the *rougarou*'s secret must be kept by its victims lest they themselves become a *rougarou*.[17]

The affinity for folklore figures in marketing local products is a trend seen throughout North America and Europe. Unibroue, a midsize brewery in Quebec, has been drawing from local folklore to name and market its beer since the early 1990s. Two of the company's more well-known examples include La Maudite, which features an iconic image of the *chasse-galerie,* and Trois Pistoles, which evokes the town known for its three-towered church whose priest is said to have asked assistance from the devil to construct. While they are not always named for specific folklore figures, other microbreweries in South Louisiana consistently evoke local geography, Louisiana French, or other cultural and ethnic markers for their craft beers. Swamp Thing, Envie, Ragin' Cajun, and Acadie Farmhouse Ale are just a few examples of how regional identity intersects with craft beer marketing. This trend is also visible in the world of cuisine in naming dishes or restaurants, such as Compère Lapin in New Orleans, which specializes in Caribbean cuisine.[18]

It would be easy to dismiss these instances of recycled folklore as superficial marketing or even cultural appropriation. However, the reason why this trend toward utilizing local folklore elements as an identity marker is so pervasive is that it consists of a direct reaction to the movement of globalization and mass production that prevailed for several decades. In the early twenty-first century, locally sourced and regional products (in the French spirit of *terroir*) became much more in demand, particularly in the United States and Canada. The value, and marketability, of local restaurants and breweries is that they represent the antithesis of multinational corporations like ConAgra, McDonald's, or Budweiser (Anheuser-Busch). Low cost, speed, and uniformity have taken a back seat—at least to some extent—to regional specialties and a curiosity for authentic "ethnic" products. In this sense, it is no surprise that so many small companies have availed themselves of local folklore as a means to market their products. Folklore, as obscure as it might seem in our contemporary era, represents the essence of a region and its communities, and this is precisely why it is an effective marketing tool.

Recycled folklore figures, as a means of staking out a regional specificity in opposition to global mass-market brands, is even more effective for a region such as South Louisiana that has already undergone a massive exploitation of the "Cajun" label—often by entities outside of the state—starting in the 1980s. One need not look far to find complete misappropriations of the term applied to fajitas, French fries, rice pilaf, and other foods. The extreme saturation of the national market with faux Cajun products has already prompted the Louisiana Department of Agriculture and Forestry to create the Certified Cajun and Certified Creole labels in order to help in-state companies to establish some visible sign of authenticity. As a more recent trend, the use of folklore figures arguably accomplishes this more effectively by moving beyond geography to express a more defined cultural identity with an authentic cultural reference.

This recycling use of folklore begs the question: "Does this still qualify as folklore at all?" The almost purely commercial use of folklore figures is reminiscent of what Richard Dorson termed as "fakelore."[19] Dorson vilified fakelore; in his mind, "fake" characters like Paul Bunyan and Pecos Bill were artificial, disingenuous, and motivated by commercialism and profit.[20] However, even in these cases, fakelore has been used to fill a regional, psychic need and to assert a specific identity.[21] We might also think of this specifically commercial use of folklore as more akin to what Priscilla Denby called "folklure" as it pertains to decorative purposes or marketing.[22]

However, it seems that the ways in which folklore has been and is being recycled in Louisiana corresponds more closely to a kind of survival or revival. Dundes draws a clear distinction between the two terms: "*Survival* implies a continuity of tradition, no matter how diminished or altered in form an item of folklore might be. *Revival* suggests discontinuity, a break in the tradition. It refers to a conscious decision to resuscitate an item of folklore that flourished in the past."[23]

The interest Louisiana businesses and writers have in drawing on folklore figures is clear. Still, we might wonder why *these* characters and not others? Why do we not see La Christine each year at Christmastime? Why are most Louisianans familiar with the *feu follet* but not the *létiche?* The *rougarou* but not the *lutin?* Why has the extensive cast of animal characters been for the most part distilled to two characters, Bouki and Lapin?

First, I would argue that the so-called folklure at play for some of these characters does not require any kind of narrative. The *rougarou* is the perfect example of this phenomenon; even in the relatively few attestations in folklore collections, there is no veritable *rougarou* narrative. By and large, *rougarou* tales are personal accounts of supposedly lived experiences. It requires no effort on the part of the consumer in terms of learning a story or comprehending its origins. Furthermore, because the notion of the werewolf is familiar to most, one need only understand that the *rougarou* is "the werewolf of Louisiana." In a second and related set of circumstances, Bouki and Lapin—even if not by those names—are perfectly recognizable to most Americans. J. C. Harris's *Uncle Remus* tales and the subsequent adaptations by Disney in *Song of the South* (1946) and others made this part of Creole and African American folklore a fixture of American culture. Again, one needs no prior knowledge of Louisiana's history or folklore to recognize Bouki and Lapin: most Americans are familiar with Brer Fox and Brer Rabbit; in Haiti, they would be recognizable as *Bouki ak Malis* and in France as *le loup et le renard*. Even those who have not been exposed to any of these folklore figures would recognize a strong similarity with another trickster rabbit of popular culture: Bugs Bunny.

It seems clear, then, that *continuity* of select elements of the oral tradition is directly related to *congruity* with the larger American folklore repertoire. Moreover, those characters that enjoy particular popularity are the ones that have no fixed narrative associated with them (for example, the *rougarou*) or require no extensive explanation to those outside the community because they are already familiar but by another name. Ironically, while folklore is consciously being used to highlight cultural specificity and instill cultural pride, be it in local commerce or children's literature, it is generally not done by using folklore figures that are most unique to French and Creole Louisiana. Rather, we mostly see characters that are easily recognizable versions of figures already present in the larger American folklore repertoire. Unfortunately, these more superficial and nonnarrative uses of folklore in marketing and branding fail to convey the sense of humor or a set of values or morals representative of a given community or region.

With regard to the study of folklore, new technology in the digital humanities, such as the *FrancOralité* platform and an ever-increasing amount of digitized and transcribed materials in archival sources, mean that much more work can be undertaken in comparative folklore research. At the same time, however, we should not look only at folklore as an indicator of the vitality of cultural communities. A marked increase in French-language cultural production in Louisiana as well as new media outlets and content suggest that French and Creole Louisiana will be retelling old stories in innovative ways as well as creating many new stories for future generations.

Notes

1. For a more complete account of folklore publications, see Ancelet, *Cajun and Creole Folktales*, xxv–xxviii.

2. Delarue and Ténèze, *Le Conte populaire français*, 7.

3. Simonsen, *Le Conte populaire*, 51.

4. Dundes, *Folklore Matters*, 57.

5. A prime example is *Gumbo Ya-Ya*, which resulted from the Federal Writers' Project. As Carl Lindahl notes: "Most of the work published by the Federal Writers ultimately displayed far more journalism than folk artistry" because it was "filled with valuable stories and impressive bits of oral history, but these tales were not rendered in the actual words of the storytellers, nor were they free of the biases of the collectors." Introduction to Lindahl, Owens, and Harvison, *Swapping Stories*, 3.

6. Marshall, "Origin and Development of Louisiana Creole French," 334.

7. Brasseaux, *Scattered to the Wind*, 1.

8. Fiehrer, "From La Tortue to La Louisiane," 1.

9. Brasseaux, *French, Cajun, Creole, Houma*, 18.

10. Hall, *Africans in Colonial Louisiana*, 161.

11. Ibid., 159.

12. Brasseaux, *French, Cajun, Creole, Houma*, 12–13.

13. Brasseaux and Conrad, *Road to Louisiana*, vii.

14. Brasseaux, *French, Cajun, Creole, Houma*, 22.

15. Hall, "Franco-African Peoples of Haiti and Louisiana," 43.

16. Parham, *American Routes*, 2.

17. Ibid., 16.

18. In addition to its use as an ethnic and cultural label, the term *Creole* also refers to the French-based Creole language (also called *kouri vini*) still spoken today by some ten thousand in Louisiana, although there is not always congruency between those who speak Creole and those who identify as Creole in a cultural or ethnic sense. Not only are there white Louisianans who

speak Creole; there are also a considerable number of self-identified Creoles who speak Louisiana French or only English.

19. Klingler and Valdman, "Structure of Louisiana Creole," 110.

20. Roosevelt, "Letter to the American Defense Society"; Blyth, "Sociolinguistic Situation of Cajun French," 31.

21. Ancelet, "Perspective on Teaching the 'Problem Language' in Louisiana," 345.

22. Sexton, "Cajun-French Language Maintenance and Shift," 37.

23. Picone, "Enclave Dialect Contraction," 123.

24. Descriptions of these experiences and their impact on collective identity are by no means meant to present an equivalency of different instances of cultural trauma (for example, slavery or the Acadian deportation). In fact, the gravity of trauma and the creation of a trauma narrative are quite unrelated. Even if thousands of individuals lose their lives or undergo intense suffering, there is no guarantee that these misfortunes will lead to the construction of a sense of shared cultural trauma. These events, however painful, remain individual historical facts unless this shared trauma is processed and interpreted on a collective level. Unlike individual trauma, collective trauma narratives hinge on the question of "not who did this to me, but what group did this to us?" Alexander, *Trauma*, 2.

25. Caruth, *Trauma*, 4.

26. Alexander, *Trauma*, 3.

27. Ibid., 4.

28. Eyerman, "Cultural Trauma," 60. The notion that slavery is traumatic for those who experience it may be obvious; however, I am interested in how this experience has played a role in collective identity for Louisiana Creoles. As Eyerman explains, "The trauma in question is slavery, not as institution or even experience, but as collective memory, a form of remembrance that grounded the identity-formation of a people."

29. Rabalais, "Mythologies Louisianaises," 7.

30. Simonsen, *Le Conte populaire*, 19.

31. Finnegan, *Oral Poetry*, 134.

32. Zumthor, *Oral Poetry*, 206.

33. Ibid., 207.

34. Bartlett, *Remembering*, 213.

35. Rubin, *Memory in Oral Traditions*, 129–30.

36. Brasseaux, *Founding of New Acadia*, 90.

37. Trépanier, "Cajunization of French Louisiana," 162–68.

38. Hall, *Africans in Colonial Louisiana*, 157.

39. Brasseaux, *French, Cajun, Creole, Houma*, 89.

40. Moreover, because the Saint-Domingue refugees were composed of roughly equal groups of White, free Creoles of color, and the enslaved, the surge of new arrivals in 1809 and 1810 that doubled the population of New Orleans at the time reinforced this nonracialized definition of *Creole*.

41. Parham, *American Routes*, 6.

42. Brasseaux, *French, Cajun, Creole, Houma*, 90.

43. Parham, *American Routes*, 16.

44. Klingler and Valdman, "Structure of Louisiana Creole," 109.

1. LAPIN AND OTHER ANIMAL TRICKSTERS

1. Ancelet, *Cajun and Creole Folktales*, xxix.

2. The trickster figure is occasionally considered somewhat of an archetype, as proposed by Carl Jung, and as such the manifestation of a universal unconscious. The archetypal quality of the trickster figure was most notably developed in Paul Radin's seminal collection of essays, *The Trickster: A Study of American Indian Mythology*. Many other scholars, including renowned mythologist Joseph Campbell, focused on Native American folklore in their treatment of the figure. More recent research, such as Hynes and Doty's *Mythical Trickster Figures* (1997) and David Williams's *The Trickster Brain* (2012), move beyond the Jungian notion of archetype to focus instead on the cultural manifestations of the trickster, which is more in line with my analyses here.

3. See Pelton, *Trickster in West Africa*.

4. Gaudet, "Bouki, the Hyena, in Louisiana and African Tales," 68.

5. Levine, *Black Culture and Black Consciousness*, 81.

6. Fortier, *Louisiana Folktales*, xviii.

7. Ibid., xvii.

8. For more information regarding the folktale's capacity to serve as a vehicle for slave narrative, see Dundes, "Making and Breaking of Friendship"; Levine, *Black Culture and Black Consciousness;* and Dorson, *American Negro Folktales* and *Buying the Wind*. Levine devotes an entire chapter to such tales in *Black Culture and Black Consciousness*, titled "The Meaning of Slave Tales," although it mostly pertains to the English-speaking colonies of the South.

9. Fortier, *Louisiana Folktales*, 32–33.

10. For all citations taken from Fortier's collections, I use his English translations.

11. Fortier, *Louisiana Folktales*, 32–33.

12. Ibid.

13. It can be presumed that Fortier, as both a linguist and folklorist, took care to accurately transcribe the tales that he collected. That being said, it is likely that on a more personal level, Fortier would have been unready or unwilling to interpret such tales as slave narratives. Fortier's political views were often slanted with the preservation of the elite Creole society in mind; however, he was at times an outspoken critic of the abolitionist movement, and some of his writing contains blatantly racist remarks.

14. Fortier, *Louisiana Folktales*, 188.

15. Ibid., 28–29.

16. Ibid.

17. Hereafter referred to by the abbreviation ATU, the *Aarne-Thompson-Uther Index* is an essential cataloging resource used by folklorists for identifying and classifying stories in the oral tradition by tale type. It is the result of the original text by Finnish scholar Antti Aarne in 1910

that was translated and expanded by the American folklorist Stith Thompson. More recently, Hans-Jörg Uther revised and developed the system in 2004. The *Motif-Index of Folk-Literature*, created by Stith Thompson, is another essential tool in folklore studies.

18. Okpewho, *African Oral Literature*, 115.

19. Fortier, *Louisiana Folktales*, xvii.

20. "Li prend couteau découpé, pas la peine. Li prend casse téte, pas la peine. Li prend lahache; li cassé lassiette, la tabe, mais tortie la resté telle. Li oua alorse c'était ein lapierre, et jisqua asteur li pas comprende comment so tortie té changé en lapierre."

21. Mercier, *L'Habitation Saint-Ybars, ou, maitres et esclaves en Louisiane*, 55.

22. Levine, *Black Culture and Black Consciousness*, 125.

23. Ibid., 123.

24. Abraham, *African Folktales*, 155.

25. Pelton, *Trickster in West Africa*, 1.

26. For a fuller analysis, see Radin, Kerényi, and Jung, *Trickster*, 63–91.

27. Levine, *Black Culture and Black Consciousness*, 105–6.

28. Bojang and Bojang, *Folk Tales and Fables from the Gambia*, 2:72–82.

29. Ibid., 2:72.

30. Fula (or *peul/peulh* in French) is related to Wolof and is the first language for most Fulani and is spoken in approximately twenty western and central African countries. Austin notes that "Fulani-speaking areas cover a vast territory, comprising a belt along the entire Sahel from Mauritania to Sudan, and falling into two large dialect areas: Pulaar in the western areas, with the Fuuta Tooro dialect spoken in Senegal and the Gambia." Austin, *One Thousand Languages*, 69.

31. Riesman, *Freedom in Fulani Social Life*, 67.

32. Bojang and Bojang, *Folk Tales and Fables from the Gambia*, 2:72.

33. Ibid., 2:78.

34. Ancelet, *Cajun and Creole Folktales*, 10–11.

35. Ibid., 11. "Là, une autre fois (ils étaient associés, tu vois), ils ont fait une récolte. Ça fait, la première année, ils ont planté des patates, juste des patates, O! C'était beau, ces lianes de patates-là." As with the excerpts from Fortier's collections, the English translations are those of the collector except where noted.

36. Abraham, *African Folktales*, 155.

37. Ancelet, *Cajun and Creole Folktales*, 11. "Tu me blufferas pas cette année. Je vas prendre ça qu'est dans la terre!"

38. There exists a sort of supernatural counterpart of *The Crop Division* classified as ATU 1030 among other tales of pacts between Man and the Devil. Ancelet suggests that there are two basic presentations of this type and notes that the version featuring humans or manlike spirits, such as Saint Michael or Satan, emphasize the hero's wit, whereas the variants casting animals, like Bouki and Lapin, highlight the stupidity of the dupe, who "chooses unwisely, motivated by greed or a misunderstanding of the true value of the shared commodity." Ancelet, *Cajun and Creole Folktales*, 10–11.

39. Claudel, *Fools and Rascals*, 29.

40. Bojang and Bojang, *Folk Tales and Fables from the Gambia*, 1:52.

41. Ibid., 1:53.

42. Ibid., 1:55.

43. Ibid.

44. Ibid., 1:56.

45. This peripheral quality of the trickster figure is consistent with Hynes and Doty's persuasion that "plurality, plurivocity, and ambiguity are essential to the trickster Gestalt." Hynes and Doty, *Mythical Trickster Figures*, 9.

46. Bojang and Bojang, *Folk Tales and Fables from the Gambia*, 1:56.

47. Ibid., 1:57.

48. Ibid., 1:58.

49. Konan, *Le Conte dans la société africaine*, 3. My translation: "En effet, le conte est le reflet de la société, de toute la société. C'est la vie de notre peuple, de notre civilisation traditionnelle avec sa structure sociale, sa vie économique, politique, son système culturel. La société que nous offre le conte est d'abord celle dans laquelle hommes et bêtes vivent en symbiose. Le conte nous fait connaître la civilisation du peuple, plus précisément sa culture, c'est-à-dire un héritage de coutumes, de connaissances lentement acquises, au cours des siècles, des croyances."

50. Levine, *Black Culture and Black Consciousness*, 90.

51. Fortier, *Louisiana Folktales*, 30. "Compair Bouki et Compair Lapin té voisin."

52. Ibid. "Qui ça qui senti si bon dans chaudière la, Compair Lapin? Oh, comme mo gagnin mal aux dents!"

53. Cazenave, *Encyclopédie des symboles*, 100. "Les dents sont le symbole le plus souvent de la vitalité, de la procréation, de la puissance et du sperme. [. . .] Rêver que les dents tombent à par ailleurs, comme le mal de dents, un rapport avec l'expression de l'impuissance."

54. Fortier, *Louisiana Folktales*, 30. "Faut to porté moin in pé!"

55. Ibid. "Oui, c'est moin qui mangé vous dézef."

56. Ancelet, *Cajun and Creole Folktales*, lxi.

57. Valdman and Rottet, *Dictionary of Louisiana French*, 323.

58. Ancelet, *Cajun and Creole Folktales*, 9. "Il y avait deux malfaicteurs, une fois. Il y en a un, son nom, c'était Bouki, et l'autre, c'était Lapin. Et Lapin était tout le temps gras. Il était en bonne condition, et Bouki était tout le temps, tout le temps maigre."

59. In Louisiana French, *malfaicteurs* refers to a scoundrel or rascal.

60. Ancelet, *Cajun and Creole Folktales*, 9. "Il y avait un beau clair de lune. Ils ont arrivé à une grosserie. Et Lapin s'est traîné dessous la grosserie. Il a arrivé droit dessous le milieu du plancher. Il y avait une planche qu'était déclouée. Ça se fait, il a poussé la planche et il s'est traîné dedans la grosserie."

61. Claudel, *Fools and Rascals*, 26.

62. Ibid., 26.

63. This cannot be known with any degree of certainty; however, many of Claudel's Avoyelles Parish informants were his own family members and of White Creole descent.

64. Claudel, *Fools and Rascals*, 26.

65. Ibid.,

66. Ibid., 27.

67. Ibid.

68. Magel, *Folktales from the Gambia*, 186.

69. Ibid., 187.

70. Ibid.

71. Gaudet, "Bouki, the Hyena, in Louisiana and African Tales," 67.

72. Levine, *Black Culture and Black Consciousness*, 82.

73. For a summary of North American attestations of ATU 15, see Ancelet, *Cajun and Creole Folktales*, 3–4.

74. Ibid., 3–5.

75. "Begun," "A quarter," "Halfway," "Three quarters," and "Finished."

76. Ancelet, *Cajun and Creole Folktales*, 4. "Là, quand ils travaillaient comme ça-là, Lapin s'avait mis comme un prêtre, tu vois? Il baptisait les enfants. Mais, ils s'avaient acheté un baril de beurre, un gros baril de beurre."

77. "Le Loup et le renard," no. 29, roll 3, Collection: Georges Arsenault. Recorded on December 31, 1971.

78. Klipple, "African Folk Tales with Foreign Analogues," 42.

79. Dennett, *Folk-Lore of the Fjort*, 90, cited in ibid., 44.

80. Nos. 6, "Bouki p'is Lapin," and 7, "Entamé, à moiquié mangé, tout mangé," in Carrière's *Tales from the French Folk-Lore of Missouri*.

81. Dennett, *Folk-Lore of the Fjort*, 92.

82. Ibid., 93.

83. Klipple, "African Folk Tales with Foreign Analogues," 213–33.

84. Ibid., 869.

85. The inquiry has been made about whether or not Fortier and Harris were aware of each other's work. In the 2011 introduction to Fortier's 1895 collection, Russell Desmond states: "It is clear that Joel Chandler Harris was unfamiliar with Alcée Fortier's work. Indeed, Harris' first published article featuring Brer Rabbit material predated Fortier's first piece with such material by eight years, and his first Uncle Remus book preceded Fortier's book publication of the tales by some fifteen years."

86. Fortier, *Louisiana Folktales*, 34. "Merci, mo bon Compair Bouki, to metté moin jisse la ou mo moman resté."

87. Claudel, "Study of Louisiana French Folktales in Avoyelles Parish," 106.

88. My transcription of "'Tit bébé godron," *French-Language Folktales, Avoyelles Parish, 1944*, collection in the Louisiana Research Collection archives of Tulane University.

89. Benwell and Stokoe, *Discourse and Identity*, 130.

90. Ibid., 138.

91. Saucier, *Folk Tales from French Louisiana*, 87.

92. Brasseaux and Conrad, *Road to Louisiana*, x.

93. At the time, St. Martin Parish included present-day Lafayette and Vermilion Parishes.

94. Foreword by Russel Desmond in Fortier, *Louisiana Folktales*, xii.

95. Levine, *Black Culture and Black Consciousness*, 83.

96. Jones, "Psychoanalysis and Folklore," 90.

97. Eyerman, "Cultural Trauma," 60.

98. Ibid., 60.

2. THE MASTER THIEF, A HUMAN TRICKSTER

1. Prassel, *Great American Outlaw*, 327.

2. Arceneaux, *Le Trou dans le mur*, contains numerous such examples based on folktales collected in Louisiana.

3. LeJeune, *Legendary Louisiana Outlaws*, 6.

4. Ibid., 8.

5. Ibid., 12.

6. Cavaglion, "Societal Construction of a Criminal as Cultural Hero," 256.

7. Hobsbawm, *Bandits*, 17.

8. Ibid., 127.

9. Seal, "Robin Hood Principle," 74–75. Seal identifies twelve narrative functions associated with the outlaw hero, including being forced to defy the law, righting wrongs, showing kindness to the poor and to women, eluding authorities with flare, and dying a brave death before ultimately returning to myth as rumors of his possible escape spread.

10. For detailed accounts of attestations, see Bolte and Polívka, *Anmerkungen Zu Den Kinder- und Hausmärchen Der Brüder Grimm*, 379–406; Cosquin, *Contes populaires de Lorraine*, 274–81; and Uther, *Types of International Folktales*, 2:243–45.

11. I use the spelling employed in the transcription or version in question.

12. Seal, *Outlaw Heroes in Myth and History*, 27.

13. See Claudel, *Fools and Rascals*, 59–60; Brandon, cited in Dorson, *Buying the Wind*, 253–56; Saucier, *Folk Tales from French Louisiana*, 50–54.

14. LeJeune, *Legendary Louisiana Outlaws*, 5.

15. Lindahl, "Who Is Jack," 380.

16. Ibid.

17. Claudel, *Fools and Rascals*, 54–57.

18. Ibid., 55.

19. Motif P251.6.1 *Three brothers*.

20. Claudel, *Fools and Rascals*, 54.

21. Ibid., 55.

22. Such carnivalesque inversion is often employed in creating Mardi Gras masks in rural Louisiana.

23. Claudel, *Fools and Rascals*, 57.

24. I refer to a sound recording collected by Lauraine Léger in 1980, but a similar transcription is found in Ancelet, *Cajun and Creole Folktales*, 51.

25. Faul, *Le Fin voleur.* "Y avait trois frères, mais y en avait deux qui étaient moyens, là y en avait un petit. Eux-autres, c'était du monde pauvre."

26. Ibid.

27. In the French American variant "Fin voleur, ou les pantoufles d'or," collected by Joseph Médard Carrière in Missouri, Fin Voleur decides to learn his trade as a thief late in the afternoon—in between the day and night—when he encounters three thieves who initiate him into their profession. Carrière, *Tales from the French Folk-Lore of Missouri,* 285.

28. Seal, *Outlaw Legend,* 6. See also Lemieux, *Les Vieux m'ont conté,* 2:171 and 11:31.

29. Propp, *Morphologie du conte,* 96.

30. The use of a pig in this scenario is found elsewhere in Acadian folklore. See "Le Fin voleur," told by Marcellin Haché, collected in 1957 by Anselme Chiasson, reel 13, no. 264, CEAAC.

31. Bakhtin, *L'Œuvre de François Rabelais,* 199.

32. Valière and Debiais, *Récits et contes populaires du Berry,* 115–17; and UPCP-Métive archives, reference DCC00005-003/ CON_CAT_21-029, collected in Vendée / Noirmoutier-en-l'Ile (canton de) / Barbâtre (La Fosse) by Providence Bouteau, told by Marguerite Morisson.

33. The orthography of this name is variable; Roclore, Roquelore, and Roquelaure are attested.

34. *Glossaire du parler français au Canada,* 556–57. Berry and Normandy are among the regions where such a pronunciation would be attested.

35. For a list of the Franco-Ontarian variants collected in the volumes of *Les Vieux m'ont conté,* see the cumulative index in Lemieux, *Les Vieux m'ont conté,* 33:319.

36. Valdman and Rottet, *Dictionary of Louisiana French,* 561.

37. Reinecke, "Louisiana's Roquelaure."

38. Perhaps as early as 1727, although the existence of several editions and the obscurity of the text's author render the original publication date unclear. Following his own archival research, George Reinecke came to a similar conclusion: "The Grand Larousse ('Roquelaure') authorizes the date 1727, but the Bibliothèque nationale in Paris contains editions ranging from 1739 to the mid-nineteenth century, many of them printed by Marteau at Cologne" (65).

39. Lindahl, "Who Is Jack," 380.

40. Haase, *Greenwood Encyclopedia of Folklore and Fairy Tales,* 683.

41. Tallemant des Réaux, *Les Historiettes de Tallemant des Réaux,* 5:291–313.

42. Robville, *Histoire curieuse du duc de Roquelaure,* vi. "Gaston, duc de Roquelaure [. . .] est un personnage populaire; les salons et les ateliers le connaissent au moins nominativement, et on le fêtera comme un ami dont on attend le retour de voyage."

43. S.L.R., *Le Momus françois,* 5–6. "Ce Duc avait de petits yeux noirs, qu'on nomme vulgairement yeux de cochon; il avait les sourcils épais et larges, le teint brun, c'est-à-dire basané; le nez plat et écrasé entre ses deux yeux, de manière qu'on aurait eu bien de la peine à le discerner."

44. Abraham, *African Folktales,* 155.

45. S.L.R., *Le Momus françois,* 4–5. "Pour ce qui est de son humeur, elle était gaie, son esprit satyrique, bouffon et ailleurs, ses manières civiles, insinuantes, aisées et nobles; [. . .] Il aimait les

plaisirs, même jusqu'à la débauche, et quelquefois jusqu'à l'excès. Il était brave comme un soldat, et généreux comme un prince, chaud au service de ses amis, [. . .] Son vice le plus dominant était le satyre ; il la poussait quelquefois si loin qu'elle dégénérait en calomnie. On peut dire que, s'il avait beaucoup de belles qualités, il avait aussi bien des défauts."

46. Houdard, "Vie de scandale et écriture de l'obscène," 57.

47. Mothu, "Trois notes sur Cyrano," 220. "Un gentilhomme d'une puissante famille, blasphémateur et débauché célèbre."

48. Howarth, *Molière,* 208. See also Morel "À propos de la 'scène du pauvre' dans 'Dom Juan.'"

49. *Dom Juan,* act 3, scene 2.

50. Howarth, *Molière,* 208.

51. Pintard, "Une Affaire de libertinage au XVIIe siècle," 22.

52. Seal, "Robin Hood Principle," 73.

53. Tallemant des Réaux, *Les Historiettes de Tallemant des Réaux,* 5:309–10. "Le chevalier de Roquelaure est une espèce de fou, qui est avec cela le plus grand blasphémateur du royaume. On dit qu'il s'est un peu corrigé. À Malte, il fut mis dans un puits, où on le laissa quelque temps par punition. À l'armée navale, le comte d'Harcourt fut sur le point de le faire jeter dans la mer avec un boulet au pied. Cela ne le rendit pas plus sage ; car quelques années après ayant trouvé à Toulouse des gens aussi fous que lui, il dit la messe dans un jeu de paume . . . , baptisa et maria des chiens, et fit et dit toutes les impiétés imaginables. On en avertit la justice. [. . .] Quelques jours après il corrompit le geôlier moyennant six cents pistoles: le geôlier se sauva avec lui, dont mal lui en prit, car le chevalier lui prit son argent, et le renvoya comme un coquin."

54. Leuven, "Roquelaure, ou l'homme le plus laid de France," 5 (act 1, scene 5).

55. Barrié, "Contes du pays du sault," 11.

56. Ibid., 11–12.

57. Decros, "Contes réunionnais, textes et traductions," 295–307.

58. Ibid., 304–7.

59. Found in Dorson, *Buying the Wind,* 254.

60. Zumthor, *Oral Poetry,* 206.

61. Orso and LaBorde Smith, "Roquelaure," 27; Saucier, *Folk Tales from French Louisiana,* 53.

62. Brasseaux, *French, Cajun, Creole, Houma,* 18–20.

63. Perrin, *Vermilion Parish,* 7–24.

64. Reinecke, "Louisiana's Roquelaure," 68. Reinecke claims that Roquelaure is "quite unlike Jean Sot, for example, who turns up in all parts of the state, or the song of the Wandering Jew, which is collected both in Avoyelles and on the prairie a hundred miles away."

65. Jean-Pierre Pichette, sound recording and transcription, "Roquelore," told by Séraphie Daigle-Martin. Centre d'Études Acadiennes Anselme Chiasson, recording 2998. Séraphie Daigle-Martin told another version of this tale, collected by Ronald Labelle, "Conte de Roquelaure (fin voleur)," Centre d'études acadiennes Anselme Chiasson, Collection Ronald Labelle, reel 186, recording 2838.

66. Pichette, "Roquelore," 2.

67. Seal, *Outlaw Heroes in Myth and History*, 25.

68. Cavaglion, "Societal Construction of a Criminal as Cultural Hero," 255.

69. Levine, *Black Culture and Black Consciousness*, 131.

70. Fortier, *Louisiana Folktales*, 88–89.

71. Levine, *Black Culture and Black Consciousness*, 127–28.

72. Ibid., 128.

73. Parsons, *Folk-Lore of the Antilles, French and English*, 2:187–89. Another Creole variant from Reunion Island is explored in the next chapter. See Decros, "Contes réunionnais, textes et traductions," 5–13.

74. See also Cosquin's *Contes populaires de Lorraine*, 274, for a variant from the Lorraine region.

75. Parsons, *Folk-Lore of the Antilles, French and English*, 2:188. "Tous les jours yo ca pa'lé la fin du moune, la fin du moune, regardé au cimitière pou' vwé comment la mort ca broulé. Ci la qui vlé rentré en Pawadis avec moin, rentré dans mon sac!"

76. Bolte and Polívka, *Anmerkungen Zu Den Kinder-und Hausmärchen Der Brüder Grimm*, 3:33.

77. See also "Les Coups de pied au cul donnés et remerciés," in D'Avallon, *Contes à rire*, 317–19); and "Conte de Raucleau," told by Maurice Motard of La Caillerie, CERDO reference LA500063, Ct. 100001 (Joceline et al.).

3. THE MANY FACES OF JEAN LE SOT

1. Campbell, *Hero with a Thousand Faces*, 49–244.

2. Parsons, "Re-Membering John the Baptist," 179.

3. Revon Reed says to this effect: "Despite all of his foolishness, Jeansotte had a certain air about him that made him different from all the other young people in the village. Maybe it was his eyes, the way he walked, or maybe his personality." Reed, *Lâche pas la patate*, 69. My translation from the French.

4. Some episodes of Jean le Sot were explored in a previous publication: Rabalais, "Les Représentations de Jean le Sot dans le contexte francophone."

5. The pronunciation of *sot* in Louisiana French is typically [sÐt], phonetically resembling the feminine form of the adjective *sotte*. The pronunciation of final [t] in the masculine form is likely a dialectal vestige originating in France, as it is also found elsewhere, notably in the Caribbean. See Parsons, *Folk-Lore of the Antilles*, pt. 1, 264.

6. For the lack of a definitive orthography, I have chosen to use the spelling employed in each of the respective tales for my analyses.

7. Thomas, "Contes de Jean-Le-Sot," 17.

8. Labre, *Dictionnaire biblique, culturel et littéraire*, 169.

9. John 1:1.

10. M. Fumeron, sound recording by anonymous collectors, UPCP-Métive/Cerdo archives, reference DCC00450-032 / CON_CAT_19-002.

11. Emile Caillon, sound recording collected by Thierry Fréret, Serge Gauthier, Equipe CPG, Dominique Simonet, and Richard Simonet, UPCP-Métive/Cerdo archives, reference DCC00251-010 / CON_CAT_20-002 / CON_CAT_26-004.

12. As a quintessential "fool," Jean le Sot is a carnivalesque rendering of the aforementioned traits associated with the biblical figures. There is certainly evidence of a tradition of religious parodies in popular culture dating back to the Renaissance and the Middle Ages. Bakhtin suggests that some early religious parodies may have been assimilated into folklore. See Bakhtin, *L'Œuvre de François Rabelais,* 12.

13. Dundes, *Morphology of North American Indian Folktales,* 62.

14. Neemann offers this definition of Dundes's *motifemes:* "The term 'motifeme' designates a tale's fundamental structural unit, specified or manifested by a motif. As such, a motifeme is to a motif as a function (in the Proppian sense) is to an action, or a phoneme to a phone." See Neemann, *Piercing the Magic Veil,* 118.

Dundes, "Structural Typology in North American Indian Folktales," 208–10. Dundes conceived a system of motifemes in order to better understand the structural typology of North American Native American folktales. The concept was not necessarily intended for analysis but rather for understanding the basic structural regularities of tale. Typical motifemes in Native American folklore include Lack (L), Lack Liquidated (LL), Interdiction (I), Violation (V), Consequence (C), and Attempted Escape (AE).

15. Dundes, *Morphology of North American Indian Folktales,* 63. These medial motifemes are: Task (or test) and Task Accomplished; Interdiction and Violation; and Deceit and Deception. The Task and Task Accomplished pair is problematized in many tales since Jean fails to complete his orders.

16. Ancelet, *Cajun and Creole Folktales,* 79–80.

17. Claudel, "Study of Louisiana French Folktales in Avoyelles Parish," 101.

18. While *traire* is typically used in most varieties of French, *tirer* is commonly used in Louisiana French for the verb "to milk."

19. This motif is prevalent in the Poitou region of France. See Nowak, *Les Contes traditionnels du Poitou,* 52–53.

20. Ancelet, *Cajun and Creole Folktales,* 79.

21. Numerous examples can be found in the UPCP-Métive/CERDO archives, including "Jean-le-Sot et la fille du roi" (Ribardière) and "Vengeance de Jean-le-Sot chez son patron" (Morin).

22. Vidaud, Pintureau, and Valière, *Paroles d'or et d'argent,* 149–54.

23. Other variants from France, particularly from Britanny, are associated with Cinderella and refer to the protagonist of ATU 513B as "Cendrillon" (masculine). In another recorded version by Vidaud, Jean le Sot offers the Virgin Mary a *pain de cendres* (ash bread). Vidaud, Pintureau, and Valière, *Paroles d'or et d'argent,* 154.

24. Ibid., 154. "Alors, tu comprends, o s'aghit pas d'être malin, o s'aghit d'être bon! Tu vés, li, eu sit bon, alors eu réussissit, et lous frères qu'atiant plus fins, atiant plus bêtes! Voilà. Et Jhean le Sot ayit la fille du roi." My translation.

25. Ancelet, *Cajun and Creole Folktales*, 37–42. This tale also formed the basis for the first French-language play performed by the troupe Nous Autres (later known as Theatre Cadien), *Jean l'Ours et la fille du roi*. Ancelet and Guidry, *Jean l'Ours*.

26. See Sidonie Giraud, sound recording collected by Jany Rouger, UPCP-Métive/Cerdo archives, reference DCC01029-009 / CON_CAT_14-011; and Métois, sound recording collected by Pierre Morin, UPCP-Métive/Cerdo archives, reference DCC00814-004 / CON_CAT_14-013.

27. Another tale that illustrates the complexity of the Jean le Sot character from the Poitou region of France is "Jean-le-Sot et la fille du roi." Contrary to the Jean Sotte of Louisiana, who repeatedly fails in his endeavors because of his literal interpretation of verbal messages, the Jean-le-Sot in this French tale proves to be a master of language. Along with his brothers, Jean-le-Sot sets off to the castle of the king's daughter, hoping to win her hand in marriage by making her say three words. Thus far, nobody is capable of causing her to say more than two words: "I brûle" (I'm burning). Jean-le-Sot has the idea to collect wood along the way and brings a rotten egg to the princess, saying to her: "Si vous brûlez, faites cuire mon œuf, faites cuire mon œuf!" (If you're burning, cook me an egg!). Disgusted by the taste of the egg, the princess exclaims: "Une belle chiée!" (This tastes like shit!), and with these three words, Jean-le-Sot wins the hand of the princess. Robert and Valière, *Récits et contes populaires du Poitou*, 1:63–64.

28. Brasseaux, "Acadian Education," 214.

29. Blyth, "Sociolinguistic Situation of Cajun French," 31.

30. Ibid.

31. Castille, *200 Lines*.

32. The enduring effects of this widespread trauma inflicted on French-speaking children in the early to mid-twentieth century prompted CODOFIL to use the slogan: "Schools have destroyed French, schools must restore it." Such slogans framed the burgeoning French-language immersion programs as the responsibility of the state to undo the damage done to the French language through the educational system. For more examples of CODOFIL slogans from the period, see Henry, "Louisiana French Movement," 190.

33. Ancelet, Edwards, and Pitre, *Cajun Country*, 220.

34. Ancelet, *Cajun and Creole Folktales*, 82.

35. In the ATU index, the model description shows that the young man pretends to only know Latin upon returning home; however, many variations are attested throughout Europe and North America. It is interesting to note the most recent folktale index contains no attestations of the tale type relating to English as the forgotten language.

36. Ancelet, *Cajun and Creole Folktales*, 82. "Mon garçon, je vois ton français commence à te revenir!"

37. Nowak, *Les Contes traditionnels du Poitou*, 60–61.

38. Ibid., 60.

39. My translation.

40. In Revon Reed's Jean Sot tale, he jokingly suggests that Jean may have gone off to college to become a professor. Barry Ancelet, who collected this particular variant, observes that Reed's

jibe "is based in part on a lack of regard for education within traditional Cajun society." See Ancelet, *Cajun and Creole Folktales*, 79.

41. Siphrone D'Entremont, sound recording collected by Helen Creighton, Centre d'études acadiennes Anselme Chiasson, reel 2, recording 20.

42. Mme Ben Benoît, "Jean-Sot et Jean-Sage," sound recording collected by Catherine Joli-coeur, Centre d'études acadiennes Anselme Chiasson, reel 560, recording 21972. This tale is also popular in western France, where at least six similar variants of 1653A *Guarding the Door* can be found in the UPCP-Métive/CERDO collection.

43. Exelda Hébert, "Jean le simple," collected by Robert Richard, Centre d'études acadiennes Anselme Chiasson, reel 96b, recording 1539.

44. Contact between Acadians and Black Creoles was significant and occurred in various social arenas. New Orleans was the port of entry for the Acadians, and many of their later settlement sites were in close proximity to Black communities west of the Crescent City (the river parishes). While rarely discussed, a majority of Acadians in river parishes owned slaves.

45. Fortier himself notes in his commentary that the story might have been included among the animal tales, although he decided to place it with the Märchen in the second part of his work. Fortier, *Louisiana Folktales*, 189.

46. Ibid., 62–63. "Tout ça yé, c'est tout mo popa, chaquéne dans yé quand yé passé dit moin: Bonjou, mo piti, alors mo croi yé tout c'est mo popa."

47. The practice of indulging in pranks on April 1 is well-known in Europe and likely goes back at least to the early sixteenth century.

48. Dundes mentions several similar examples of such sexual imagery in folklore. See Dundes, "Psychoanalytic Study of the Grimms' Tales," 114–17.

49. Dundes, "April Fool and April Fish," 98.

50. As we have seen, the Jean le Sot character's fickle relationship with nature and animals is a common trait in many variants, including the greasing of cracks in the ground, brooding eggs, and so forth.

51. Fortier, *Louisiana Folktales*, 62–64.

52. Ibid., 64–65. "Mais pou qui to prend moin, Jean Sotte, ou ça to déja tendé ein n'homme accouché? Mo pensé to oulé foute toi dé moin."

53. Ibid., 64–67.

54. Ibid. "Pas blié moin quand ta marié avec fille lé roi, voyé chercher moin et na fait bon zaffaire."

55. Ibid. "Qui ça qui bon matin marché en haut quatre pattes, a midi en haut dé pattes, et lé soir en haut trois pattes?"

56. Ibid., 68–69. "C'est ein piti moune qui marché en haut quatre pattes. Quand li vini grand li marché en haut dé, et quand li vini vié li bligé prend ein baton pour apiyer li, ça fait trois pattes."

57. Ibid. "Mo oua ein mort qui té apé porté trois vivants et apé nourri yé. Mort la té pas touché la terre ni li té pas dans ciel, dis moin qui c'est ou ben mo va prend vous place avec vous fortine."

58. Ibid. "Mo choal mouri en haut ein pont, mo jété li dans la rivière et quand li té apé dérivé carencros posé en haut li et mangé li dans dolo. Li té pas touché la terre ni li té pas dans ciel."

59. Bakhtin, *L'Œuvre de François Rabelais*, 368. "Le détrônement carnavalesque accompagné de coups et injures est de même un rabaissement et un ensevelissement. Chez le bouffon, tous les attributs royaux sont renversés, intervertis, le haut mis à la place du bas: le bouffon est roi du 'monde à l'envers.'"

4. *UN SACRÉ CONTE*

1. Dubois, Leumas, and Richardson, *Speaking French in Louisiana*, 137.

2. Ancelet, "Ôte voir ta sacrée soutane," 150.

3. Dubois, Leumas, and Richardson, *Speaking French in Louisiana*, 35.

4. Ancelet, "Le Rôle des religieux dans la préservation du français," 399.

5. Ibid., 402.

6. Carroll, "Were the Acadians/Cajuns (Really) 'Devout Catholics,'" 325.

7. Gaudet, "Cultural Catholicism in Cajun-Creole Louisiana."

8. Ancelet, "Ôte voir ta sacrée soutane" 91.

9. Brasseaux, *Founding of New Acadia*, 155.

10. Ancelet, "Ôte voir ta sacrée soutane," 92.

11. Rabalais, *Finding Cajun*.

12. Ancelet, "Ôte voir ta sacrée soutane," 92.

13. Ancelet, "Le Rôle des religieux dans la préservation du français," 398.

14. Chatelain, "Question pour l'évêque et la corneille," September 4, 2018.

15. Daron Burrows perceives the "stereotype" of the priest in medieval fabliaux in *Stereotype of the Priest*.

16. Ancelet, "Ôte voir ta sacrée soutane," 92.

17. Bakhtin, *Dialogic Imagination*, 52.

18. Bakhtin, *L'Œuvre de François Rabelais*, 368.

19. Jean Arceneaux is the creative and literary alter ego of folklorist Barry Ancelet.

20. Ancelet found the tale amusing and indicative of the kind of anticlerical humor that characterizes a particular subset of Louisiana's folklore repertoire. It was not until some four decades later that his colleague Monica Wright, a medievalist, who was proofreading the text before its publication, alerted him to a nearly identical fabliau from thirteenth-century France.

21. Eichmann, Introduction, 5.

22. Deschênes, "Le Prêtre mis à nu," 34; Rossi, *Fabliaux érotiques*, 158.

23. Arceneaux, *Le Trou dans le mur*, 101.

24. Uther, *Types of International Folktales*, 2:215. Many attestations of ATU 1423 exist in folklore as well as one well-known literary example in Boccaccio's *Decameron* (7.9).

25. Eichmann, *Cuckolds, Clerics, and Countrymen*, 43.

26. Eichmann, Introduction, 7; Eichmann, *Cuckolds, Clerics, and Countrymen*, 44.

27. Eichmann, Introduction, 6.

28. Such adaptations are in line with what Paul Zumthor refers to as *false reiterability* in oral contexts. According to Zumthor, false reiterability is only achieved by one of two ways: *archiving* (which stops the currency of orality at a single performance) and *memorization*. Concerning the latter, a narrative can only survive through continuous oral transmission, which occurs only so long as it remains relevant to its social context. Therefore, *signified* motifs, actions and "functions" (to use Vladmir Propp's term) remain intact while discourse or other *signifiers* adapt to their new social environments. See Zumthor, *Oral Poetry,* 197.

29. Rossi, *Fabliaux érotiques,* 30. "Garin préfère prendre le contre-pied de la littérature courtoise, en joignant à ses *contrafacta* une subtile satire des mœurs, où le contraste entre la 'noblesse,' qu'incarnent le plus souvent les personnages féminins, et la 'vilanie' des nouveaux riches est au centre de la vision de l'auteur."

30. Arceneaux, *Le Trou dans le mur,* 99. "Elle, a trouvait le prêtre de son goût, elle aussi, et alle aurait aimé essayer de le rencontrer pour un tit élan."

31. Ibid., 100. "C'est vrai, bèbe. On est juste après manger comme nous-autres t-à l'heure."

32. Michel Zink, cited in Rossi, *Fabliaux érotiques,* 8. "Histoire de la sexualité et histoire de la littérature, enfin, s'éclairent mutuellement."

33. Deschênes, "Le Prêtre mis à nu," 36.

34. My translation from the Old French (lines 79–81).

35. Nykrog, *Les Fabliaux,* 110.

36. Eichmann, Introduction, 7.

37. Ibid., 7–8.

38. Burrows, *Stereotype of the Priest,* 16.

39. Hutton, "La Stratégie dans les fabliaux," 112.

40. Robert and Valière, *Récits et contes populaires du Poitou,* 1:85.

41. Told by Anita Dieumegard in Saint-Genis-de-Saintonge, collected by Jean-Louis Neveu and Patricia Jeannaud, CERDO collection, reference DCC00263-023 / CON_CAT_27-002.

42. Ancelet, "Ôte voir ta sacrée soutane," 96.

43. One example is told by Mrs. Barbot in the Vienne region. Collected by Michel Valière, CERDO collection, reference DCC01332-002 / CON_CAT_32-010.

44. Collected by Barry Ancelet, Archives of Cajun and Creole Folklore, University of Louisiana at Lafayette, AN1-163. My translation of the French.

45. Despite the candor between the two men, the priest addresses the man with the informal pronoun *tu* (you), while the man refers to the priest as *vous* (you)—a sign of respect or formality in the Francophone world, but in Louisiana, where the *vous* pronoun is relatively rare, it can also be a sign of hostility or distancing from the interlocutor.

46. Ancelet, *Cajun and Creole Folktales,* 79.

47. Chatelain, *Graines de parasol,* 45.

48. This name brings to mind the Louisiana French phrase "(être sur le) *ratata,*" meaning to be all dressed up.

49. Bakhtin, *Rabelais and His World,* 410.

50. Brasseaux, "Immoral Majority in French Colonial Louisiana," 274.

51. Conrad, "How Acadian Is Acadiana," 155.

52. Collected by Barry Ancelet, Archives of Cajun and Creole Folklore, University of Louisiana at Lafayette, AN1-119, 20:43–22:07.

53. Ibid., 22:20. My translation of the French.

54. Persels and Ganim, "Scatology, the Last Taboo," xiii.

55. Bakhtin, *Rabelais and His World*, 370.

56. Ibid., 410.

57. Pasquier, "Les Confrères et les pères," 159–60.

58. Ibid., 147.

59. Ibid., 148.

60. Trappey, "Creole Folklore in Phonetic Transcription," 5.

61. Ibid.

62. Ibid.

63. Pasquier, "Les Confrères et les pères," 159.

5. BAYOU BELLES

1. While I mean to only examine tales that were collected from oral sources and not literary renditions supposedly based on folk narratives, this approach is not to be confused with an exceedingly traditionalist methodology predicated on supposedly "pure" or "uncontaminated" tales transmitted solely through oral cultures. Recent scholarship has shown that tales in printed form were available to those of modest means as early as the fifteenth century in Italy.

2. Bottigheimer, *Fairy Tales*, 7.

3. Ibid., 9.

4. Ancelet, *Cajun and Creole Folktales*, xxv.

5. Saucier, *Folk Tales from French Louisiana*, 15.

6. Fortier's *Louisiana Folktales* (1895) contains a section of "Märchen," although they do not bear a great resemblance to archetypical fairy tales such as *Cinderella*.

7. Trépanier, "French Louisiana at the Threshold of the 21st Century," 98.

8. Dorais, "Les Francophones des Avoyelles: des Cadjins comme les autres," 3.

9. Ibid., 16.

10. Calvin Claudel's informants in Avoyelles Parish, for example, are exclusively women.

11. Lieberman, "Some Day My Prince Will Come," 385.

12. Fortier, *Louisiana Folktales*, 68–75.

13. Ancelet, *Cajun and Creole Folktales*, 42–51; and Saucier, *Folk Tales from French Louisiana*, 19–21.

14. Popular in the oral tradition of Europe, the tale tells of a woman whose husband is sent off to war. In his absence, the king makes repeated and unwanted advances on the woman. Rejected, the king seeks revenge and sends a letter to the husband claiming that his wife is an adulteress and that the child she bears is not his. Geneviève escapes and lives for years in a

cave with her son, fed by the milk of a doe. Eventually, the husband returns, learns the truth, and the treacherous king is punished. The origin and historicity of this tale is not entirely clear, although it seems to trace its origin to Marie de Brabant, wife of Louis IV, who was beheaded by her husband in 1256 after being accused of infidelity.

15. Another widely held theory is that the tale is based on a supposedly historical individual alive during the first century BCE. A Greek courtesan (*hetaira*) named Rhodopis was enslaved in Egypt. One day she lost a shoe while bathing in a river, and an eagle snatched it, brought it to Memphis, and released it in the lap of the king. The enamored king sent men everywhere to find the woman who owned the sandal. However, as Labelle and other contemporary scholars have noted, the lost shoe motif is practically the only element shared with ATU 510A. It is more likely that the tale originated in China and was brought to Greece much later.

16. Labelle, "Le Conte de Cendrillon," 16.

17. Ibid., 17. Labelle states that the large majority of North American variants of ATU 510A were collected in Acadia, despite the overall collection of folklore in Quebec being around five times greater.

18. Perrault, *Complete Fairy Tales*, 130.

19. Hannon, *Fabulous Identities*, 64. Hannon goes on to say: "It is well known that, during the second half of the century, marriages between men of the high nobility and daughters of the newly ennobled or the wealthy were not uncommon. Nobles sought to provide for their increasingly expensive life style, while the commoners they wed sought the prestige conferred by a title."

20. Bottigheimer, *Fairy Tales*, 11–12.

21. Ibid., 10.

22. In Léon Pineau's *Conte du Poitou*, "La Cendrouse" features a wealthy family with no instance of death or remarriage. The mother and father are simply the biological parents of all three daughters.

23. In many ways, this distinction is what prompted the creation of Belmont and Lemirre's 2008 anthology of *Cinderella* tales *Sous la cendre*. This collection of tales told by the storytellers themselves differs greatly from Alan Dundes's earlier work *Cinderella: A Casebook* (1983), which emphasizes the literary fairy tale across various countries and time periods.

24. At seventy-four years of age, it is likely that Lacour's parents or grandparents would have emigrated from Europe.

25. Saucier, "Histoire et traditions de la paroisse des Avoyelles," 366. My English translation.

26. Ibid., 367.

27. There is at least one instance of this retort from the Poitou region of France. See Pineau, *Contes du Poitou*, 119.

28. Saucier, "Histoire et traditions de la paroisse des Avoyelles," 367.

29. Motif Z71.1 *Formulistic number: three.*

30. Claudel, "Study of Louisiana French Folktales in Avoyelles Parish," 178.

31. Comeaux, "Cajun Dancehall," 142.

32. Motifs B421 *Helpful dog* and B211.1.7 *Speaking dog.*

33. Bettelheim, *Uses of Enchantment*, 238.

34. According to Bettelheim's reasoning, even tales of sibling rivalry actually hinge on a confrontation between the heroine and her mother. As one matures, it is easier on a psychological level to manage a confrontation with the mother by "splitting" her image. In this sense, the deceased biological mother, the wicked stepmother, and even the wolf disguised as grandmother in *Little Red Riding Hood* are all of parts of the mother figure. By separating the different facets, a child's psyche is able to maintain the ideal mother of her childhood while coming to terms with the humanity and character faults that all humans possess.

35. This formula has also been attested in Martinique and Dominica. See Parsons, *Folk-Lore of the Antilles*, pt. 1, 26:362 and 477.

36. Bettelheim, *Uses of Enchantment*, 241.

37. Motifs: F311.1 *Fairy godmother*, F861.4.3 *Carriage from pumpkin*, D315.1 *Transformation: rat to person*, and D397 *Transformation: lizard to person*.

38. Saltzman, *Cendrillon*. "L'Prince l'a pris et l'a mariée et ses sœurs étaient très jalouses de elle."

39. Brandon, "Mœurs et langue de la paroisse Vermilion en Louisiane," 2:470.

40. Ancelet, *Cajun and Creole Folktales*, 60–62.

41. Lanclos, *Les Contes à Mémère*, 31–34.

42. While ATU 709 is certainly well known in France and elsewhere in the Francophone world as *Blanche neige*, Perrault did not include any version in his *contes*.

43. Uther, *Types of International Folktales*, 2:384.

44. Zipes, *Oxford Companion to Fairy Tales*, 573.

45. Claudel, "Study of Louisiana French Folktales in Avoyelles Parish," 184.

46. Dorais, "Les Francophones des Avoyelles," 3.

47. National Weather Service, "NWS LIX—Snow Climatology."

48. Rölleke, "Weiß—Rot—Schwarz," 215.

49. Pastoureau, *Rouge*, 17.

50. Motif Z65.1 *Red as blood, white as snow.* Often from blood on snow as a suggestion, a wish is made for a child (wife) with skin like snow and cheeks like blood. (Sometimes hair black as a raven.)

51. Claudel, "Study of Louisiana French Folktales in Avoyelles Parish," 184. "She placed her finger into the snow; the blood and the snow came together. It made a very beautiful color."

52. Pastoureau, *Rouge*, 148–55.

53. The storyteller specifies "eight or nine years of age." In the Grimms' version, the girl is seven years old, a significant number in biblical numerology as it implies completion or perfection. The implication is that the girl is now entering womanhood and is thus an increasing threat to the stepmother.

54. Motif L55 *Stepdaughter heroine.*

55. Motif S322.2 *Jealous mother casts daughter forth.*

56. Unlike other variants, including that of the brothers Grimm, the stepmother does not eat the heart and tongue.

57. Motif F451.5.1.2 *Dwarfs adopt girl as sister.*

58. Motif D1311.2 *Mirror answers questions.*

59. Claudel, "Study of Louisiana French Folktales in Avoyelles Parish," 187. I have modified slightly Claudel's English translation.

Claudel's translation of *effet* is "quarters." Although the context seems clear here, no other attestation of such a usage of *effet* could be found. The literal meaning is likely to be closer to "of everything that is in the land" (316).

60. S111.4 *Murder with poisoned apple.*

61. Grimm and Grimm, *Grimm's Complete Fairy Tales*, 192.

62. Takenaka, "Realization of Absolute Beauty," 507.

63. Claudel, "Study of Louisiana French Folktales in Avoyelles Parish," 191.

64. Motif F852.1. *Glass coffin* is absent here; the coffin's material is unspecified.

65. Claudel, "Study of Louisiana French Folktales in Avoyelles Parish," 193.

66. Motif Q414.4 *Punishment: dancing to death in red-hot shoes.*

67. Fortier, *Louisiana Folktales*, 56–61.

68. Schmidt, "Snow White in Africa," 269.

69. Chatelain, *Folk-Tales of Angola*, 30.

70. Schmidt, "Snow White in Africa," 271.

71. Ibid., 270. Only one example in Tanzania could be found in which the heroine's host removed the poisoned combs and revived her.

72. Parsons, *Folk-Lore of the Antilles*, 2:181–82.

73. Ancelet, *Cajun and Creole Folktales*, 37–42.

74. Claudel, "Study of Louisiana French Folktales in Avoyelles Parish," 202–3.

75. Motif K2011 *Wolf poses as grandmother and kills child* is modified here since wolves are generally not found in Louisiana; localization is required.

76. This ending is similar to Perrault's version; however, this is almost certainly coincidental. Neither this nor any other tales in Claudel's collection bears any strong resemblance to Perrault's texts beyond the basic structure of the tale type. Moreover, Alan Dundes has shown that Perrault's is an exception even in the French tradition because the heroine is generally saved in oral sources. See Dundes, *Little Red Riding Hood*, 13.

77. The character Tiana was inspired by chef Leah Chase of Dooky Chase's Restaurant in New Orleans.

6. MYSTERY, MAGIC, AND CURSES

1. Lieberman, "Some Day My Prince Will Come."

2. Uzee, *Lafourche Country*, 84.

3. Bruce Duthu compiled the most consequential collection of the Houma oral tradition for *Louisiana Folklife* journal in 1979. Duthu, himself a member of the Houma Native American community, provides numerous *rougarou* and *lutin* tales transcribed in English translation.

4. One finds the spelling *loutain* as well, for example in Duthu's transcription. It is unclear whether this represents a regional pronunciation or simply an approximation of the sound as interpreted by the collector. I maintain the conventional French orthography here.

5. Sébillot, *Le Folklore de la Bretagne*, 2:35.

6. Duthu, "Folklore of the Louisiana Houma Indians," 13–14.

7. Ibid.

8. Mould, *Choctaw Tales*, 173.

9. Dardar, *Istrouma*, 176.

10. These similarities are illustrated by the word *houma* (red or Red Nation) itself, which finds its Choctaw equivalent in the name of the state of Oklahoma (red people). Choctaw pedagogy material has also been used in Houma language revitalization efforts.

11. Mould, *Choctaw Tales*, 174.

12. Ibid., 175.

13. Ibid., 144.

14. Jolicoeur, *Les Plus belles légendes acadiennes*, 43.

15. Ibid., 50.

16. Duthu uses the spelling *loutain*.

17. Duthu, "Folklore of the Louisiana Houma Indians," 12–13.

18. Mould, *Choctaw Tales*, 142.

19. Brasseaux, *French, Cajun, Creole, Houma*, 69.

20. Lindahl, McNamara, and Lindow, *Medieval Folklore*, 440.

21. Ibid., 441.

22. For a full account of the history and etymology related to the werewolf, see Summers, *Werewolf in Lore and Legend*.

23. Ibid., 222.

24. Ancelet, *Cajun and Creole Folktales*, 158–59.

25. Dupont, *Légendes des ancêtres québécois*, 55.

26. Segura and Rodrigue, *Bayou*.

27. Amoss, *Loup Garou*.

28. Caparroy, *Poésie francophone de Louisiane à la fin du XXe siècle*.

29. *Gumbo Ya-Ya*, 191.

30. Doherty, "Le Loup-garou en Louisiane," 81–82.

31. Sing, "Mission mitchif."

32. Sarrazin, Kraus, and Krintzman, "Werewolves on Bayou Lafourche," 34–35.

33. Motif Z72.1 *A year and a day*.

34. Lindahl, Owens, and Harvison, *Swapping Stories*, 273–74.

35. O'Connor, *Blessed and the Damned*, 36.

36. *Encyclopedia of World Religions*, 663.

37. *Lagasse, "Limbo," Columbia Encyclopedia*.

38. O'Connor, *Blessed and the Damned*, 36.

39. Ibid., 115.

40. *Catechism of the Catholic Church*, 320.

41. Brandon Collection, interview with Henry Saltzman, BR1-015. My transcription of the audio recording.

42. Bourque, "Cauchemar and Feu Follet," 78–79.

43. Pluquet, *Essai historique sur la ville de Bayeux*, 327.

44. Omens, *Omens and Superstitions*, 57.

45. Souvestre, *Les Derniers paysans*, 43; my translation. "Une vingtaine de petites formes blanches et gracieuses, après s'être élevées sur le marais, grandirent subitement en prenant l'apparence d'une flamme bleuâtre et se mirent à danser sur la cime des roseaux. 'Tu vois que les létiches sont des follets, dit-il à Étienne, nous sommes ici dans leur royaume.'"

46. Longfellow, *Evangeline*, 13.

47. Ancelet, Edwards, and Pitre, *Cajun Country*, 3.

48. Brasseaux, *French, Cajun, Creole, Houma*, 45–46.

49. Cameron, *Longfellow's Reading in Libraries*.

50. Ancelet, Edwards, and Pitre, *Cajun Country*, 3.

51. Brasseaux, *In Search of Evangeline*, 9–11.

52. *Gumbo Ya-Ya*, 191–92.

53. Griolet, *Mots de Louisiane*, 102. Theriot gave this description in 1974 at the age of sixty-five. My translation. "Les vieux Nègres avec leur vaudou parlaient des létiches: un bébé qu'est mort avant être baptisé, ça fait un létiche."

54. This has been the case with Bouki, the *rougarou*, and the *fifolé* explored later in this chapter.

55. Ancelet, *Cajun and Creole Folktales*, 157.

56. Ibid., 156.

57. Lindahl, Owens, and Harvison, *Swapping Stories*, 272.

58. Robicheaux, interview with Jimmy and Felicien Verret et al.

59. Duthu, "Folklore of the Louisiana Houma Indians," 10–11.

60. Ibid., 11.

61. O'Connor, *Blessed and the Damned*, 121.

62. Sébillot, *Le Folk-Lore de France*, 2:435.

63. Ancelet, *Cajun and Creole Folktales*, 157–59. The Ancelet Collection contains a version more typical in Louisiana featuring a hunter who is condemned for hunting on a Sunday (motif E.501).

64. For an English translation of many of these folktales, see *Costello, C'est ça yé dit*.

65. Jarreau, "Creole Folklore of Pointe Coupee Parish," 57.

66. In Louisiana Creole as well as other French-based Creole languages, rounded vowels often become more closed. Thus, vowels like [y] and [ø] typically shift to [i] and [e], respectively.

67. From Lavergne, "Phonetic Transcription," 34, quoted in Neumann-Holzschuh, *Morceaux choisis du folklore louisianais*, 77. My English translation.

68. Similar to motif H1118.1 *Task: counting the seeds in a package of mustard.*

69. Neumann-Holzschuh, *Morceaux choisis du folklore louisianais*, 64.

70. Motif F491.3.3 *Steel protects a person from Will-o'-the-Wisp.*

71. In Matthew 13.31–32, Jesus shares the parable of the "smallest of seeds" that grows into a strong tree where birds may perch, a metaphor for faith.

72. Chireau, *Black Magic*, 12.

73. Lavergne, "Phonetic Transcription," 6.

74. Ibid., 7.

75. Chireau, *Black Magic*, 86.

76. Lavergne, "Phonetic Transcription," 13–14, cited in Neumann-Holzschuh, *Morceaux choisis du folklore louisianais*, 59–60.

77. Because Louisiana Creole uses the neuter third-person pronoun *li* for men and women, the *fifolé*'s gender is unclear until the end of the tale (*nhomme la trapé vié fome*).

78. My translation.

79. Richard Dorson even includes one variant from his fieldwork among African Americans in Michigan, in *American Negro Folktales*, 246–47.

80. Puckett, *Folk Beliefs of the Southern Negro*, 155.

81. *Gumbo Ya-Ya*, 250.

82. Durrant and Bailey, *Historical Dictionary of Witchcraft*, 167.

83. Parsons, *Folk-Lore of the Antilles*, pt. 1, 26:512.

84. Ibid., 26: 510–12.

85. Anatol, *Things That Fly in the Night*, 45.

86. Ibid., 42.

87. An alternative pronunciation [kuÐmÐl] has prompted some to suggest that the term is derived from the French *couche mal* (bad sleep). I argue that this is extremely unlikely as this phrase is not an idiomatic expression in French. Moreover, the shift from [Ð] to [u] is common in Louisiana French (for example, *beaucoup* pronounced [buku]) as is the confusion of two liquid consonants—that is, a substitution of a postvocalic [r] for [l]. Not to mention, the original meaning of *cauchemar* is precisely the mysterious experience of sleep paralysis.

88. Sharpless and Doghramji, *Sleep Paralysis*, 3.

89. Hufford, *Terror That Comes in the Night*.

90. Sharpless and Doghramji, *Sleep Paralysis*, 217–25.

91. Joe K K and Zydeco Force, *Kush-Mal*. See also the 2016 short horror film *Kooshma* by Chelsea Charles.

92. Roberts, "Contemporary Cauchemar," 15.

93. CNRS, "Cauchemar."

94. Valdman and Rottet, *Dictionary of Louisiana French*, 457.

95. *Glossaire du parler français au Canada*, 508. *Pesant* is also attested in Francophone Canada.

96. Davies, "Nightmare Experience," 184.

97. Sharpless and Doghramji, *Sleep Paralysis*, 19.

98. Roberts, "Contemporary Cauchemar," 19.

99. Bourque, "Cauchemar and Feu Follet," 76.

100. Rickels, "Some Accounts of Witch Riding," 2–3.

101. Wing et al., "Sleep Paralysis in the Elderly."

102. Jiménez-Genchi et al., "Sleep Paralysis in Adolescents."
103. Rickels, "Some Accounts of Witch Riding," 3.
104. Ibid., 6–7.
105. Bourque, "Cauchemar and Feu Follet," 71–73.
106. Lanclos, personal interview.
107. Miles, *Christmas in Ritual and Tradition*, 319.
108. Ibid., 227.
109. Deiler, *Settlement of the German Coast of Louisiana*, 11.
110. Ibid., 16–17.
111. Bloch-Raymond, "Leaving Alsace Lorraine and Blending into Louisiana."
112. Bloch, "Mercy on Rude Streams," 84.
113. Fabacher, personal interview.
114. McCord, "Historical and Linguistic Study," 69.
115. Broussard, "Madame Grands Doigts."
116. David Lanclos, personal interview.
117. Miles, *Christmas in Ritual and Tradition*, 207–8.
118. Agbenyega, Tamakloe, and Klibthong, "Folklore Epistemology," 120.

EPILOGUE

1. Ancelet, *Cajun and Creole Folktales*, xxvii.
2. This is not to fall prey to the long-standing practice of folklore scholars to focus on specific (and very limited) definitions of folklore—for example, animal tales or *Märchen*—that would result in a static definition of culture and pessimistic outlook of the culture's vitality. The distinction I would draw here is one related to genre or medium. Stand-up comics' material represents original content created by individuals and performed before an audience with limited capability to interact with the artist.
3. De Caro, *Folklore Recycled*, 4.
4. Duthu, "Folklore of the Louisiana Houma Indians," 7–10.
5. None are found in the collections of Ballowe or Duthu.
6. Admittedly, the discrepancy between these figures' present popularity and their scarcity in past folklore collections could be explained by other factors. Perhaps by chance the folklorist did not happen to find any attestations during their fieldwork, for example, or perhaps they were deemed less interesting than other tales.
7. Taylor, *Rougarou*; Charles, *Kooshma*; see also Dytania Johnson's books *Kooshma: The Origin* (2018) and *Kooshma: Reborn* (2019).
8. This book actually consists of Creole animal tales. The book was later translated into French by Earlene Broussard. See Soper, *Contes populaires cadiens*.
9. Spillman, *Compère Lapin voyageur*.
10. Landry, *Madame Grand Doigt*.
11. Guidry, *B pour bayou*.

12. Ancelet, *Qui est le plus fort;* and *Cajun and Creole Folktales,* 26–29. A variant of ATU 2031 *Stronger and Stronger.*

13. Ancelet, *Jean-le-Chasseur et ses chiens,* 1. For example: "Et elle, alle aimait son fils avec tout son cœur. Lui, il aimait beaucoup faire la chasse ça y-eux donnait de la viande à manger. I chassait souvent avec ses trois chiens."

14. Rougarou Fest, https://rougaroufest.org/.

15. The proceeds of the festival go to the nonprofit South Louisiana Wetlands Discovery Center.

16. Rougarou Beer (retired), Tin Roof Brewing Company, https://www.tinroofbeer.com/brew /rougarou-retired/.

17. Sugarshine, Donner-Peltier Distillers, http://www.dpdspirits.com/home/products/sugar shine/.

18. Turgeon, "Les Produits du terroir," 478.

19. Dorson, "Fakelore."

20. Alan Dundes takes a more nuanced stance and recognizes the manufactured aspects of much of what we generally consider to be authentic—for example, the supposedly authentic folk narratives collected by the brothers Grimm. See Dundes, "Nationalistic Inferiority Complexes and the Fabrication of Fakelore."

21. Ibid., 13.

22. Denby, "Folklore in the Mass Media," 115.

23. Dundes, "Nationalistic Inferiority Complexes and the Fabrication of Fakelore," 6; my emphasis.

Bibliography

ARCHIVAL SOURCES

Barry Jean Ancelet Collection. Sound recordings. Center for Louisiana Studies, University of Louisiana at Lafayette, accession numbers AN1-119, AN1-163.

Georges Arsenault Collection. "Le Loup et le renard," told by Alyre Maddix. Centre d'études acadiennes Anselme Chiasson, 1971, no. 29, roll 3.

Elizabeth Brandon Collection. "Cendrillon," told by Lucille Saltzman. Sound recording. Archives de folklore et d'ethnologie de l'Université Laval, reference F208.

———. Interview with Henry Saltzman. Sound recording. Center for Louisiana Studies, University of Louisiana at Lafayette, accession number BR1-015.

Bruce Duthu Collection. Sound recordings, Center for Louisiana Studies, University of Louisiana at Lafayette, accession numbers DU3-001–DU3-025.

Thierry Fréret, Serge Gauthier, Equipe CPG, Dominique Simonet, and Richard Simonet. "Jean-le-Sot, le chien et les oies," told by Emile Caillon. Sound recording. UPCP-Métive/CERDO archives, reference DCC00251-010 / CON_CAT_20-002 / CON_CAT_26-004.

M. Fumeron. Sound recording by anonymous collectors. UPCP-Métive/CERDO archives, reference DCC00450-032 / CON_CAT_19-002.

Catherine Jolicoeur Collection. Sound recording, "Jean-Sot et Jean-Sage," told by Mme Ben Benoît, Centre d'études acadiennes Anselme Chiasson, reel 560, recording 21972.

Ronald Labelle Collection. "Conte de Roquelaure (fin voleur)," told by Séraphie Daigle-Martin. Centre d'études acadiennes Anselme Chiasson, reel 186, recording 2838.

Lauraine Léger Collection. "Le Fin voleur," told by Stanislaus Faul, 1980. Sound recording. Centre d'études acadiennes Anselme Chiasson, reel 57, recording 1909.

Jean-Louis Neveu and Patricia Jeannaud. "Prêtre caché dans l'armoire et le forgeron," told by Anita Dieumegard. Sound recording. CERDO collection, reference DCC00263-023 / CON_CAT_27-0.

———. "Sacristain et le vin de messe de monsieur le curé," told by René Belloteau. Sound recording. CERDO collection, reference DCC00263-022 / CON_CAT_27-012.02.

Jean-Pierre Pichette Collection. "Roquelore," told by Séraphie Daigle-Martin. Sound recording and transcription. Centre d'études acadiennes Anselme Chiasson, recording 2998.

"Conte de Raucleau," told by Maurice Motard of La Caillerie. CERDO collection, reference LA500063, Ct. 100001 (Joceline et al.).

Robert Richard Collection. "Jean le simple," told by Exelda Hébert. Sound recording. Centre d'études acadiennes Anselme Chiasson, reel 96b, recording 1539.

Earl Robicheaux Collection. "Interview with Jimmy, Felicien Verret et al." Sound recording. Center for Louisiana Studies, University of Louisiana at Lafayette, accession number RO3-004.

PUBLISHED WORKS

Abraham, Roger. *African Folktales*. New York: Pantheon, 1983.

Agbenyega, Joseph, Deborah Tamakloe, and Sunanta Klibthong. "Folklore Epistemology: How Does Traditional Folklore Contribute to Children's Thinking and Concept Development?" *International Journal of Early Years Education* 25, no. 2 (2017): 112–26.

Alexander, Jeffrey C. *Trauma: A Social Theory*. Cambridge: Polity, 2012.

Amoss, Berthe. *The Loup Garou*. Gretna, LA: Pelican Publishing, 1979.

Anatol, Giselle Liza. *The Things That Fly in the Night: Female Vampires in Literature of the Circum-Caribbean and African Diaspora*. Critical Caribbean Studies. New Brunswick, NJ: Rutgers University Press, 2015.

Ancelet, Barry, ed. *Cajun and Creole Folktales: The French Oral Tradition of South Louisiana*. Jackson: University Press of Mississippi, 1994.

———. *Cajun and Creole Music Makers / Musiciens Cadiens et Créoles*. Jackson: University Press of Mississippi, 1999.

———. *Jean-le-Chasseur et ses chiens: un conte cadien (d'après la version d'Edouard Dugas)*. Moncton, NB, and Lafayette: Éditions Bouton d'or Acadie and University of Louisiana at Lafayette Press, 2016.

———. "Ôte voir ta sacrée soutane: Anti-Clerical Humor in French Louisiana." In *Mardi Gras, Gumbo, and Zydeco: Readings in Louisiana Culture*, edited by Marcia Gaudet and James McDonald, 91–98. Jackson: University Press of Mississippi, 2003.

———. "A Perspective on Teaching the 'Problem Language' in Louisiana." *French Review* 61, no. 3 (1988): 345–56.

———. *Qui est le plus fort?* Moncton, NB, and Shreveport, LA: Bouton d'Or and Tintamarre, 2014.

———. "Le Rôle des religieux dans la préservation du français: l'exception Louisianaise." *Port Acadie* 24–26 (2013): 395–403.

Ancelet, Barry, and Richard Guidry. *Jean l'Ours et la fille du roi: pièce acadienne-louisianaise en trois actes en français de la région.* Lafayette: Center for Louisiana Studies, 1979.

Ancelet, Barry Jean, Jay Dearborn Edwards, and Glen Pitre. *Cajun Country.* Jackson: University Press of Mississippi, 1991.

Arceneaux, Jean. *Je suis Cadien.* Translated by Sheryl St. Germain. Merrick, NY: Cross-Cultural Communications, 1994.

———. *Le Trou dans le mur: fabliaux cadiens.* Acadie tropicale. Moncton, NB: Éditions Perce-Neige, 2012.

Austin, Peter. *One Thousand Languages: Living, Endangered, and Lost.* Berkeley: University of California Press, 2008.

Ballowe, Hewitt L. *Creole Folk Tales: Stories of the Louisiana Marsh Country.* Baton Rouge: Louisiana State University Press, 1948.

Bakhtin, Mikhail. *The Dialogic Imagination.* Edited by Michael Holquist. Austin: University of Texas Press, 1981.

———. *L'Œuvre de François Rabelais et la culture populaire au Moyen Âge et sous la Renaissance.* Translated by Andrée Robel. Paris: Gallimard, 1970.

———. *Rabelais and His World.* Translated by Hélène Iswolsky. Bloomington: University of Indiana Press, 1984.

Barrié, Paul. "Contes du pays du sault." *Folklore revue d'ethnographie méridionale* 126, no. 2 (1967): 11–12.

Bartlett, Frederic C. *Remembering: A Study in Experimental and Social Psychology.* Cambridge: Cambridge University Press, 1995.

Bettelheim, Bruno. *The Uses of Enchantment: The Meaning and Importance of Fairy Tales.* Vintage Books ed. New York: Vintage Books, 2010.

Bloch, Anny. "Mercy on Rude Streams: Jewish Emigrants from Alsace-Lorraine to the Lower Mississippi Region and the Concept of Fidelity." *Southern Jewish History* 2 (1999): 81–110.

Bloch-Raymond, Anny. "Leaving Alsace Lorraine and Blending into Louisiana: The Issue of Belonging and Loyalty to Host and Home Countries." Paper presented at colloquium on the Alsace-Lorraine Jewish Experience in Louisiana and the Gulf South. Historic New Orleans Collection. New Orleans, November 13, 2009. http://anny-bloch.fr/ArticlesGb/leaving.html.

Blyth, Carl. "The Sociolinguistic Situation of Cajun French: The Effects of Language Shift and Language Loss." In *French and Creole in Louisiana,* edited by Albert Valdman, 25–46. New York: Plenum Press, 1997.

Bojang, Dembo Fanta, and Sukai Mbye Bojang. *Folk Tales and Fables from the Gambia*. Vol. 1. Gambia: Educational Services, 2009.

———. *Folk Tales and Fables from the Gambia*. Vol. 2. Gambia: Educational Services, 2011.

Bolte, Johannes, and Georg Polívka. *Anmerkungen Zu Den Kinder-und Hausmärchen Der Brüder Grimm*. Vol. 3. Hildesheim: G. Olms, 1963.

Bottigheimer, Ruth B. *Fairy Tales: A New History*. Albany, NY: Excelsior Editions / State University of New York Press, 2009.

Bourque, Darrell. "Cauchemar and Feu Follet." *Louisiana Folklore Miscellany* 2, no. 4 (1968): 69–84.

Brandon, Elizabeth. "Mœurs et langue de la paroisse Vermilion en Louisiane." PhD diss., Université Laval, 1955.

Brasseaux, Carl A. "Acadian Education: From Cultural Isolation to Mainstream America." In *The Cajuns: Essays on Their History and Culture*, edited by Glenn Conrad, 212–24. Lafayette: Center for Louisiana Studies, 1978.

———. *Cajuns: Essays on Their History and Culture*, edited by Glenn Conrad, 212–24. Lafayette: Center for Louisiana Studies, 1978.

———. *The Founding of New Acadia: The Beginnings of Acadian Life in Louisiana, 1765–1803*. Baton Rouge: Louisiana State University Press, 1987.

———. *French, Cajun, Creole, Houma: A Primer on Francophone Louisiana*. Baton Rouge: Louisiana State University Press, 2005.

———. "The Immoral Majority in French Colonial Louisiana." *Proceedings of the Meeting of the French Colonial Historical Society* 10 (1985): 273–74.

———. *In Search of Evangeline: Birth and Evolution of the Evangeline Myth*. Thibodaux, LA: Blue Heron Press, 1988.

———. *Scattered to the Wind: Dispersal and Wanderings of the Acadians, 1755–1809*. Louisiana Life Series, no. 6. Lafayette: Center for Louisiana Studies, University of Southwestern Louisiana, 1991.

Brasseaux, Carl, and Glenn Conrad. *The Road to Louisiana: The Saint-Domingue Refugees, 1792–1809*. Translated by David Cheramie. Lafayette: University of Louisiana at Lafayette Press, 1992.

Broussard, Lizzie. "Madame Grands Doigts." *Country Roads*, October 1, 2011. https://countryroadsmagazine.com/art-and-culture/people-places/madame-grands-doigts/.

Burrows, Daron. *The Stereotype of the Priest in the Old French Fabliaux: Anticlerical Satire and Lay Identity*. Bern: Peter Lang, 2005.

Cameron, Kenneth. *Longfellow's Reading in Libraries: The Charging Records of a Learned Poet Interpreted*. Hartford, CT: Transcendental Books, 1973.

Camoin, Cécilia. *Louisiane: la théâtralité comme force de vie.* Lettres francophones. Paris: PUPS, 2013.

Campbell, Joseph. *The Hero with a Thousand Faces.* 2nd ed. Princeton, NJ: Princeton University Press, 1973.

Caparroy, Jean-François. *Poésie Francophone de Louisiane à la fin du XXe siècle: complexité linguistique et clandestinité dans les oeuvres de Jean Arceneaux, David Cheramie et Déborah Clifton.* Collection "Documents pour l'histoire des francophonies," vol. 42. Brussels: PIE Peter Lang, 2017.

Carrière, Joseph Médard. *Tales from the French Folk-Lore of Missouri.* Evanston: Northwestern University, 1937.

Carroll, Michael. "Were the Acadians/Cajuns (Really) 'Devout Catholics'?" *Studies in Religion / Sciences religieuses* 31, nos. 3–4 (2002): 323–37.

Caruth, Cathy, ed. *Trauma: Explorations in Memory.* Baltimore: Johns Hopkins University Press, 1995.

Castille, Hadley. *200 Lines: I Must Not Speak French.* Sound recording. Ville Platte, LA: Flat Town BMI, 1991.

Catechism of the Catholic Church. Washington, DC: United States Catholic Conference, 2000.

Cavaglion, Gabriel. "The Societal Construction of a Criminal as Cultural Hero: The Case of the 'Brinks Truck Theft.'" *Folklore* 118, no. 3 (2007): 245–60.

Cazenave, Michel. *Encyclopédie des symboles.* Paris: Librairie générale française, 1996.

Certeau, Michel de, Dominique Julia, and Jacques Revel. *Une Politique de la langue: la Révolution française et les patois: l'enquête de Grégoire.* Collection Folio Histoire 117. Paris: Gallimard, 2002.

Charles, Chelsea. *Kooshma.* Film. Horror, 2016.

Chatelain, Héli. *Folk-Tales of Angola: Fifty Tales, with Ki-Mbundu Text, Literal English Translation, Introduction, and Notes.* Memoirs of the American Folklore Society. Boston: American Folklore Society, 1894.

Chatelain, Jude. *Graines de parasol.* Shreveport, LA: Tintamarre, 2012.

———. "Question pour l'évêque et La Corneille." Personal correspondence (email), September 4, 2018.

Chireau, Yvonne Patricia. *Black Magic: Religion and the African American Conjuring Tradition.* Berkeley: University of California Press, 2003. https://doi.org/10.1525/california/9780520209879.001.0001.

Claudel, Calvin. *Fools and Rascals.* Baton Rouge: Legacy, 1979.

———. "A Study of Louisiana French Folktales in Avoyelles Parish." PhD diss., University of North Carolina, 1947.

CNRS. "Cauchemar." *Centre national de ressources textuelles et lexicales.* https://www
.cnrtl.fr/etymologie/cauchemar.

Comeaux, Malcolm. "The Cajun Dancehall." In *Accordions, Fiddles, Two Step and Swing:
A Cajun Music Reader,* 139–51. Lafayette: Center for Louisiana Studies, 2006.

Conrad, Glenn. "How Acadian Is Acadiana?" *Attakapas Gazette* 21, no. 4 (1986): 148–67.

Cosquin, Emmanuel. *Contes populaires de Lorraine: comparés avec les contes des autres
provinces de France et des pays étrangers; et précédés d'un essai sur l'origine et la propagation des contes populaires européens.* Vol. 2. Paris: F. Vieweg, 1886. https://gallica
.bnf.fr/ark:/12148/bpt6k1157368.image.

Costello, Brian J. *C'est ça yé dit: Creole Folk Tales, Superstitions, Remedies, Customs,
Nicknames and Linguistic Peculiarities of Pointe Coupee Parish, Louisiana.* New Roads,
LA: New Roads Printing, 2004.

Dardar, T. Mayheart. *Istrouma: A Houma Manifesto / Manifeste Houma.* Translated by
Clint Bruce. Shreveport, LA: Les Cahiers du Tintamarre, 2014.

D'Avallon, Cousin. *Contes à rire, ou recueil amusant.* Paris: Chez Corbet Ainé, 1825.

Davies, Owen. "The Nightmare Experience, Sleep Paralysis, and Witchcraft Accusations." *Folklore* 114, no. 2 (2003): 181–203.

De Caro, Frank. *Folklore Recycled: Old Traditions in New Contexts.* Jackson: University
Press of Mississippi, 2013.

Decros, Marie-Christine. "Contes réunionnais, textes et traductions." Master's thesis,
Centre Universitaire de la Réunion, 1978.

Deiler, J. Hanno. *The Settlement of the German Coast of Louisiana and the Creoles of
German Descent.* Philadelphia: Americana Germanica Press, 1909.

Delarue, Paul, and Marie-Louise Ténèze. *Le Conte populaire français: catalogue raisonné
des versions de France.* Complete edition, including all 4 vols., 1976–85 Paris: Maisonneuve et Larose, 2002.

Denby, Priscilla. "Folklore in the Mass Media." *Folklore Forum* 4, no. 5 (1971): 113–25.

Dennett, Richard. *The Folk-Lore of the Fjort.* London: Publications of the Folk-Lore Society,
1898.

Deschênes, Sarah. "Le Prêtre mis à nu: étude de la poétique du personnage dans les
fabliaux érotiques (XIIe–XIVe siècles)." Master's thesis, McGill University, 2012.

Doherty, Rachel. "Le Loup-garou en Louisiane: de la légende à la littérature contem-
poraine." *Rabaska* 17 (2019): 69–84.

Dorais, Louis-Jacques. "Les Francophones des Avoyelles: des Cadjins comme les autres?" Working paper. *Projet Louisiane* 9 (1980): 1–21.

Dorson, Richard M. *American Negro Folktales: Collected with Introduction and Notes.*
Mineola, NY: Dover Publications, 2015.

———. *Buying the Wind: Regional Folklore in the United States.* Chicago: University of Chicago Press, 1991.

———. "Fakelore." *Zeitschrift Für Volkskunde,* no. 65 (1969): 56–64.

Dubois, Sylvie, Emilie Gagnet Leumas, and Malcolm Richardson. *Speaking French in Louisiana, 1720–1955: Linguistic Practices of the Catholic Church.* Baton Rouge: Louisiana State University Press, 2018.

Dundes, Alan. "April Fool and April Fish: Towards a Theory of Ritual Pranks." *Folklore Matters,* 98–111. Knoxville: University of Tennessee Press, 1989.

———. *Folklore Matters.* Knoxville : University of Tennessee Press, 1996. https://archive .org/details/folklorematters0000alan.

———, ed. *Little Red Riding Hood: A Casebook.* Madison: University of Wisconsin Press, 1989.

———. "The Making and Breaking of Friendship as a Structural Frame in African Folk Tales." In *Structural Analysis of Oral Tradition,* edited by Pierre Maranda and Elli Köngäs Maranda, 171–87. Philadelphia: University of Pennsylvania Press, 1971.

———. *The Morphology of North American Indian Folktales.* Folklore Fellows Communications 195. Helsinki: Suomalainen Tiedeakatemia, 1964.

———. "Nationalistic Inferiority Complexes and the Fabrication of Fakelore: A Reconsideration of Ossian, the Kinder- und Hausmärchen, the Kalevala, and Paul Bunyan." *Journal of Folklore Research* 22, no. 1 (1985): 5–18.

———. "Psychoanalytic Study of the Grimms' Tales: 'The Maiden without Hands' (AT 706)." *Folklore Matters,* 112–50. Knoxville: University of Tennessee Press, 1989.

———. "Structural Typology in North American Indian Folktales." *The Study of Folklore,* 206–15. Englewood Cliffs, NJ: Prentice-Hall, 1965.

———. *The Study of Folklore.* Englewood Cliffs, NJ: Prentice-Hall, 1965.

Dupont, Jean-Claude. *Légendes des ancêtres québécois.* Sainte-Foy, Quebec: Éditions J.-C. Dupont, 2008.

Durrant, Jonathan B., and Michael David Bailey. *Historical Dictionary of Witchcraft.* 2nd ed. Historical Dictionaries of Religions, Philosophies, and Movements. Lanham, MD: Scarecrow Press, 2012.

Duthu, Bruce. "Folklore of the Louisiana Houma Indians." *Louisiana Folklife* 4, no. 1 (1979): 1–33.

Eichmann, Raymond, ed. *Cuckolds, Clerics, and Countrymen: Medieval French Fabliaux.* Translated by John DuVal. Fayetteville: University of Arkansas Press, 1982.

———. Introduction. In *Cuckolds, Clerics, and Countrymen: Medieval French Fabliaux,* edited by Raymond Eichmann, translated by John DuVal, 1–12 Fayetteville: University of Arkansas Press, 1982.

Encyclopaedia Britannica. *Encyclopedia of World Religions*. Chicago: Encyclopaedia Britannica, 2006. http://public.eblib.com/choice/publicfullrecord.aspx?p=361916.

Eyerman, Ron. "Cultural Trauma: Slavery and the Formation of African American Identity." In *Cultural Trauma and Collective Identity*, edited by Ron Eyerman, Jeffrey C. Alexander, Bernhard Giesen, Neil J. Smelser, and Piotr Sztompka, 60–111. Berkeley: University of California Press, 2004.

Fabacher, Philip. Personal interview, December 5, 2019.

Fiehrer, Thomas. "From La Tortue to La Louisiane: An Unfathomed Legacy." In *The Road to Louisiana: The Saint-Domingue Refugees, 1792–1809*, edited by Carl A. Brasseaux and Glenn R. Conrad, 1–30. Lafayette: Center for Louisiana Studies-University of Southwestern Louisiana, 1992.

Finnegan, Ruth. *Oral Poetry: Its Nature, Significance, and Social Context*. Bloomington: Indiana University Press, 1992.

Fortier, Alcée. *Louisiana Folk-Tales: In French Dialect and English Translation*. Boston: Houghton Mifflin for the American Folklore Society, 1895.

———. *Louisiana Folktales: Lapin, Bouki, and Other Creole Stories in French Dialect and English Translation*. Introduction to new edition by Russell Desmond. Lafayette: University of Louisiana at Lafayette Press, 2011.

Gaudet, Marcia. "Bouki, the Hyena, in Louisiana and African Tales." *Journal of American Folklore* 105, no. 415 (1992): 62–72.

———. "Cultural Catholicism in Cajun-Creole Louisiana." *Louisiana Folklore Miscellany* 15 (2000): 3–20.

Glossaire du parler français au Canada. Quebec: Presses de l'Université Laval, 1968.

Grimm, Jacob, and Wilhelm Grimm. *Grimm's Complete Fairy Tales*. San Diego: Canterbury Classics, 2011.

Griolet, Patrick. *Mots de Louisiane: étude lexicale d'une francophonie*. Romanica Gothoburgensia 30. Gothenburg: Acta Universitatis Gothoburgensis, 1986.

Guidry, Richard. *B pour bayou: un abécédaire cadien*. Lafayette: University of Louisiana at Lafayette Press, 2019.

Gumbo Ya-Ya: A Collection of Louisiana Folk Tales. 1st paperback ed. Gretna, LA: Pelican Publishing, 1987.

Haase, Donald. *The Greenwood Encyclopedia of Folklore and Fairy Tales*. Westport, CT: Greenwood, 2008.

Hall, Gwendolyn Midlo. *Africans in Colonial Louisiana: The Development of Afro-Creole Culture in the Eighteenth Century*. Baton Rouge: Louisiana State University Press, 1992.

———. "The Franco-African Peoples of Haiti and Louisiana: Population, Language, Culture, Religion, and Revolution." In *Revolutionary Freedoms: A History of Survival,*

Strength and Imagination in Haiti, edited by Cécile Accilien, Jessica Adams, and Elmide Méléance, 41–47. Coconut Creek, FL: Caribbean Studies, 2006.

Hannon, Patricia. *Fabulous Identities: Women's Fairy Tales in Seventeenth-Century France.* Faux Titre 151. Amsterdam: Rodopi, 1998.

Harris, Joel Chandler. *Uncle Remus, His Songs and His Sayings: The Folk-lore of the Old Plantation.* New York: D. Appleton and Company, 1880.

Henry, Jacques M. "The Louisiana French Movement: Actors and Actions in Social Change." In *French and Creole in Louisiana,* edited by Albert Valdman, 183–213. New York: Plenum Press, 1997.

Hobsbawm, Eric. *Bandits.* Harmondsworth: Penguin, 1972.

Houdard, Sophie. "Vie de scandale et écriture de l'obscène: hypothèses sur le libertinage de mœurs au XVIIe siècle." *Tangence* 66 (2001): 48–66.

Howarth, William. *Molière: A Playwright and His Audience.* Cambridge: University of Cambridge Press, 1982.

Hufford, David. *The Terror That Comes in the Night: An Experience-Centered Study of Supernatural Assault Traditions.* Publications of the American Folklore Society, vol. 7. Philadelphia: University of Pennsylvania Press, 1982.

Hutton, Gabrielle. "La Stratégie dans les fabliaux." *Reinardus* 4, no. 11 (1991): 111–17.

Hynes, William J., and William G. Doty, eds. *Mythical Trickster Figures: Contours, Contexts, and Criticisms.* 1st paperback ed. Tuscaloosa: University of Alabama Press, 1997.

Jarreau, Lafayette. "Creole Folklore of Pointe Coupee Parish." Master's thesis, Louisiana State University, 1931.

Jiménez-Genchi, Alejandro, Víctor Ávila-Rodríguez, Frida Sánchez-Rojas, Blanca Vargas Terrez, and Alejandro Nenclares-Portocarrero. "Sleep Paralysis in Adolescents: The 'A Dead Body Climbed on Top of Me' Phenomenon in Mexico." *Psychiatry and Clinical Neurosciences* 63 (2009): 546–49.

Joe K K, and Zydeco Force. *Kush-Mal.* Maison de Soul, 1995.

Jolicoeur, Catherine. *Les Plus belles légendes acadiennes.* Montreal: Stanké, 1981.

Jones, Ernest. "Psychoanalysis and Folklore." In *The Study of Folklore,* edited by Alan Dundes. Englewood Cliffs, NJ: Prentice-Hall, 1965.

Klingler, Thomas, and Albert Valdman. "The Structure of Louisiana Creole." In *French and Creole in Louisiana,* edited by Albert Valdman, 109–44. New York: Plenum Press, 1997.

Klipple, May. "African Folk Tales with Foreign Analogues." PhD diss., University of Indiana, 1938.

Konan, Koffi. *Le Conte dans la société africaine.* 1979. CEAAC, Louise St.-Laurent Collection.

Labelle, Ronald. "Le Conte de Cendrillon: de la Chine à l'Acadie sur les Ailes de la tradition." *Rabaska* 15 (2017): 7–28.

Labre, Chantal. *Dictionnaire biblique, culturel et littéraire*. Paris: Colin, 2002.

Lagasse, Paul. "Limbo." *The Columbia Encyclopedia*. Columbia University Press, 2018.

Lanclos, David. *Les Contes à Mémère: A Collection of Folktales from the Pecanière Community*. Pecanière, LA: La Crête du coq, 2010.

———. Personal interview, September 28, 2018.

Landry, Yvette. *Madame Grand Doigt*. Lafayette: University of Louisiana at Lafayette Press, 2016.

Lavergne, Remi. "A Phonetic Transcription of the Creole Negro's Medical Treatments, Superstitions and Folklore in the Parish of Pointe Coupee." Master's thesis, Louisiana State University, 1931.

LeJeune, Keagan. *Legendary Louisiana Outlaws: The Villains and Heroes of Folk Justice*. Baton Rouge: Louisiana State University Press, 2016.

Lemieux, Germain. *Les Vieux m'ont conté: contes franco-ontariens*. 33 vols. Montreal: Éditions Bellarmn; and Paris: Maisonneuve et Larose, 1973–93.

Leuven, Adolphe de. "Roquelaure, ou l'homme le plus laid de France." *Le Magasin théatral, choix de pièces nouvelles jouées sur tous les théatre de Paris* 15 (1837).

Levine, Lawrence W. *Black Culture and Black Consciousness: Afro-American Folk Thought from Slavery to Freedom*. 30th anniversary ed. Oxford: Oxford University Press, 2007.

Lieberman, Marcia. "'Some Day My Prince Will Come': Female Acculturation through the Fairy Tale." *College English* 34, no. 3 (1972): 383–95.

Lindahl, Carl. "Who Is Jack? A Study in Isolation." *Fabula* 29, no. 1 (1988): 373–82.

Lindahl, Carl, John McNamara, and John Lindow, eds. *Medieval Folklore: A Guide to Myths, Legends, Tales, Beliefs, and Customs*. Oxford: Oxford University Press, 2002.

Lindahl, Carl, Maida Owens, and C. Renée Harvison, eds. *Swapping Stories: Folktales from Louisiana*. Jackson: University Press of Mississippi in association with Louisiana Division of the Arts, Baton Rouge, 1997.

Longfellow, Henry. *Evangeline*. Boston: Houghton Mifflin, 1886. https://www.loc.gov/item/26000864/.

Mabire, Jean. *Légendes traditionnelles de Normandie*. Saint-Malo, France: Éditions de l'ancre de marine, 1997.

Magel, Emil A., ed. *Folktales from the Gambia: Wolof Fictional Narratives*. 1st ed. Washington, DC: Three Continents Press, 1984.

Marshall, Margaret. "The Origin and Development of Louisiana Creole French." In *French and Creole in Louisiana*, edited by Albert Valdman, 333–49. New York: Plenum Press, 1997.

McCord, Stanley Joe. "A Historical and Linguistic Study of the German Settlement at Roberts Cove, Louisiana." PhD diss., Louisiana State University, 1969.

Mercier, Alfred. *L'Habitation Saint-Ybars, ou, maitres et esclaves en Louisiane*. 1st ed. Shreveport, LA: Editions Tintamarre: Cahiers du Tintamarre, 2003.

Miles, Clement A. *Christmas in Ritual and Tradition, Christian and Pagan*. London: T. Fisher Unwin, 1912.

Morel, Jacques. "À propos de la 'scène du pauvre' dans 'Dom Juan.'" *Revue d'histoire littéraire de la France* 72, nos. 5–6 (1972): 939–44.

Mothu, Alain. "Trois notes sur Cyrano." *La Lettre clandestine* 14 (2006): 213–24.

Mould, Tom, ed. *Choctaw Tales*. Jackson: University Press of Mississippi, 2004.

National Weather Service. "Baton Rouge Area, LA (1892–Present) Measurable Snow Events." https://www.weather.gov/lix/snowcli.

Neemann, Harold. *Piercing the Magic Veil: Toward a Theory of the Conte*. Biblio 17 116. Tübingen: Gunter Narr, 1999.

Neumann-Holzschuh, Ingrid. *Morceaux choisis du folklore louisianais: matière pour l'étude diachronique du créole de la Louisiane*. Hamburg: Buske, 2011.

Nowak, Éric. *Les Contes traditionnels du Poitou: les histoires extraordinaires en poitevin et en français*. Romorantin, France: Communication-presse-édition, 2011.

Nykrog, Per. *Les Fabliaux: étude d'histoire littéraire et de stylistique médiévale*. Copenhagen: Munksgaard, 1957.

O'Connor, Anne. *The Blessed and the Damned: Sinful Women and Unbaptised Children in Irish Folklore*. Oxford: Peter Lang, 2005.

Okpewho, Isidore. *African Oral Literature: Backgrounds, Character, and Continuity*. Bloomington: Indiana University Press, 1992.

Omens and Superstitions: Curious Facts and Illustrative Sketches. Edinburgh: William P. Nimmo, 1868.

Orso, Ethelyn, and Ethel LaBorde Smith. "Roquelaure: An Acadian Trickster." *Louisiana Folklore Miscellany* 3, no. 3 (1973): 25–31.

Parham, Angel Adams. *American Routes: Racial Palimpsests and the Transformation of Race*. New York: Oxford University Press, 2017.

Parsons, Elsie Clews. *Folk-Lore of the Antilles, French and English*. Vol. 1. Memoirs of the American Folklore Society. New York: G. E. Stechert, 1933.

———. *Folk-Lore of the Antilles, French and English*. Vol. 2. New York: American Folklore Society, 1936.

Parsons, Mikeal. "Re-Membering John the Baptist." In *Redeeming Men: Religion and Masculinities*, edited by Stephen Blake Boyd, Mark W. Muesse, and W. Merle Longwood, 176–86. Louisville: Westminster John Knox Press, 1996.

Pasquier, Michael. "Les Confrères et Les Pères: French Missionaries and Transnational Catholicism in the United States, 1789–1865." PhD diss., Florida State University, 2007.

Pastoureau, Michel. *Rouge: histoire d'une couleur.* Paris: Seuil, 2016.

Pelton, Robert D. *The Trickster in West Africa: A Study of Mythic Irony and Sacred Delight.* Hermeneutics, Studies in the History of Religions 8. Berkeley: University of California Press, 1980.

Perrault, Charles. *The Complete Fairy Tales.* Oxford: Oxford University Press, 2010.

Perrin, Warren A. *Vermilion Parish.* Images of America. Mt. Pleasant, SC: Arcadia Publishing, 2011.

Persels, Jeff, and Russell Ganim. "Scatology, the Last Taboo." *Fecal Matters in Early Modern Literature and Art.* Faculty Publications, Modern Languages and Literatures 6 (2004).

Picone, Michael. "Enclave Dialect Contraction: An External Overview of Louisiana French." *American Speech* 72, no. 2 (1997): 117–53.

Pineau, Léon. *Contes du Poitou.* Edited by Françoise Morvan. Rennes: Ouest-France, 2006.

Pintard, René. "Une Affaire de libertinage au XVIIe siècle: les aventures et les procès du Chevalier de Roquelaure." *Revue d'histoire de la philosophie et d'histoire générale de la civilisation* 5 (1937): 1–24.

Pluquet, Frédéric. *Essai historique sur la ville de Bayeux et son arrondissement.* Caen: T. Chalopin, 1829.

Prassel, Frank Richard. *The Great American Outlaw: A Legacy of Fact and Fiction.* Norman: University of Oklahoma Press, 1993.

Propp, Vladimir. *Morphologie du conte.* Translated by Marguerite Derrida, Tzvetan Todorov, and Claude Kahn. Points essais 12. Paris: Seuil, 1973.

Puckett, Newbell. *Folk Beliefs of the Southern Negro.* Chapel Hill: University of North Carolina Press, 1926.

Rabalais, Nathan. *Finding Cajun.* Documentary, 2019.

———. Introduction. In *Mythologies louisianaises: folklore contemporain du XXIe siècle,* edited by Jonathan Mayers. New Orleans: Paper Machine, 2018.

———. "Les Représentations de Jean le Sot dans le contexte francophone." *Port Acadie* 31 (2017): 7–22.

Radin, Paul, Karl Kerényi, and C. G. Jung. *The Trickster: A Study in American Indian Mythology.* New York: Schocken Books, 1972.

Reed, Revon. *Lâche pas la patate.* Montreal: Parti pris, 1976.

Reinecke, George. "Louisiana's Roquelaure: The Spanish Soil Trick, and 'Le Momus François.'" *Louisiana Folklore Miscellany* 3, no. 4 (1975): 65–69.

Rickels, Patricia. "Some Accounts of Witch Riding." *Louisiana Folklore Miscellany* 2, no. 1 (1961): 1–17.

Riesman, Paul. *Freedom in Fulani Social Life: An Introspective Ethnography.* Chicago: University of Chicago Press, 1977.

Robert, Catherine, and Michel Valière. *Récits et contes populaires du Poitou.* Vol. 1. Paris: Gallimard, 1979.

Roberts, Katherine. "Contemporary Cauchemar: Experience, Belief, Prevention." *Louisiana Folklore Miscellany* 13 (1998): 15–25.

Robville, T. de. *Histoire curieuse du duc de Roquelaure, surnommé l'homme le plus laid et le plus gai de France.* Paris: Le Bailly, 1861.

Rölleke, Heinz. "Weiß—Rot—Schwarz: 'Die Drei Farben der Poesie.'" *Fabula* 54, nos. 3–4 (2013): 214–34.

Roosevelt, Theodore. "Letter to the American Defense Society." American Defense Society, January 5, 1919.

Rossi, Luciano, ed. *Fabliaux érotiques: textes de jongleurs des XIIe et XIIIe siècles.* Le livre de poche lettres gothiques 4532. Paris: Libraire générale française, 1993.

Rubin, David C. *Memory in Oral Traditions: The Cognitive Psychology of Epic, Ballads, and Counting-Out Rhymes.* New York: Oxford University Press, 1995.

Sarrazin, Jean, Laura Kraus, and Donald Krintzman. "Werewolves on Bayou Lafourche." *Louisiana Folklore Miscellany* 2, no. 4 (1968): 34–44.

Saucier, Corinne. *Folk Tales from French Louisiana.* Baton Rouge: Claitor's Publishing, 1962.

———. "Histoire et traditions de la paroisse des Avoyelles en Louisiane." PhD diss., Université Laval, 1949.

Schmidt, Sigrid. "Snow White in Africa." *Fabula* 49, nos. 3–4 (2008): 268–87.

Seal, Graham. *Outlaw Heroes in Myth and History.* Anthem World History. London: Anthem Press, 2011.

———. *The Outlaw Legend: A Cultural Tradition in Britain, America, and Australia.* Cambridge: Cambridge University Press, 1996.

———. "The Robin Hood Principle: Folklore, History, and Social Bandit." *Journal of Folklore Research* 46, no. 1 (2009): 67–89.

Sébillot, Paul-Yves. *Le Folk-lore de France.* Vol. 2. Paris: Guilmoto, 1905.

———. *Le Folklore de la Bretagne.* Vol. 2. Paris: Maisonneuve et Larose, n.d.

Segura, Chris, and George Rodrigue. *Bayou.* Baton Rouge: Inkwell Publications, 1984.

Sexton, Rocky. "Cajun-French Language Maintenance and Shift: A Southwest Louisiana Case Study to 1970." *Journal of American Ethnic History* 19, no. 4 (2000): 24–48.

Sharpless, Brian A., and Karl Doghramji. *Sleep Paralysis: Historical, Psychological, and Medical Perspectives.* Oxford: Oxford University Press, 2015.

Simonsen, Michèle. *Le Conte populaire.* 1st ed. Littératures Modernes 35. Paris: Presses universitaires de France, 1984.

Sing, Pamela. "Mission mitchif: courir le rougarou pour renouveler ses liens avec la tradition orale." *International Journal of Canadian Studies / Revue internationale d'études canadiennes*, no. 41 (2010): 193–212.

S.L.R. *Le Momus françois, ou les aventures divertissantes du duc de Roquelaure, suivant les mémoires que l'auteur a trouvés dans le cabinet du Maréchal D'H. . . .* Cologne: Pierre Marteau, 1781.

Soper, Celia. *Contes populaires cadiens.* Translated by Earlene Broussard. Gretna, LA: Pelican Publishing, 1997.

Souvestre, Émile. *Les Derniers paysans.* Paris: Michel Lévy Frères, 1851.

Spillman, Mary Susan Fitch. *Compère Lapin voyageur.* 1st ed. Shreveport: Les Cahiers du Tintamarre, 2013.

Summers, Montague. *The Werewolf in Lore and Legend.* 1933. Reprint, Mineola, NY: Dover, 2003.

Takenaka, Nanae. "The Realization of Absolute Beauty: An Interpretation of the Fairy-tale Snow White." *Journal of Analytical Psychology* 61, no. 4 (2016): 497–514.

Tallemant des Réaux, Gédéon. *Les Historiettes de Tallemant des Réaux: mémoires pour servir à l'histoire du XVIIe siècles.* Vol. 5. Brussels: J. P. Meline, 1834.

Taylor, Catherine. *Rougarou.* Short film, 2016.

Thomas, Gerald. "Contes de Jean-Le-Sot." *Bulletin de la Société d'études folklorique du Centre-Ouest* (1972): 3–62.

Trappey, Adam Shelby Holmes. "Creole Folklore in Phonetic Transcription." Master's thesis, Louisiana State University, 1916. https://digitalcommons.lsu.edu/gradschool_disstheses/8208/.

Trépanier, Cécyle. "The Cajunization of French Louisiana: Forging a Regional Identity." *Geographical Journal* 157, no. 2 (1991): 161–71.

———. "French Louisiana at the Threshold of the 21st Century." PhD diss., Pennsylvania State University, 1988.

Turgeon, Laurier. "Les Produits du terroir, version Québec." *Ethnologie Française* 40, no. 3 (2010): 477–86.

Uther, Jans-Jörg. *The Types of International Folktales: A Classification and Bibliography.* Vol. 2. Helsinki: Academia Scientiarum Fennica, 2011.

Uzee, Philip D., ed. *The Lafourche Country: The People and the Land.* Lafayette: Center for Louisiana Studies, University of Southwestern Louisiana, 1985.

Valdman, Albert, and Kevin J. Rottet, eds. *Dictionary of Louisiana French: As Spoken in Cajun, Creole, and American Indian Communities.* Jackson: University Press of Mississippi, 2010.

Valière, Michel, and Geneviève Debiais. *Récits et contes populaires du Berry*. Paris: Gallimard, 1980.

Vidaud, Marie, Nicole Pintureau, and Michel Valière. *Paroles d'or et d'argent*. La Couronne: Centre départemental de documentation pédagogique de la Charente, 1994.

Wing, Yun-Kwok, Helen Chiu, Today Leung, and Jana Ng. "Sleep Paralysis in the Elderly." *Journal of Sleep Research* 8, no. 2 (1999): 151–55.

Zipes, Jack, ed. *The Oxford Companion to Fairy Tales*. Oxford: Oxford University Press, 2000.

Zumthor, Paul. *Oral Poetry: An Introduction*. Translated by Kathryn Murphy-Judy. Theory and History of Literature, vol. 70. Minneapolis: University of Minnesota Press, 1990.

Index

Note: Page numbers in italic refer to figures.

Aarne, Antti, 189n17

Aarne-Thompson-Uther Index (ATU), 116, 189n17; 6 *Animal Captor Persuaded to Talk*, 23; 9B "In the Division of the Crop the Fox Takes the Corn," 29–30, 32; 15 *The Theft of Butter (Honey) by Playing Godfather*, 41–43, 46, 48; 41 *The Wolf Overeats in the Cellar*, 32, 35–36; 175 *The Tarbaby and the Rabbit*, 43–44, 46, 52, 181; 300–749 "Magic Tales," 116; 312 *Barbe bleue* (Bluebeard), 119; 333 *Little Red Riding Hood*, 136–37; 410 *Sleeping Beauty*, 136; 425 *La Belle et la bête* (Beauty and the Beast), 119; 510A "Cinderella," 120–26, 129, 203n15, 203n17; 510B "Peau d'Âne" (Donkey Skin), 120; 513B "The Land and Water Ship," 78–79, 90, 197n23; 565 *The Magic Mill*, 126; 709 *Snow White*, 126–36, 204n42; 853 *Hero Catches the Princess with Her Own Words*, 79; 883A "Sainte Geneviève" or "Geneviève de Brabant," 119; 1006 *Casting Eyes*, 74; 1030 *The Crop Division*, 190n38; 1204 *Fool Keeps Repeating His Instructions So As to Remember Them*, 74; 1291B "Filling Cracks with Butter," 90; 1360C "Old Hildebrand," 105; 1423 *Enchanted Pear Tree*, 99, 200n24; 1525 *The Master Thief*, 51–55, 57, 62, 64, 70–71, 90; 1535 *The Rich Peasant and the Poor Peasant*, 57, 70; 1628 *The Learned Son and the Forgotten Language*, 82; 1653 *The Robbers under the Tree*, 84; 1691A "Hungry Suitor Brings Food from Home," 84; 1696 *What Should I Have Done*, 83–84, 90; 1737 *The Parson in the Sack to Heaven*, 69; 1738C "Chalk Marks on Heaven's Stairs," 106; 1777A "I Can't Hear You," 106. *See also* motifs

Abbeville, Louisiana, 125, 138

Acadiana region, 35, 92, 94, 109, 140, 179

Acadian deportation (*Grand dérangement/ Great Upheaval*), 6–7, 10, 49, 65–66, 71, 95, 109, 146

Acadians: in Canada, 73, 83–84, 93, 97, 135, 143, 154–56; Catholicism and, 92–96, 104–5, 108, 113–14; Creole and Cajun terminology and, 14–16; Jean le Sot tales, 73; *létiche* and, 154–55

Acadia Parish, 97, 173

adaptations, 3, 11–14, 48, 65, 139–40

adultery, 98–107, 109, 154, 202n14

African American folklore: Christian symbolism in, 162; cultural trauma and, 11; magical figures, 162–65; in popular culture, 185; trickster figures, 25–27

African American identity, 8, 16

African folklore: didactic, 23, 27–29, 48; fairy tales and, 133–34; influence on Black

African folklore (*continued*)
Creole oral tradition, 1–2, 4, 7, 12, 19, 27, 42, 84–85, 165; society and nature in, 33; trickster figures, 12, 17–28, 48; types and motifs, 46–47. *See also* West African connection to Louisiana

Afro-Caribbean oral tradition, 162, 165–66, 176. *See also* Antilles; Caribbean folklore

agency, 54, 101, 119, 124, 136

agricultural imagery, 41, 83

Ajapa (trickster figure), 25

All Saints' Day, 92

Alsace-Lorraine, 173

Amoss, Berthe, 146

Anansi (trickster figure), 19

Ancelet, Barry: *Cajun and Creole Folktales* (1994), 3, 15, 16, 18, 29, 35, 41, 43, 61, 78, 93–95, 98, 104, 106, 108, 113, 117, 119, 125, 137, 179–82, 190n38, 198n40, 200n20, 207n63; *Jean-le-Chasseur et ses chiens*, 182; *Qui est le plus fort?*, 181

Anglo-Americanization, 8–10, 79–83, 118, 178–79. *See also* English language

Angola, 134

Angoumois Province, France, 155

animal tales, 17–18, 21–26, 134–35, 180

animal trickster figures, 17–49; in Black Creole folktales, 20–25, 37, 45; cleverness of, 13, 19, 21–22, 25, 29, 35, 46, 48; compared to human tricksters, 69–70 (*see also* Master Thief tales); localization in, 21–22; morals, 21–26, 49; in popular culture, 185; poverty and, 39, 49; slave narratives, 17, 21–26, 47–48; specificity in, 17; theft of food, 24, 27–29, 32, 34–43; traditions influencing, 17–28, 48; in White Francophone folktales, 28, 35, 44–45, 47–49

Anjou Province, France, 155

anthropomorphizing, 17, 21

anticlericalism: carnivalesque and, 97–98, 102, 108, 110, 197n12; distinct from apathy,

95; in Francophone world, 97; in French Louisiana folklore, 92, 97–114, 149; in South Louisiana, 92–95; violence in, 103–5, 107, 114. *See also* Catholicism

Antilles, 69, 70, 73, 84, 90, 165. *See also* Afro-Caribbean oral tradition; Caribbean folklore

April Fool's Day, 86, 199n47

Arceneaux, Jean, 81, 98–101, 138, 147

archetypes, 52, 189n2. *See also* fool archetype; trickster figures

Archives de folklore et d'ethnologie, Université Laval, 4

Arnaudville, Louisiana, 171

Ascension Parish, 173

Atchafalaya, 117

Aunis Province, France, 155

Austin, Peter, 190n30

authenticity, 183–84, 210n20

authority figures: anticlerical humor and, 96–98 (*see also* anticlericalism); in educational system, 81; in Master Thief tales, 50–53, 55, 58, 61–68; mistrust of, 96, 114

Auvergne, France, 73

Avoyelles Parish, 3, 14, 36, 45–46, 66, 77, 107, 109, 123–27, 131, 136–37, 202n10; immigration history, 117–18, 126–27

Bakhtin, Mikhail, 41, 55, 89, 97, 110, 197n12

Balfa, Dewey, 1

Ballowe, Hewitt L., 180

bals de maison (house dances), 123

Bambara, 7

baptism, 140, 149–61, 166

Barrié, Paul, 64

Bartlett, Frederic, 13–14

Basile, Giambattista, 115, 120, 124, 126

Bayou (1984), 146

beauty, female, 119–20, 128–29, 133–34

Beauty and the Beast, 119

Belmont, Nicole, 203n23

Bettelheim, Bruno, 4–5, 124–25, 140, 204n34

biblical passages, 39, 74

Black Creole folktales: animal tricksters, 20–25, 37, 45 (*see also* animal trickster figures); anticlerical, 111–13; Bouki and Lapin stories, 18 (*see also* Bouki and Lapin); fairy tales, 133–35; Fortier's attitudes toward, 20; Jean Sotte tales, 84–89; magical figures, 156–57, 160–67. *See also* African American folklore; African folklore; Afro-Caribbean oral tradition

Black Creoles/Creoles of color: Acadians and, 199n44; African American identity and, 8, 16; Catholicism, 93; Creole identity, 15–16; cultural contact with White Francophone communities, 48–49; from Saint-Domingue, 188n40; West African culture and, 7 (*see also* West African connection to Louisiana)

black humor, 77, 90, 107

blasphemy, 61–62, 69

blood-on-snow motif, 127–28

Bluebeard, 119

"Blue Dog," 146

Boccaccio, 200n24

bohpoli, 142–44, 159

Bojang, Dembo Fanta and Sukai Mbye, 27, 29, 30, 36, 39

Bonhomme Janvier, 171

Bottigheimer, Ruth, 116, 121

Boudreaux jokes, 179

bouki, meaning of, 19–20, 70

Bouki ak Malis (Bouki and Malice), 19–20, 185

Bouki and Lapin: Black Creole folklore and, 84; dupe-and-trickster, 18–20, 27–49, *38,* 40, 67, 146, 184–85; episodic structure, 74; in Jean le Sot tales, 85, 87–89; popularity of, 180; regional identity and, 137. *See also* Lapin

"Bouki et Lapin et le 'tit bébé Godron" (Bouqui, Lapin, and the Tar Baby), 44–45

"Bouqui et Lapin dans la boucanière" (Bouqui and Lapin in the Smokehouse), 36–39

Bouton d'Or Acadie, 181

B pour bayou (Guidry), 181

Brabant, Marie de, 203n14

Brandon, Elizabeth, 3, 51, 65–66, 117, 125, 137, 152

brandons, 159

Brasseaux, Carl, 95, 104, 108, 112, 113, 155

Breaux Bridge, 94, 156

Brer Rabbit, 17, 18, 27, 40, 44, 45, 47, 185, 192n85

"Brer Turtle," 46

Breton legends, 151

briar patch motif, 40, 44–46, 52, 68–69

Brittany, 155

Brothers Grimm. *See* Grimm, Jacob and Wilhelm

Broussard, James, 3, 112, 160

Bugs Bunny, 185

Cajun and Cajun country: Acadians and, 6; magical figures, 139, 141, 143–44; as marketing label, 182–84; use of term, 14–16. *See also* French folktales in Louisiana; White Francophone communities

Cajun Comic Relief, 179

Cajun Folktales (Soper), 137, 181

Cajun (Louisiana Regional) French, 118

Campbell, Joseph, 72, 189n2

Canada, 6; Acadian communities, 73, 83–84, 93, 97, 135, 143, 154–56; Catholic Church and, 93; Francophone publication, 181; magical figures, 141, 143. *See also* Quebec

canevas commun, 4, 11, 138. *See also* Delarue, Paul

Cannon, Cheryl, 141

Capuchin monks, 54

Carencro, Louisiana, 82

Caribbean folklore, 4, 18, 69–71, 135, 162. *See also* Afro-Caribbean oral tradition; Antilles carnival, 97

carnivalesque, 41, 55, 83, 89; anticlerical humor and, 97–98, 102, 108, 110–11, 197n12; Mardi Gras and, 193n22

Carrière, Joseph Médard, 42–43, 194n27

Carroll, Michael, 108

Caruth, Cathy, 10

Castille, Hadley, 81

Catalon, Inez, 157–59, 182

Catholicism: Acadians and, 92–96, 104–5, 108, 113–14; Afro-Caribbean motifs and, 162; apathy and, 95, 104; baptism, 140, 149–61, 166; Cajun and Creole religiosity in South Louisiana, 15, 92–95; cultural, 114; education and, 80; hierarchy in, 106; magical figures and, 169–70 (*see also* magical figures); official laws and, 50; Protestants and, 109–10; slavery and, 111–13. *See also* anticlericalism

cauchemar or *koushma* (nightmare), 156, 167–71, *168*, 180, 208n87

Cecilia, Louisiana, 96

Celtic tradition, 151

Cendrillon (masculine), 197n23

"Cendrillon," 119–26

Center for Louisiana Studies, University of Louisiana at Lafayette, 4

Centre d'études, de recherche et de documentation sur l'oralité, Parthenay, France, 4

Centre d'études acadiennes Anselme Chiasson (CEAAC), Université de Moncton, New Brunswick, 4, 42, 84, 104

Centre national de la recherche scientifique (CNRS), 2–3

CERDO archives. *See* UPCP-Métive/CERDO, Parthenay, France

Charente-Maritime, France, 156

Charentes Province, France, 105

chasse-galerie (Wild Hunt), 160, 183

Chateaubriand, François-René de, 155

Chatelain, Jude, 107–9

Cheramie, David, 147

Chiasson, Anselme, 93

"Chien avec tigue" (The Dog and the Tiger), 21–22, 48

children: didactic tales for, 139–40, 144, 149, 170–71, 174–76; magical figures and, 139–40, 143–44, 149–77; sleep paralysis, 169–70; unbaptized, 140, 149–60, 166

children's genre, folklore as, 140–41

children's literature, 179–82

China, 119–20

Choctaw oral tradition, 142–44, 176, 206n10

Christianity, 208n71. *See also* anticlericalism; Catholicism; Protestants

Christine, la, 171–75, 184

Christkind figure (Christine), 172–73

Christmas figures, 171–75, 184

Cinderella, 115, 119–26, 129, 197n23, 202n6, 203n23

class distinctions, 54, 100–103, 120–21, 136, 203n19. *See also* kings and queens; nobility; social hierarchy and status

Claudel, A. E., 44–45, 123, 126

Claudel, Calvin, 3, 15, 30, 32, 36, 44, 51, 53–54, 77, 117, 123, 126, 133, 136–37, 180, 191n63, 202n10, 205n59, 205n76

cleverness: of animal tricksters, 13, 19, 21–22, 25, 29, 35, 46, 48; anticlerical humor and, 103–4, 113, 114; in Jean le Sot tales, 78, 86–89; Master Thief tales and, 62, 67–69. *See also* wit

Clifton, Deborah, 147

Clovis Crawfish series, 181

clumsiness, 12, 74, 137

code-switching, 45

collective memory, 4, 48. *See also* cultural (collective) trauma

colors, motifs using, 127–28, 131, 133–34, 204n50

Compagnie des Indes, 173
"Compair Bouki, Compair Lapin et dézef zozo" (Bouki, Lapin, and the Bird's Eggs), 33–35
Compair Bouki and Compair Lapin, 85, 87–89. *See also* Bouki and Lapin
comparative methodologies, 4–5
compère, 27
Compère Lapin (restaurant), 183
Compère Lapin voyageur (Spillman), 138, 181
"Confession d'ein vié esclave" (Confession of an Old Slave), 112–13
Congo folktales, 41, 42–43, 46
Conjure, 162
Conrad, Glenn, 109
contes d'animaux, 17. *See also* animal trickster figures
cornandons, 141
Cosquin, 54
Costello, Brian, 3
Côte des Allemands (German Coast), 173–74
Counter-Reformation, 151
Creighton, Helen, 83–84
Creole, use of term, 14–16
Creole architecture, 130
Creole Folk Tales (1948), 180
Creole folktales in Louisiana: aesthetics, 128; animal tricksters, 17–41; collections of, 3, 18; Master Thief, 51. *See also* Black Creole folktales
Creole identity, 8, 14–16. *See also* Black Creoles/Creoles of color; White Creoles
Creole language (*kouri vini*), 8–9, 20, 187n18, 207n66, 208n77; code-switching between French and, 45; discrimination against speakers of, 79–81; folklorists and, 112
Creuse region, France, 160
criminality, 51–54. *See also* Master Thief tales; theft
culards, 159
cultural appropriation, 183
cultural identity, 1–4, 8; French language in public education and, 79–89; marketing and, 182–83; performance of, 45–46; regional, 4, 137–38, 140–41, 182–83; terminology and language, 14–16
cultural (collective) trauma, 6, 9–11; adaptations and, 48; creation of, 188n24; fool archetype and, 11, 81, 90; fool narratives and, 90; prisming and, 81–82, 84, 90; punishments for speaking French and, 8–10, 79–81; of slavery, 26–27, 44, 47–48, 188n28; trickster figure and, 11, 48
cunning, 28. *See also* trickster figures
Cut Off, 149

Daigle, Lazard, 61
Daigle-Martin, Séraphie, 66
"Dans la grosserie" (In the Grocery Store), 35–37
Dardar, T. Mayheart, 142
death: of dupe, 29, 34, 52, 68–69, 136–37; at end of folktales, 29, 35; in fairy tales, 128, 131–37; of fathers, 54–55; of trickster, 43. *See also* punishment; violence
Decameron (Boccaccio), 200n24
Delarue, Paul, 4
Denby, Priscilla, 184
Dennett, Richard, 42–43, 46
"Der Meisterdieb" (The Master Thief), 52, 54, 61, 69. *See also* Grimm, Jacob and Wilhelm
Deshotels, Edward, 35
Deshotels, Elby, 35–36, 78
Desmond, Russell, 192n85
Dictionary of Louisiana French, 56
didactic tales, 27, 33, 139–40, 144, 149, 170–71, 174–76
diglossia, 83
disequilibrium, 75
disguises, 52, 55, 105. *See also* physical appearance

Disney productions, 115, 137, 140, 185

Dominica, 166

Dom Juan (Molière), 61–62

Donner-Peltier Distillers, 182

Dorson, Richard, 7, 18, 26, 184, 208n79

Doty, William G., 189n2, 191n45

dracs, 141

DuBourg, Louis William, 111

Dundes, Alan, 26, 36, 37, 75, 86, 90, 184, 197n14, 199n48, 203n23, 205n76, 210n20

dupe-and-trickster tales. *See* Bouki and Lapin; trickster figures

Du Prestre qui fouti la dame au vilain. See Le Prestre ki abevete

Duthu, Bruce, 3, 143, 159, 180, 205n3, 206n4

Easter Bunny, 144

Éditions Tintamarre, 181

education, formal, 8–10, 54, 79–89

English language, folktales in, 2–3, 44, 45, 51. *See also* Anglo-Americanization

equilibrium, 75

ermine, 153

Eshu (trickster figure), 19

ethical tensions, 53, 175. *See also* morals

ethnicity, terminology for, 14–16

European folklore, 135; animal trickster tales, 17, 21; Christmas figures, 171; infidelity in, 202n14; magical figures, 145, 158; Master Thief tales, 68–69; Old Hag, 167; types and motifs, 46–47. *See also* Francophone folklore

Evangeline (Longfellow), 94, 154–56

Evangeline Parish, 14, 35, 97, 109

fabliaux, medieval, 98–105, 114, 200n15, 200n20

fadets, 141

fairy tales, 115–38; "Cendrillon," 119–26; future of, 137–38; literary, 5, 115–17, 121, 125, 181, 202n1, 203n23; poverty and, 121, 125; representation of women in, 118–35; "Snow Bella," 126–35; trickster figures and, 122–23

false reiterability, 13, 65, 90, 201n28. *See also* Zumthor, Paul

False River, Louisiana, 163–65

"The Farm," 30

Faul, Stanislaus, 54

Federal Writers' Project, 187n5

Félicien (Master Thief), 69

Festival International de Louisiane, 94

Festivals Acadiens et Créoles, 94

Fête-Dieu, 94

Fêtes des fous (Feast of Fools), 97

feu follet (will-o'-the-wisp), 150, 151, 153, 157–62, 165, 167, 177, 184

fifolé, 160–66, *161*, 176–77, 208n77

"Fifolé," 160

"Fillèle Compair Lapin" (Compair Lapin's Godchild), 44–46

films, 180–81

Fin voleur, 54–55

"Fin Voleur" (Daigle), 61

"Fin voleur, ou les pantoufles d'or," 194n27

folk laws, 50–53

folklore: analysis of, 3–5, 11–14, 47; as children's genre, 140–41; contemporary uses of, 178–85, 209n2; terminology, 14–16. *See also* animal trickster figures; anticlericalism; Creole folktales in Louisiana; fairy tales; French folktales in Louisiana; Jean le Sot tales (Foolish John); magical figures; Master Thief tales; oral tradition

folklore collections, 3

Folk-lore de France (Sébillot), 160

Folklore of the Antilles, French and English (Parsons), 165

folklore studies, 2–4, 140–41, 185

Fontenot, Mary Alice, 181

food: lack of, in Jean le Sot tales, 75–77, 90; slave tricksters and, 68; theft of, in animal trickster tales, 24, 27–29, 32, 34–43. *See also* gluttony; starvation

fool archetype: carnivalesque reversal of power and, 89, 197n12; collective trauma and, 11, 81, 90; lack of heroic traits, 79; trickster figure and, 85–86. *See also* Jean le Sot tales

Fortier, Alcée: *Louisiana Folktales* (1895), 3, 15, 18, 20–23, 28, 33, 44–48, 68, 84–85, 90, 94, 111, 119, 133–34, 137, 178, 180, 189n13, 192n85, 199n45, 202n6

France, immigration from, 117–18, 154–55. See also *specific regions in France*

Francophone folklore (France and North America): animal trickster tales, 18; anti-clerical humor, 98–111, 114; fairy tales, 135; Jean le Sot tales, 72–73, 79, 89–91; magical figures, 147; Master Thief tales, 55–56, 63–64, 66–71 (*see also* Roquelaure); un-baptized souls and, 151. *See also* French folktales in Louisiana; White Francophone communities

Francophone publications, 181–82

FrancOralité (digital humanities platform), 185

Franc voleur, 53

Franklin College of Opelousas, 80

"Frank Rascal," 53–54

freedom, 24–25, 62–63, 67–69

French colonial period, 1, 5–7, 70

French folktales in Louisiana: animal tricksters, 41–49; collections of, 3; English translations of, 2; fairy tales, 121–26; magical figures, 139–47; Master Thief, 51–57, 61–62, 64–71; regional identity and, 140–41

French language: Avoyelles Parish dialect, 118; Cajun (Louisiana Regional French), 118; Catholic Church and, 93–94; code-switching between Creole and, 45; discrimination against speakers of, 8–10, 79–81; folklore in (*see* Francophone folklore; French folktales in Louisiana); poetic

movement, 147; preservation of, 181, 198n32; pronouns, 201n45

French Revolution, 95

Fulani, 27, 190n30

Gambia, 28. *See also* Senegambia

Garin (Guérin), 98–103

Gascony, France, 58, 73

"Gatta Cenerentolla" (Cat Cinderella), 120

Gaudet, Marcia, 94–95

gender norms, 166

generosity, 61, 72, 78, 171

"Geneviève de Brabant," 179

Germanic oral tradition, 127, 172–74

ghosts, 154, 156, 162, 169, 175. *See also* magical figures

globalization, 183–84

gluttony, 31–36, 39–41

gobelins, 141

Graines de parasol (Chatelain), 107

Grand dérangement (Great Upheaval). *See* Acadian deportation

Greece, 120

greed, 33, 37, 39, 52, 56

Grémillon family, 118

Grimm, Jacob and Wilhelm, 5, 52, 61, 69, 119, 126, 127, 130–33, 178, 204n53, 204n56

Groulx, Lionel, 93

Guadeloupe, 69, 70, 135

Guidry, Richard, 181

Guillory, Burke, 109–10

gullibility, 28, 52, 99, 137

Gumbo Ya-Ya, 147, 156, 165, 187n5

Haiti, 19–20, 185. *See also* Saint-Domingue Revolution

Halloween, 182

Harcourt, count of, 62–63

"The Hare and Hyena in the Well," 39–40

"Hare Gets Hyena and Elephant to Work on His Farm," 27

Harris, Joel Chandler, 11, 18, 27, 185, 192n85

hashok okwa hui'ga, 142

Hébert, Exelda, 84

Hébert-Collins, Sheila, 138, 181

Henri IV, 57–58

heresy, 104

heroes, 78–79, 135. *See also* outlaw heroes

hexendrücken (witch pressing), 169

Histoire curieuse du duc de Roquelaure (Robville), 58, 60

Histoires, ou contes du temps passé (Perrault), 115, 137

historical figures, 55–58, 61–62, 64, 67. *See also* Roquelaure

Historiettes (Tallemant des Réaux), 58, 62, 70

homophones, 107

Houma oral tradition, 3, 139, 141–44, 158–59, 176, 180, 205n3, 206n10

human tricksters, 50–51, 69–71. *See also* Master Thief tales

Hutton, Gabrielle, 104, 114

hyena and hare tales, 19–20, 27–35, 40, 44, 48, 70, 84–85. *See also* Bouki and Lapin

"The Hyena and the Hare," 30–33, 39

"Hyena in the Well," 34

Hynes, William J., 189n2, 191n45

identity. *See* cultural identity

ignorance, 81–82

illayés, 159

immigration history, 4–11, 117–18, 126–27, 154–55, 173–74; Acadian deportation, 6–7, 10, 49, 65–66, 71, 95, 109, 146; Saint-Domingue refugees, 1–2, 7–8, 15, 20, 47, 188n40. *See also* slavery

incubi, 167

infant mortality, 150–53

infidelity, 98–107, 170, 202n14

intellectualism, 50

intelligence, 33, 35, 40, 44, 86, 89

intensification, 24, 32, 41, 128

Irish folklore, 151, 158

Isleño communities, 18

jack-o'-lantern, 157, 162

Jack tales, 57, 72

Jammes, Jean-Marie, 94

Jarreau, Lafayette, 117, 160

Jaulin, Yannick, 179

Jean de l'Ours (John the Bear), 72, 78–79, 87, 90. *See also* Jean le Sot tales

"Jean des Pois Verts" (John Green Peas), 67–69

Jean-le-Chasseur et ses chiens (Ancelet), 138, 182

"Jean le Simple," 84

"Jean le Sot," 83–84

"Jean le Sot, Jean le Fin, Jean le Rusé," 78

Jean le Sot tales (Foolish John): affinity with nature, 75–77, 124, 199n50; in Black Creole tradition, 84–89; Bouki and Lapin in, 85, 87–89; carnivalesque reversal of power and, 89, 197n12; cleverness and, 198n27; education, language, and identity, 79–89, 198n40; literal interpretations of words, 74, 107; marginalized communities and, 73; Master Thief and, 84–85, 87–88, 90; morals, 78; motifs in French, Acadian, and Louisiana variants, 73–79, 83–91, 146; name variations, 72–73; religious parodies and, 197n12; as underdog protagonist, 136

Jean L'Esprit (Clever John), 89

"Jean l'Ours et la fille du roi," 78, 135

Jean-sans-peur (Fearless John), 72. *See also* Jean le Sot tales

"Jean Sot à l'école," 82

Jean Sot et le beurre, 76

Jean Sot or Sotte. *See* Jean le Sot tales

"Jean Sotte," 85–90

Jews, 173, 195n64

Jim Crow laws, 15

John (apostle), 73–74

John Paul II, Pope, 151

John slave trickster cycle, 68–69, 72

John the Baptist, 73

jokes, 105, 179

Jolicoeur, Catherine, 3, 84, 94, 143

Jolie Blonde and the Three Héberts (1999), 138

Judeo-Christian tradition, 39

Jung, Carl, 52, 189n2

justice, 50–51, 132–33

Kaplan, Louisiana, 157

Kinder- und Hausmärchen (Brothers Grimm), 126

kings and queens: in fairy tales, 130–33, 135–36; in Jean le Sot tales, 78–79, 84–89; in Master Thief tales, 51–53, 55, 58, 61, 63–66, 68; priests and, 93, 95. *See also* class distinctions; nobility; social hierarchy and status

Klipple, May, 42–44, 48

Kooshma (2016), 180, 208n91

korils, 141

korrigans, 141

koushma. See *cauchemar (koushma)*

kowi anukasha, 142–43

"Kush-Mal" (song), 167

Labelle, Ronald, 203n15, 203n17

"La Cendrouse," 203n22

Lafayette Parish, 47, 106, 117, 118, 140, 158, 192n93

La Fille du prêtre (The Priest's Daughter), 111

LaFleur, Amanda, 181

La Fontaine, Jean de, 17

Lafourche Parish, 143, 144

Lanclos, David, 126, 171, 174

Lang, Andrew, 119

languages: discrimination against French and Creole speakers, 8–11, 79–81, 90; education and identity and, 79–89; ethnic communities and terminology, 14–16. *See also* Anglo-Americanization; Creole

language (*kouri vini*); English language; French language

Lapin, 18–20, 69, 114. *See also* Bouki and Lapin

La Rochelle, France, 156

Latiolais, Martin, 29, 41, 125–26

Laurentides, 147

Lavergne, Remi, 163

Law, John, 173

laws, 50–53

"Le Chien étrange" (The Strange Dog), 180

"Le Fin voleur," 179

Le Fin voleur/Le Franc voleur, 51. *See also* Master Thief tales

Legba (trickster figure), 19

"Le Gros baril de beurre" (The Big Barrel of Butter), 41–42

"Le Loup et le renard," 42

"Le Mari trompé" (The Cheated Husband), 105

Lemieux, Germain, 56

Lemirre, Élisabeth, 203n23

Le Momus françois, 57, 58, 61, 65, 66–67

Leonville, Louisiana, 171

Le Prestre ki abevete, 98–107

Le Prêtre crucifié (The Crucified Priest), 103

Le Prêtre teint (The Painted Priest), 103

"Lé Roi Pan" (King Peacock), 133–35

Le Roy, Sieur Antoine, 58

Les Derniers paysans (Souvestre), 154

Les Vieux m'ont conté (Lemieux), 56

létiche, 153–57, 177, 184

"Le Trou dans le mur" (The Hole in the Wall), 98–107

"L'Évêque et le corbeau" (The Bishop and the Crow), 107–8

Levine, Lawrence, 7, 18, 26, 40, 67–68

l'exception louisianaise (the Louisiana exception), 93–94

Lieberman, Marcia, 119, 140

limbo, 150–51, 160

liminality, 31, 36–37, 40, 54, 85, 131, 177

Lindahl, Carl, 180, 187n5

literal meaning of words, 74, 107

literary fairy tales, 5, 115–17, 121, 181, 202n1, 203n23

Little Red Riding Hood, 136–37, 204n34

localization, 11–12, 42, 205n75; in animal trickster tales, 21–22; in fairy tales, 123, 127, 130, 133, 136; magical figures and, 176; in Master Thief tales, 54, 65

local products, 183–84

Lomax, Alan, 94

Longfellow, Henry Wadsworth, *Evangeline,* 94, 154–56

lost objects, 77, 78, 203n15

Louisiana Department of Agriculture and Forestry, 183–84

Louisiana Folklore Miscellany (journal), 180

Louisiana Purchase (1803), 79, 92

Louisiana Research Center, Tulane University, 4

Louisiana State Constitution (1921), 80, 90

Louisiana State University, 112, 160

Louisiana Territory, 42, 66, 112

Louisiana Writers' Project, 165

Louis XIV, 57, 63

loumerotte, 160

loup et le renard tales (the wolf and the fox), 19, 40–42, 85, 185. *See also* wolves

Loup Garou (1979), 146

loup-garou (rougarou), 139–41, 144–49, *148,* 162, 176–77, 179–80, 182, 184–85

Luther, Martin, 172

lutin (elf), 139, 141–44, 159, 162, 177, 184

lycanthropy, 145. *See also* werewolves

Madame Grand Doigt (Landry), 181

Madame Grands Doigts (Lady Long Fingers), 140, 174–76, 181

magic: in fairy tales, 115–16, 119, 121–25; in Master Thief tales, 55

magical figures, 139–77; didactic uses of, 139–40, 144, 149; in popular culture, 182.

See also *cauchemar;* Christine, la; *feu follet; fifolé; létiche; loup-garou (rougarou); lutin;* Madame Grands Doigts

magic mirror motif, 129–32, 134

malaprops, 74

Mali, 7

Malice, 114

Mamou, Louisiana, 109

Manitoba, 147

Mansura, Louisiana, 117

Mardi Gras, 92, 97, 193n22

marginalization, 10–11, 40, 50, 54, 73, 91, 123–24

"Mariaze Djabe" (The Devil's Wedding), 119

marketing, 179–80, 182–84

Maroon spaces, 24–25

marshes, 146, 153–54, 156–59, 176

Mary (Virgin), 78, 92, 153, 197n23

Master Thief tales: authority figures in, 50–53, 55, 58, 61–68; characteristics of, 61; disguises, 55; Jean le Sot and, 84–85, 87–88, 90; localization, 54; magic, 55; morals, 53–54; poor communities and, 50–55; poverty and, 50–55, 70, 121; Roquelaure, 52, 55–67, *59, 60,* 69–71, 135, 195n64; social hierarchy in, 135. *See also* outlaw heroes

maubeh, 27

medieval fabliaux, 98–105, 114, 200n15, 200n20

medieval legends, 119

memorization, 13–14

Mercier, Alfred, 25, 111

Métis, 147

microbreweries, 182–83

"The Millionaire, His Daughter, and Her Suitors," 79

missionary priests, 95–96, 112

Missouri, 73, 148

Molière, 61–62

monarchy. *See* kings and queens

morals: animal trickster tales, 21–26, 49; in fairy tales, 118–19, 123; in Jean le Sot tales, 78; magical figures and, 139–40, 149, 176–77; Master Thief tales, 53–54; morbid endings and, 29 (*see also* death); prisming and, 12–14; psychology of, 140. *See also* ethical tensions

motifemes, 75, 90, 197nn14–15

Motif-index of Folk-Literature (Thompson), 128, 190n17

motifs: D712.4 *Disenchantment by drawing blood*, 148; D1181 *Magic needle*, 162; D1311.2 *Mirror answers questions*, 134; E.501 (condemned hunter), 146; E742.2 *Soul as will-o'-the-wisp. Appears as a ball or fire or a figure in a fiery garment*, 158; F491.1 *Will-o'-the-Wisp leads people astray*, 157; F491.3.2 *Power of Will-o'-the-Wisp over person neutralized if person sticks his knife into the ground*, 157–58, 160; F491.3.3 *Steel protects person from Will-o'-the-Wisp*, 158; G60 and C221.3.1 *Tabu: eating animal's genitals*, 40; G60 *Human flesh eaten unwittingly*, 32; G229.1.1. *Witch who is out of skin is prevented from reentering it when person salts or peppers skin*, 163–64; J1731.9.1 *Ignorance of which part of plant is the fruit (crop)*, 30; J2030 *Absurd inability to count*, 143; J2259*(p) *Fool's action based on pun*, 74, 77, 89, 107; J2460 *Literal obedience*, 74, 89, 107; K171.1 *Deceptive crop division*, 29, 190n38; K581.2 *Briar-patch punishment for rabbit*, 40, 44–46, 48, 68–69; K842 *Dupe persuaded to take prisoner's place in a sack: killed*, 52, 63, 65, 66, 68–69; K981 (truth test), 43; K.1020.1, in *The Wolf Overeats in the Cellar*, 32; K1856.1 *Human flesh substituted for eaten (lost) meat*, 32; K2011 *Wolf poses as grandmother and kills child*, 205n75; M301.12 *Three Fates*, 54; S111.3 *Murder with poisoned comb*, 130–31; Z65.1.1

Red as blood, white as snow, (and black as a raven), 127–28, 204n50; Z65.1 *Red as blood, white as snow*, 204n50

Mounier, Brenda, 181

Muskogean language group, 143

mysterious creatures and phenomena, 149, 176–77. *See also* magical figures

mythological figures, 26, 67

name-giving motif, 41–43

narrative structures, 74–75, 77, 90

Native American oral tradition, 189n2; magical figures, 145; motifs in, 197n14; trickster figures, 17, 21, 26. *See also* Choctaw oral tradition; Houma oral tradition

Native Americans in Louisiana, 6

nature: affinity with, 75–77, 124, 129, 199n50; mysterious phenomena in, 176–77; society and, 33

"Neige casse la patte de la froumi" (The Snow Breaks the Ant's Foot), 181

New Brunswick, 67, 143

New Orleans, 3, 137; Acadians in, 199n44; refugees from Saint-Domingue in, 7–8, 47

New Year's Day, 172, 174

"Ngana Fenda Maria," 134

Night Hag, 167. *See also* cauchemar

nobility, 100–103, 120–21, 136, 203n19. *See also* class distinctions; social hierarchy and status

Normandy, France, 153–56

Norse mythology, 127

Nous Autres (theater), 135

Nova Scotia, 143, 155

numerology, 153, 204n53

Ogo-Yurugu (trickster figure), 19

Okpewho, Isidore, 23

Old Hag, 167. *See also* cauchemar

Omens and Superstitions, 154

ondoiement (lay baptism), 151–53

Opelousas, Louisiana, 173

oppression, 8, 54, 169; resistance against, 67–69

oral history, 3, 81, 93, 112, 173, 178–79

oral tradition: analytic approach to, 4–5; complexity of, 2; contemporary uses and future of, 137, 178–85, 201n28; disappearance of, 3, 178; literary fairy tales and, 114–16 (*see also* literary fairy tales); performance of identity, 45–46; proximity with audience, 72, 91. *See also* adaptations; intensification; localization; prisming; repetition; specificity

Ossun, Louisiana, 81

otherness, 45, 58

outlaw heroes, 50–53, 62, 67, 193n9. *See also* Master Thief tales

outsiders, 21, 91, 96

Owens, Maida, 180

Pa Janvier, 140, 171

Papa Noël, 171

Paris, France, 82–83

Parsons, Elsie Clews, 69, 165

patois, 8

Paul Bunyan, 184

Pays de Sault, 64

peasants, 100–103

Pecanière, Louisiana, 126, 171

Pecos Bill, 184

Pelzmärtte (Skin Martin), 175

Pentamerone (*Tale of Tales,* Basile), 120, 126

Perceval legend, 127

Perchta, 171

Père Noël, 171–72

Perrault, Charles, 5, 115, 119–21, 123–25, 137, 204n42, 205n76

Perronet, Father, 96

pesadela, 169

pesant (heaviness), 168. See also *cauchemar*

Petit Jean. *See* Ti-Jean/'Tit Jean/Petit Jean (Little John)

physical appearance: in fairy tales, 119–20, 128–29, 133–34; of trickster figures, 58, 61. *See also* beauty, female; disguises

Pichette, Jean-Pierre, 66

Pineau, Léon, 1, 178, 203n22

Pitre, Loulan, 149

Plaquemine, Louisiana, 173

Pointe Coupée Parish, 7, 47, 53, 160–66, *161*

Poitevin-Saintongeais dialect, 79, 82

Poitou-Charentes, 82–83

Poitou Province, France, 73, 77, 105–6, 109, 155, 160

popular culture: fairy tales in, 115; folklore in, 179–85; in France, 70; images of Louisiana in, 139; magical figures and, 167; as resistance, 83

Poste des Avoyelles, 117

poverty: animal tales and, 39, 49; fairy tales and, 121, 125; Master Thief tales and, 50–55, 70, 121

power: reversal of, 55, 89, 97–98, 102, 110–11; sexuality and, 40; wit and, 114 (*see also* cleverness; wit)

priests: attitudes toward, 95–96; corruption and, 106; enslaved people and, 111–13; as folklore figures, 96–114; missionary, 95–96, 112. *See also* Catholicism

The Princess and the Frog (2009), 137

prisming, 12–14; collective trauma and, 81–82, 84, 90

pronouns, 201n45, 208n77

Propp, Vladimir, 55, 201n28

Protestants, 109–10, 172–73

psychoanalytical approach, 4–5, 140

Pubnico West, Nova Scotia, 83

punishment: in animal tales, 38–40, 46; in fairy tales, 132–33; magical figures and, 146, 149, 170, 176–77; of priests in anticlerical tales, 103–7, 114; for speaking French, 8–10, 79–81

puns, 74, 107

Quebec, 2, 93, 95, 147, 148

Qui est le plus fort? (Ancelet), 181

"The Rabbit and the Antelope," 42–43

Rabelaisian humor, 110

race, 8, 15–16. *See also* Black Creoles/Creoles of color; White Creoles; White Francophone communities

Radin, Paul, 189n2

realism, 29

Red River, 117

Reed, Revon, 75–77, 83, 87, 196n3, 198n40

regional identity, 4, 137–38, 140–41, 182–83

Reinecke, George, 56–57, 66, 194n38, 195n64

religious parodies, 197n12. *See also* anticlericalism

repetition, 3, 11–12, 24, 105, 130

restoration tales, 121

Reunion Island, 64

revival, 184

Révolution tranquille (Quiet Revolution), 93, 95

Richard, Clotilde, 82–83

Richard, Larrell, 81

Richibucto, New Brunswick, 84

Rickels, Patricia, 169–70

riddles, 74, 88

Rinzler, Ralph, 94

rise tales, 121, 136

Roberts Cove, 173

Robin Hood legend, 51

Robville, T. de, 58, *60*

Roclore/Roclos. *See* Roquelaure (Roclore or Roclos)

Rodrigue, George, 146

"Roklor é le roi" (Roklor and the King), 64

Roman Catholic Church. *See* Catholicism

Roman de Renart, 17, 29, 42

Roosevelt, Theodore, 9

rôquelaure, 56

Roquelaure (Roclore or Roclos), 51–52, 55–71, *59, 60,* 135–36, 195n64

Roquelaure, noble family, 57–58, 61–62, 64

Roquelaure, ou l'homme le plus laid de France (1863), 63, 65

rougarou. *See* loup-garou (*rougarou*)

Rougarou (film, 2016), 180

"Rougarou" (Sweet Crude), 182

Rougarou Fest, 182

rural Francophone Louisiana: baptism in, 150; carnival and, 97–98, 193n22; commerce, 130; Creoles, 16; French language and, 8–9; French popular culture and, 70; house dances, 123; living conditions, 50, 52, 77, 79, 84, 90, 107, 112, 124, 142; mysterious natural phenomena in, 176; Saint-Domingue refugees in, 47; social structure, 100

sack exchange motif, 52, 63, 65, 66, 68–69

Saint-Domingue Revolution, 1–2, 7–8, 15, 20, 47, 188n40. *See also* Haiti

Saint-Malo, France, 155, 156

Saint Nicholas, 172, 175

Saintonge Province, France, 155

St. Bernard Parish, 18

St. Charles Parish, 173

St. James Parish, 7, 47, 65–66, 173

St. John the Baptist Parish, 7, 173

St. Landry Parish, 45, 97, 171

St. Martin Parish, 45, 47, 157, 192n93

Saltzman, Henry, 152–53

Saltzman, Lucille, 125

salvation, 150–51

Santa Claus, 141, 144, 171

satire, 61

Saucier, Corinne, *Folk Tales from French Louisiana* (1962), 3, 15, 46, 51, 79, 94, 117, 119, 121, 137, 180

Scandinavian folklore, 151

scatalogical tales, 55, 110–11

"Schizophrénie linguistique," 81

Schmidt, Sigrid, 135

Schmutzli, 171, 175

"Schneewittchen," 130–33, 204n53, 204n56

Schwarzpeter, 175

Seal, Graham, 193n9

Sébillot, Paul-Yves, 160

Segura, Chris, 146

Senegambia, 7, 27–28, 30

sexuality, 40, 55, 86–87, 98–107

shape-shifters, 143, 145, 161

Shreveport, Louisiana, 173

sibling rivalry, 124, 204n34

skin motif, 160–61, 163–66

slave narratives: animal trickster tales, 17, 21–26, 47–48; Master Thief genre and, 67–69. *See also* Black Creole folktales

slavery, 2, 4, 7–8, 10–11, 89, 199n44; cultural trauma of, 26–27, 44, 47–48, 188n28; magical figures and, 160–62; morality and survival, 25–27, 67–69; priests and, 111–13. *See also* West African connection to Louisiana

sleep paralysis, 167–70, 208n87. See also *cauchemar*

"Snow Bella," 126–36

Snow White, 115, 126–36

social hierarchy and status, 53, 100–103, 118, 120–21, 133, 135–36. *See also* class distinctions; kings and queens; nobility

Song of the South (1946), 185

Soper, Celia, 137, 181

sortrets, 141

soucouyant (sukuyan), 165–66, 176

souris de Noël (Christmas mouse), 171, 175

South Africa, 42

Souvestre, Émile, 154

Spanish colonial period, 6–7, 65–66, 92

Spanish folklore, 18

Spanish soil trick, 63–69

specificity, 4, 11, 17

Spillman, Susan, 18, 138, 181

spirits, 149–67. *See also* magical figures

stand-up comedy, 179, 209n2

starvation, 34, 39, 40

strength, physical, 21–22, 25, 27, 34, 49, 69, 124

Study of Louisiana French Folktales (1947), 180

superstition. *See* magical figures

survival, 25–27, 52, 67–69, 184, 201n28

swamp gases, 157–59

Swapping Stories (1997), 180

Sweet Crude (band), 182

Swiss Germans, 173

Tallemant des Réaux, Gédéon, 58, 62, 70

tall tales, 179

Tanzania, 205n71

tar baby story, 11, 44–46

Terrebonne Parish, 143, 144

teus, 141

Théâtre Cadien, 135

theft, 27–30, 54, 67–69. *See also under* food; Master Thief tales

Thevis, Peter, 173

Thibodaux, Louisiana, 182

Thibodeaux jokes, 179

Thomas Aquinas, Saint, 151

Thompson, Stith, 190n17. *See also Aarne-Thompson-Uther Index* (ATU)

Ti-Jean/'Tit Jean/Petit Jean (Little John), 68, 72, 79, 90, 136. *See also* Jean le Sot tales

Tin Roof (microbrewery), 182

"'Tit Chapilon Rouge," 136–37

Todorov, Tzvetan, 100

"Tortie" (The Tortoise), 22–25, 30, 48

'T Pousette et 'T Poulette (2001), 138

transgressions, 12, 37–38, 46, 51, 131, 176. *See also* adultery; didactic tales; morals; punishment

Trappey, Adam Shelby Holmes, 112

trauma. *See* cultural (collective) trauma

Trent, Council of, 151

trickster figures, 19, 84–85, 189n2; clergy as, 114; collective trauma and, 11, 48; death of,

43; death of dupe and, 29, 34, 52, 68–69, 136–37; dupe-and-trickster tales, 18–23, 27–31, 33–40, 48, 98, 190n38, 191n45; in fairy tales, 122–23; fool archetype and, 85; magical, 141–42; malice of dupe and, 44, 48; physical appearance of, 52, 58, 61; slave trickster cycle (John), 68–69. *See also* animal trickster figures; Master Thief tales

truth tests, 43

Tulane University, 4, 20

"200 lignes," 81

unbaptized children, 140, 149–60, 166

Uncle Remus (Harris), 18, 27, 185, 192n85

unconventionality, 73

underdog protagonists, 49, 136

Unibroue (brewery), 182–83

universality, 4

Université Laval, 2

University of Louisiana at Lafayette Press, 181

Un Tour de Roquelaure (1799), 65

UPCP-Métive/CERDO, Parthenay, France, 74, 79, 105, 106

uses of enchantment, 139–40

Uther, Hans-Jörg, 190n17. See also *Aarne-Thompson-Uther Index* (ATU)

vampire-like figures, 142, 163, 166–67

Vatican Council, Second (1962–65), 94

Vermilion Parish, 3, 47, 65–66, 125, 152, 158, 192n93

Verret, Felicien, 158

Verret, Jimmy, 158

Verret, John, 158

Vicksburg, Mississippi, 173

Vidaud, Marie, 78

Vienne Province, France, 106

violence, 103–5, 107, 114. *See also* death; punishment

voodoo, 137, 147, 156

Weihnachtsmann, 171

werewolves, 145–47, 161–62, 185

West African connection to Louisiana, 1–2, 7, 19, 42. *See also* African folklore; Senegambia; slavery

White Creoles, 15–16, 20, 191n63; anticlerical tales, 107, 111; in Avoyelles Parish, 46, 107, 109; Catholicism, 93, 111; Creole identity, 15–16; hyena and hare tales, 28

White Francophone communities: animal trickster tales, 28, 35, 44–45, 47–49; cultural contact with Black Creole communities, 48–49; magical figures and, 144; use of term, 15. *See also* French folktales in Louisiana

Wild Hunt, 160

Winnebago Hare Cycle, 26

wit, 26, 28, 52, 62–63, 67–69, 87, 114. *See also* cleverness; trickster figures

witches, 163, 165, 169, 174

Wolof language, 19–20, 70, 190n30

wolves, 46, 136–37, 145, 147, 205n75. See also *loup et le renard* tales (the wolf and the fox); werewolves

women: in fairy tales, 118–35; gender norms and, 166; informants, 202n10. *See also* beauty, female; sexuality

Works Progress Administration, 147

Yeh-hsien, 119–20

Yoruba culture, 25

Zumthor, Paul, 13, 65, 135, 201n28

Zydeco Force & Joe K K, 167

www.ingramcontent.com/pod-product-compliance
Lightning Source LLC
Chambersburg PA
CBHW031546260326
41914CB00002B/289